# Savor the ... of e...

Experience a neighborhood of unparalleled diversity in the Phoenix metro area. Scott Communities builds extraordinary homes with unique characteristics including:

◆ Six distinct floor plans with sixteen color packages
◆ Finished basements
◆ Detached bungalow-style guest houses
◆ Craftsman, Spanish Eclectic, Northern European, and Arizona Ranch architectural styles.
◆ Front porches

The community of Agritopia charms its residents and visitors with parks, tree-lined streets, and a neighborhood design reminiscent of those found in the 1920s. Excellent freeway access from its Gilbert location allows easy travel to any destination.

2754 East Valencia Street
Gilbert, Arizona
480-279-0285
www.scottcommunities.com

SCOTT COMMUNITIES

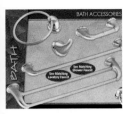

## Bath Accessories

## Laminate Flooring

Minka Aire

## Ceiling Fans with Light Kits

## Door Handles, Knobs, & Locks
## Entry, Privacy, Passage, Dummy

## Various Vessel Sinks

## Outdoor Lighting

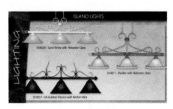

## Island Lights

## Vanities

**New inventory daily!**

HOME IMPROVEMENT WAREHOUSE

# 602-275-3315
www.constructionlots.com

## Where to Live in Phoenix and the Valley of the Sun

Published by NEXZUS Publishing Group,LLC, PO Box 44990, Phoenix, AZ, 85064-4990 in association with Barbican Publishing, Auckland, New Zealand.

Phone: 602.241.0800
Email: publisher@nexzuspub.com
Website: www.wheretolivebooks.com

ISBN 0-9777005-0-X

| | |
|---|---|
| Publishers | Andrew Waite and Stephen Hart |
| Associate Publisher | James Hodgson |
| Managing Editor | Nancy Lucas |
| Senior Writer | Scott C. Seckel |
| Writers | Teresa Bitler<br>Helene Lesel |
| Researcher | Julian King |
| Photography | Mike Baxter, www.BaxterImaging.com |
| Map Creation | Mike Gushock |
| Director of Advertising Sales | Lisa Kandel |
| Director of Sales Operations | Alan Goodyke |
| Associate Publisher – Tucson | Laura Castillo |
| Design | Liesl Strauss<br>Sid Roy |
| Imaging | Image Centre |

Our sincere thanks and gratitude to the many industry sources, local authorities and individuals interviewed for this book. A complete list of contributors is shown on page 288. Our special thanks to Arizona State University Real Estate Center for their invaluable contribution. Thanks also to our primary sponsors, Alpine Associates, Alpine Lending, and The Mark Bosworth Companies and Property Performers for their support.

Cover image: Camelback mountain silhouetted by a spectacular sunset. Custom home by Phoenix Smith. Cover image by Mike Baxter.

# One Call
## DOES IT ALL...

[Al]pine Lending is the **SINGLE SOURCE for all your Real Estate Financial needs!** We've [ma]de it simple for Realtors and their clients by [co]mbining the services of 3 powerful companies [t]o one easy call.

### [FI]NANCING THROUGH ALPINE LENDING

[Wh]ether your client needs financing for a condo, [s]ingle family home or a commercial space, [Al]pine Lending is committed to finding the [pe]rfect loan product. With access to more than [?0] mortgage lenders nationwide, Alpine Lend-[ing] offers thousands of programs to "custom [tail]or" a lending plan for your needs with:

NEW HOME AND CONDOMINIUM PURCHASES
HOME IMPROVEMENT LOANS
HOME EQUITY LINES OF CREDIT
REFINANCE PROGRAMS
DEBT CONSOLIDATION
1ST AND 2ND MORTGAGES

### TITLE & ESCROW Services from Stellar Title

Alpine Lending guides you painlessly through the title and escrow process with the help of their sister company, Stellar Title. A national full service title firm, Stellar Title can produce your title commitments in 24 to 48 hours.

### APPRAISAL SERVICES From EMI

No need to find an outside appraisal company. Alpine Lending provides quick and accurate service through their affiliation with EMI Appraisals. No more waiting for weeks to get the appraisal back!

By combining the services of all 3 companies allows for a quick, easy, smoother process, and... happy customers!

**ALPINE LENDING**
HOME LOANS

# Are you tired of wasting your time and energy trying to find a rental home that works for you and your lifestyle?

What if there were an easier solution that gives you the home you want without the hassle and headache?

"You can buy it in any color, as long as it's black."

## Henry Ford

### Henry Ford could have been in real estate

Are you frustrated with the limited selection of quality homes available from most property management companies? Tired of calling dozens of individual homeowners trying to find the right house for you? Stop wasting your precious time, money and energy and let GoRenter.com do the work for you.

### The Valley's Largest Selection

Talk to one person one time and get everything you need. With hundreds of quality single-family homes available for lease and lease-purchase throughout the Valley you get the home you want, when you want it. Your time is valuable. Invest it wisely.

### Quick And Easy Qualifying

Nobody's perfect. We understand. That's why we created our quick and easy qualification process. That means even with a bankruptcy or other credit bruises you can still qualify for your next home today. We even have a no qualifying program on select homes Valleywide where your down payment is your qualification. Why worry whether you can get the home you want today? GoRenter.com has your next home now with quick and easy qualifying.

## Flexible Lease-Purchase Program

Do you want the option of home ownership? Our flexible lease-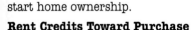 may be the perfect fit for your needs. If you think home owners your future let one of our lease-purchase experts show you how to start on that journey today. With as little as $1,000 down and payments that may be a lot lower than a mortgage payment you can be in your new home today. Our lease-purchase program is the perfect way for you to start home ownership.

## Rent Credits Toward Purchase

On our exclusive lease-purchase program you build value in your home from the very first day. We value win/win relationships and we want to give you a reward

for contributing to a winning partnership. For every month that you make your scheduled payment on time we will give you half of your payment as credit towards purchase and closing costs on our lease-purchase program. We make it easy for you to build value in your next home.

## "No Qualifying" Financing On Purchase

On our exclusive lease-purchase program it's so easy for you to get financing on your home. When you make each of your scheduled rent payments on time you are automatically qualified for financing on your new home. We really do value win/win relationships that much. When you show your

commitment to a successful partnership, you are rewarded. It's that simple.

## Convenient Valley Locations

With 2 Valley locations and more on the way, you get the convenience you deserve for your busy life. Our regional experts can also give you the information you need to make a great living decision in the area of your choice.

# Call Today!
# 623.773.2905 or 480.275.2200
# Se Habla Español - 623.773.2908

HOMEAMERICA
PROPERTY MANAGEMENT LLC

GoRenter.com is sponsored by Home America Property Management, LLC
9501 W. Peoria Ave. • #106 • Peoria • AZ • 85345
14301 N. 87th St. • #118 • Scottsdale • AZ • 85260
www.GoRenter.com

Lic# LC 549202000

where to live in
**PHOENIX**
and the Valley of the Sun

*Continued on page 10*

# Imagine finding both style and value under one roof.

You're in for a few nice surprises when you visit a Meritage Homes community. You'll see floorplans with a lot more flair and extra features than you'd expect. And when you find out you can afford a more stylish home than you thought, that may be the best surprise of all. Visit one of our communities today, and get ready to be pleasantly surprised. Meritage Homes, where a heritage of Arizona homebuilding excellence remains the cornerstone of every new home we build.

Ask**Meritage**Homes.com
877-Ask-Meritage
click or call 24/7 for current or future sales information

**Meritage**Homes®

MeritageHomes-Phx.com

# Contents

# No matter where you live, there's always a shopping Nirvana near you.

# Letter from the Publishers

*Where to Live in Phoenix and the Valley of the Sun* is for people who are moving here from across the sea, across the country or across town. It's also for residents who are curious about other parts of the Valley. It's a must-have resource book packed with facts, figures, insights and opinions that help answer that crucial question: Where should I live in this vast metropolis?

You can spend hours surfing the Internet, driving the town, poring over visitor guides, contacting chambers of commerce and talking to real estate agents. We've already done it so you don't have to. We put all we learned from them, and from many other sources, in the pages of this book and organized it so it's easy to use.

It's for both newbies and natives. But mostly it's for the individual or family with specific needs and wants. It is designed to help you match the city or neighborhood that suits you best. We don't promote one place over another. We don't care where you live, as long as it's a good fit for you. And we're not trying to sell you anything – except for this book!

You may still want to consult the same sources we did to reach your final decision. But this book will help you narrow down your options and ask more informed questions.

*Where to Live in Phoenix and the Valley of the Sun* will save you time, money and aggravation. It will lead you to parts of the Valley you may have overlooked. It will lead you to suitable neighborhoods and to the type of home you want and can afford.

In our experience, well-informed people buy the best homes in the best areas at the best prices. This book will provide you with everything you need to know to make smart buying and selling choices and find the home that is perfect for you.

**Andrew Waite**

**Stephen Hart**

# How to use this Book

*Where to Live in Phoenix and the Valley of the Sun* is split into a number of geographical areas – Phoenix (Central, East, West, North, and South), Mesa, Scottsdale, East Valley, Northeast Valley, West Valley and Northwest Valley. Each area is, in turn, divided into cities, towns and neighborhoods. To find the place you are interested in, either refer to the Contents pages or use the index at the back of the book.

Within each city, or neighborhood, we look at the character of the area, the people who live there, types of homes, real estate trends and typical prices, as well as the amenities you can find there – schools, leisure facilities, shopping and dining.

Towards the back of the book, you'll find more fascinating facts – a comprehensive list of the major schools, house prices, crime statistics and demographic data for the whole of the Valley.

**Our Star Ratings:** Where to Live editors have awarded the areas and their amenities a star rating from one to five, based on desirability, house prices, personality and general access to amenities.

**Maps:** Each area has its own map, which graphically illustrates the boundaries of the areas we describe.

**Prices:** Home and rental prices quoted in the *At a Glance* boxes are anecdotal and are based on interviews with real estate agents and analysis of the MLS database of houses for sale. Prices shown in the statistics section are provided by Arizona State University Real Estate Center, based on actual, recorded sales for the third quarters of 2004 and 2005.

**Who Lives Where?** Obtained from the 2000 US Census Web site www.census.gov. Neighborhood data within the Phoenix, Mesa and Scottsdale sections were extracted by mapping the zip codes, census tracts or census blocks that make up the neighborhood. The information is intended as a general approximation only and no guarantees can be made regarding accuracy. Population data includes the percentage of: White (alone), Hispanic or Latino (all races combined), Black or African American (alone), American Indian and Alaskan Native (alone), Asian (alone) or other. The 'median' value is the middle value in each case.

**Population & Demographic Data:** We identify the race, median age, and median income of people who live in each of the areas. This has been compiled from analysis of census data (2000) by the US Government and complemented, where possible, by more recent data provided in annual population estimates from the US Census Bureau and local city sources.

**School Listings:** Our tables enable you to search for schools by city or neighborhood and to check their achievement profiles. Provided by the Department of Education, AZ Learns 2004-05.

**Crime Data:** City by city data showing reported crimes in 2004, provided by Access Integrity Unit of the Arizona Department of Public Safety.

# Phoenix & The Valley of the Sun — An Overview

*"God bless the fact we live in Phoenix, Arizona."*

*- Mayor Paul Johnson, at the dedication of Sunnyslope High School's mascot, Victor the Viking, May 1, 1992.*

Phoenix is aptly named. Fly over the Salt River Valley today, and most of what you see didn't exist before World War II. Much of the fifth-biggest city in the country didn't exist even 15 years ago. It's probably the only city of its size on Earth with huge chunks of vacant land on the main thoroughfare. Phoenix arose from desert dust overnight and spread its wings. There are entire new-born cities in this Valley. To a newcomer, all of it looks brand-new, as if there is no history.

The truth is, few places are so closely tied to their past. The 131-mile long canal system which delivers water to Valley homes and swimming pools was excavated from canals dug by the Hohokam Indians about 1,700 years ago. Today executives meet in gleaming towers 26 miles from shamans chanting in teepees. There are Ahwatukee homes with petroglyph-covered boulders in backyards. If you have a big enough lot in the middle of the city, you're allowed to have horses or livestock. (One Scottsdale man living amidst suburbia has buffalo on his property.) If you have a revolver, you're allowed to wear it holstered and walk down the street. Phoenix doesn't preserve its history. It lives it.

Phoenix constantly arises from ashes. The city was founded in the 1860s. Building materials were scarce to non-existent then; people lived in tents or wikieups or adobes, almost all of which have sunk back into the sands. (The Valley's oldest building is the Casa Vieja in Tempe, built in 1871.) It's not like Boston or Philadelphia, where 200 year-old buildings lay about everywhere. Newness is a Phoenix tradition. It's not uncommon to visit a sandwich shop you haven't been to in six months, only to find it's been torn down. Bad areas in Los Angeles are always going to be bad areas. In Phoenix, everything gets better.

The city's setting is basin-and-range topography typical of the Southwest. The correct name for the area is the Salt River Valley; Valley of the Sun is a modern appellation. Moving clockwise, the Valley's surrounding ranges begin with Black Mountain to the north, the Continental Mountains to the north-northeast, the McDowell Mountains to the northeast, Red Mountain, the Usery and Superstition Mountains to the east, the Santans south-southeast, South Mountain to the south, the Estrellas to the southwest, the White Tanks to the west, and the Hieroglyphic Mountains to the northwest.

There are also 14 mountains, buttes, and hill groups in the middle of the Valley. Metro Phoenix began to spill beyond its physical boundaries in the 1990s.

Average annual temperature is 72.6F. The average high is 85 degrees. In a good year about eight inches of rain falls. How's the heat? Let the fact we've provided an entire article on it speak for itself.

You won't find statues of the local founding fathers. Phoenix was founded by a violent, drug-addicted, Civil War veteran and an outcast alcoholic English aristocrat. Jack Swilling fought for both sides, once shot and scalped a man on the main street of Wickenburg in the middle of the day, and died in territorial prison, where he was locked up for robbing a stagecoach. Darrell Duppa was exiled because he killed a fellow army officer in a duel. In Arizona, where he was constantly drunk, he accidentally shot a white woman held hostage by Apaches during a raid. When General William Sherman visited Phoenix after the Civil War, a group of dignitaries met him at the train station. They told the general the area was a paradise, lacking only water and a goodly measure of the better part of society. Sherman looked around and said, "Hell labors under precisely the same handicaps."

The caliber of both inhabitants and living standards has improved vastly since the days of the Old West. Innovative, creative, can-do people like Phoenix. There's not an entrenched establishment resistant to new faces, ideas, and energy. You can also move here and the neighbors aren't calling your mother because you didn't go to mass on Sunday. People come here to escape and live the life they want to live. In the Valley, people only care about what you do, not who you are or where you're from.

Arizona was the second fastest-growing state during the 1990s (Nevada was tops). It became the last continental state to be admitted to the Union, on Valentine's Day 1912. In 1910 about 45,000 people lived in the Valley. Most of Arizona's roads weren't paved.

During World War II thousands of pilots and GIs trained here. Throughout five years of European and Pacific mud, they

thought about Phoenix's sun and palms. When the war ended, veterans poured into the Valley.

By 1950 the metro Phoenix population exploded to 332,000. Developers began mass-production housing. From then to now, the lowest percentage change in the greater Phoenix area per decade has been 41 percent. (From 1950 to 1960 the Valley grew 100 percent.)

Phoenix isn't a retirement home. About 3.4 million people live in the Valley of the Sun, and they're all on the move. More than 50 percent of the population is between 18 and 54 years of age, which is younger than the national average.

Phoenix Sky Harbor International Airport is the fifth busiest in the U.S. and the world for passenger traffic for takeoffs and landings, handling more than 36 million travellers in 2000.

Technology is a $50 billion industry. World-class companies like Intel, Avnet, Motorola, AlliedSignal, Honeywell and Boeing have corporate and regional headquarters here. Industry giants like American Express, Phelps Dodge, Sumitomo Sitix, Prudential, Charles Schwab and the Mayo Clinic all have major operations in Phoenix.

Phoenix tops the nation's cities in growth, the U.S. Census announced last summer. Almost 30,000 people moved here, more than to Los Angeles, San Antonio, or Las Vegas, the runners-up. (Suburban Gilbert and Chandler were fourth and seventh respectively in the rankings.) The state Department of Economic Security, the agency responsible for official projections, expects Arizona will continue to grow at its present rate of three to 3.5 percent per year.

They're coming from California, where they've decided commuting two hours from a $575,000 rundown tract house in an Orange County ghetto is not how they want to live. They're coming from the Midwest because they always have; one too many Wisconsin winters and anyone would rather be out by the pool in Tempe with bikinis and palm trees. Retirees still come here. The past decade's boom has brought in twentysomethings with retro tastes who've lunged for poolside Scottsdale 1960s condos. That's nudged retirees out; south Scottsdale went from nearly-deads to newlyweds in a decade. People who want Sun Belt living without hurricanes are opting to move somewhere windows are tinted, not boarded-up.

Another reason a lot of people move here is to start their lives again. Something went wrong, like a divorce or a bankruptcy. They rent an apartment or buy a house here, a place where they don't have any relatives or acquaintances, and get a new job, make new friends (kind of like Darrell Duppa).

There are Mexicans from Chiapas or Nayarit who come to work, earn a stake, and return home. There are refugees: Vietnamese boat people who survived attacks by pirates, Afghans, Somalis, Russians, young Sudanese who escaped slavery in another desert on the other side of the world. In the beginning America was the world, John Locke said. Now the American West is the world for those who need a second chance.

They all move here for jobs, the weather, and big, cheap houses in a booming metropolis which gets better every day. The quality of life is outstanding in terms of leisure, convenience, quality, and efficiency. Compare the wide, bright well-stocked aisles of Albertsons to cramped, dark, dirty New York stores. Neighborhood streets are new and clean, with rows of spotless houses. Most things work, people are usually on time, and Christmas brunch on the lawn beats a white Christmas any day.

Arizona home builders want everyone to have a home. One hundred and nine new homes are built every day in metropolitan Phoenix.

A report issued last year by the independent, non-partisan Brookings Institution think tank, projected the state to have the second-fastest growth rate in the country, with the construction of nearly 2.1 million new housing units by 2030. That's about as many units as currently exist in Arizona today.

Metro Phoenix has been the number one housing market in the West for a decade and number two in the nation. Home builders have been at maximum production for the past decade. Almost every national homebuilder is already here. To accommodate these throngs, instant cities for as many as 45,000 people are being built every year. You'll read about areas in this book which got their first grocery stores within the past two years. Areas with unpaved roads where flooding can cut you off from the outside world still exist in view of the bright lights of downtown.

Housing variety is wide. Historic cottages covered in ivy. Immense Spanish Colonial Revival mansions on manicured lawns. Golf course patio homes with rabbits nibbling greens. Big lazy old ranch homes on large lots with pools and citrus orchards. Properties where you can have a horse, a couple of cows, or even a flock of sheep within sight of skyscraper penthouses. Roomy comfortable production homes in the suburbs with swimming pools for kids to run wild in during the Fourth of July. Sleek steel and glass masterpieces

perched on mountainsides with infinity pools cascading toward city lights.

Dozens of high rises are being built in five urban cores, mostly Phoenix and Tempe. They range from the high $100,000s to more than $4 million. Some have sold out before groundbreaking. They have private elevators, fireplaces, and maid's quarters.

Master-planned communities become more elaborate with each generation of building. Amenities can be mind-boggling: lakes for boating and fishing, climbing walls, concierges, water parks for kids, tennis, golf, and parks. There aren't many places in the country where a young family can buy so much new home for so little money.

The freeway system is excellent, if a bit overloaded during rush hours. Everyone praises the network (except for the 101 in Scottsdale, a perpetual Formula One event). You can cover ground quickly. The views are amazing and the walls and shoulders are landscaped and decorated with art. It's also rubberized in most of the Valley. You can stand in backyards 100 feet from five lanes of traffic and hear birds. (This also makes frontage properties excellent buys.) The state transportation department holds popular parties on freeway segments before they're opened to traffic.

Public buses are as sadistically slow and tortuous as the freeways are swift and excellent. There's a longstanding joke that the only people who walk in Phoenix are escaped criminals and dogs. The good news is a light rail system is currently being built between Phoenix and Mesa through Tempe. It'll be open for riders in 2008. Extensions to northwest Phoenix, Glendale, and north Phoenix will be built over the next 20 years.

This is a dynamic, vibrant place brimming with excitement and opportunity. To paraphrase Thomas Paine, here you have it in your power to begin the world again.

# Attention Real Estate Investors...
## Are Your Real Estate Investments Keeping You Up At Night?
### Discover What Home America Property Management Can Do For You.

**Dear Real Estate Investor,**

Do ever wonder what the secrets of the real estate pros are? Professional property management with Home America is like having insider information for your real estate investments. No more worrying about your portfolio or your decisions. Let us show you how our valuable services can help you sleep at night...

**Professional Management Doesn't Cost...It Pays**

Do you think professional property management costs too much money? Home America was created by investors, for investors. You take your money seriously and expect your partners to do the same. That's why we created our exclusive Accountable Management System™. If it's not good enough for our own investments, it's not good enough for yours.

**Over 100 Years Of Combined Experience**

Experience matters. So many things can happen that impact your investment. Let's face it, when everything goes just right you don't need much experience to make real estate work. But when you hit that first eviction, or a challenging vacancy or difficult market you'll want our experience on your side. Experience from both a management and investor perspective. Why rely on luck when you can be backed by over 100 years of quality experience?

**Unique Insights Through Proprietary Data**

With nearly 1,500 single-family homes under management, we gain data and valuable insights the average investor just can't get. If you're a serious investor you can't afford not to have this strategic insight incorporated into your investment portfolio. That's the advantage of a company created by investors for investors. It's the little things like this that pay such huge dividends.

**Win/Win/Win Relationships**

At Home America we know our Accountable Management System™ isn't for everyone, so we carefully screen our prospective partners for relationships that will work. One of the ways we keep our fees so low is we focus heavily on win/win/win relationships between you, your tenant and us from the beginning. So while our program isn't a perfect fit for everyone, our relentless pursuit of winning relationships serves you and your investment.

**Total Investor Services**

At Home America we can manage the entire investment experience for you. As a full-service brokerage we can assist you in selling existing properties, evaluating and acquiring new properties and managing your entire portfolio. Why use a regular real estate agent for your critical real estate transactions? The experts at Home America are there for you at every step of your investment experience.

**Exclusive Rent Guarantee**

We're so confident we will rent your home...we guarantee it. The exclusive Home America Rent Guarantee is the best way we know of to put our money where our mouth is. If we don't rent your market-ready home in a reasonable amount of time your management is free. Call for all the details.

**Absolutely Hands Down The Best Advertising Exposure Anywhere**

Like any business, sales and marketing is a huge part of your real estate investment. Why settle for cheap, ineffective advertising? At Home America we're committed to providing the most visibility and most opportunities to rent your investment property. No one else can give your home the attention of full-page newspaper ads, prime television commercials, drive time radio spots, and over 30,000 page views each week on the internet. If there's a way to get your home seen, you can bet that we'll be there for you.

**Increase Your Cash Flow**

Our unique lease-purchase program can increase your investment return substantially. Created to allow maximum investment flexibility and improved returns, the Home America lease-purchase is a win/win opportunity for both you and your tenant. Put more cash in your pocket and get a tenant who is motivated to take care of your investment like her own. The Home America lease-purchase program gives the best to both of you.

**Worry-Free Investing**

Real estate is a big-time investment. Why stay up nights worrying about your investment portfolio? Whether it's a vacancy or insecurity about the stability of your portfolio, professional property management from Home America lets you sleep at night knowing your investment is managed by the pros. To find out if our Accountable Management System™ is right for you call Home America Property Management today...it could be the best call you ever make for your real estate investments.

Lic# LC 549202000

9501 W. Peoria Ave. • #106 • Peoria • AZ • 85345
623.776.2320 • fax 623.776.2162

14301 N. 87th St. • #118 • Scottsdale • AZ • 85260
480.275.2200 • fax 480.588.5609

HomeAmericaPM.com • info@HomeAmericaPM.com

# Living & Investing in the Valley of the Sun

## Why live in Phoenix?

Most cities around the world have a core central business district and ever less-densely populated suburbs as you move away from that one center, but not Phoenix. Phoenix is really a conglomeration of many towns and cities, Scottsdale, Tempe, Glendale, Chandler, Peoria, Paradise Valley and Sun City, to name a few. It's a true megalopolis that's been dubbed the "Valley of the Sun."

It's often said that 100 homes are built in greater Phoenix every day. Visitors are astounded to learn this, and can only visualize it after a day spent driving around and seeing the incredible scale of construction that is going on. This massive growth is not new. Since 1991, 503,000 homes have been built in the Valley of the Sun, which works out to pretty close to 100 homes per day for the last 14 years.

One of the most alluring things about Phoenix is the benign climate. Yes, it gets hot in the middle of the summer, but for most of the year it is heaven on earth. Why shovel snow and put up with drizzle when you can have 350 sunny days a year?

Another aspect that draws people is price. Despite the run-ups in real estate values, you can still buy a new, four- or five-bedroom house for much less than what a tiny (and older) two-bedroom cottage would cost in most parts of California. And, there is space, great real estate laws, beautiful scenery, a great job infrastructure, and of course the weather, although I may have mentioned that already!

## Where in Phoenix?

As with any other city, some suburbs are more desirable than others. Remember two things, though. First, a "less desirable" part of Phoenix may still be a much better place to live than a "more desirable" town back east. The eastern town will be covered in snow four months of the year and probably has a steel mill that's been shuttered for years. It's all relative. Second, mediocre suburbs are being transformed into up-market neighborhoods with the continued influx of residents, jobs, opportunities and creativity. The historic districts of Central Phoenix are a case in point. Long a motley collection of dilapidated eyesores, in the last few years these areas have become desirable and even "in" places to live.

In terms of capital growth, some suburbs of the megalopolis have grown by a massive 40 percent in the last 12 months, and other suburbs by a paltry 25 percent. However, even the "lousy" 25 percent increase is nearly three times the national average of about 9.7 percent.

What matters most is whether you are close to where you will be working and playing, and whether your house and community feel like home. The fact that people live all over the Valley reflects that these factors vary widely from person to person.

## Where do tenants want to live?

I can usually convince someone looking for a home to let their personal preference for style, proximity to facilities, and price, determine where they should live. Most

people "know" when they are in the right area. I have more difficulty convincing people about my views on where they should buy investment real estate.

To set the scene for my theory, let me remind you of two features of real estate that set it apart from other investment vehicles. First, unlike the stock market, which is very efficient (you pay the same price for a stock whether you or the stock is in Phoenix, Helsinki, Montevideo or Singapore), the real estate market is very inefficient. This means that a property may be put on the market at a price based on the opinion of a single real estate agent, appraiser, or seller. Sometimes they choose a price that the market determines to be too high (and never sells at that price), and sometimes they choose a price that is too low (and sells within six hours). The point: while it is impossible to buy stock at a price substantially below what others are willing to pay, it is possible to buy real estate at a price much lower than you could sell it for the next day.

The second feature (relevant to this discussion) that sets real estate apart from stock is that once you have bought a stock, there is nothing you can do to that stock to increase its value other than hope and pray. With real estate, however, once you have bought it, there are many things you can do to increase its value (capital value as well as rental value) without even spending much money.

What do these points add up to? I do not believe that there is one suburb, area, town or city in Phoenix where investors should invest exclusively. Tenants are inspired to rent in all areas, as suits their needs geographically and financially. Wiser than investing in the "best investment area," I believe it's best to use two of the great advantages of real estate over other investments: find a property that

is (for whatever reason, don't even question why) on the market for less than true market value, or a property where you can massively increase the value with just a nominal outlay of time and money.

If you follow this advice and end up with 10 houses spread out all over the city, congratulations! You have spread your risks. Financial planners are always telling you to diversify (usually into investments that generate commissions for them!). I agree. Diversify your real estate across many parts of the Valley. Get some residential, some commercial, some hospitality, and some specialist real estate. Diversify in real estate!

By investing in Phoenix, you are already enjoying the benefits of catching the rise of the second fastest growing city on this planet. Rather than sweat over which suburb is best, find a house with an angle — at a discount to market or with some potential for increasing its value — and then go out and do it again and again.

Life is short. If you've spent five minutes reading this article, then another home has been completed and occupants moved in somewhere in the Valley. (It happens every 4.8 minutes to be exact, based on an eight-hour working day). How many more homes need be built before you decide to get some for yourself?

© 2006 Dolf de Roos
*Dolf has been to over 90 countries, and lived in over a dozen. He chooses to live in Phoenix. He is also the author of the New York Times bestseller Real Estate Riches — How to Become Rich using your Banker's Money (Wiley & Sons). More information is available at www.dolfderoos.com.*

*Turn-Key Real Estate Investments ...*

# Without the Work.

## NO MORE LOOKING, WATCHING, OR WAITING FOR THE RIGHT INVESTMENT OPPORTUNITY

Choose from dozens of available properties and invest with confidence. Continue to enjoy worry-free returns, with a track record unmatched in the industry. Call us today to find out just how easy earning hassle-free cash flow every month can be.

- No property management worries
- 10% annual returns
- Earn fixed monthly income, no fluctuation
- Compounding annual appreciation
- Purchase 30%* or more below market value
- Invest from $50,000 to $5,000,000
- Satisfies 1031 Exchange
- IRA and 401k funds can be used
- 1-5 year terms
- Financing options available

Call **602.481.2990** TODAY
or visit us online at **www.RedDoorGroupInc.com**

1520 West Osborn Road
Suite 8
Phoenix, AZ 85015

# REDDOOR
GROUP, INC.

*On average. There are risks with investment ownership. Red Door Group does everything possible to minimize these risks, and prevent loss of investor capital. As with all investments, it is important to understand risks before making an investment decision.

# Hot Tips For Phoenix Buyers

Buying a house may be the biggest investment you will ever make. It's complicated and expensive. It can be very stressful. Here is a guide that explains the process step-by-step. With a little help you can take ownership of your dream home with your sanity and bank account intact — and reap the benefits for a lifetime.

## Check Your Credit

Several months before applying for a mortgage or even looking for a property, check out your credit rating for unsuspected problems or errors. A new law allows consumers to check their credit reports annually at no charge. A good resource for free credit reports can be found at www.annualcreditreport.com.

Why check your credit? To be sure no one else has tapped into your identity, charged purchases against your credit or borrowed money in your name. Your credit should be clean and without blemishes caused by late payments, lawsuits, evictions, etc.

What if you're the cause of the low score? Clean up your act, and solve the debt problems creditor by creditor. Why should you care about your score? To secure the best loan rates, you'll need a high credit score. The higher the credit rating, the lower the interest rate you'll have to pay.

## PITI Me?

Now that you're ready to move forward, time to take two steps back. Some people pick a neighborhood and start searching for a home, only to discover they've wasted their time, since prices for homes in the area were simply too high. Had they taken the time to pre-qualify themselves for a mortgage, they would have spared themselves the aggravation and embarrassment of looking for something out of their price range.

**Price Range?** Buyers often mistakenly assume the loan amount is all they have monthly to pay. Not quite. The monthly payout includes four components, known in the industry as PITI: Principal, Interest, Taxes and Insurance. Let's take a look at what they mean to your wallet.

**Payment and Interest.** It looks like one number, but don't let the monthly payment amount fool you — it's actually two sums in one. The interest portion of the loan is one and the principal (or actual payback) amount on the loan is the second component. Your payment equals both amounts lumped into one (Principal + Interest = Monthly Payment). At first, you'll be paying mostly interest, and very little principal. Loans come in all sizes, shapes and amortizations, but more on that later.

**Taxes.** Usually due twice a year, the deduction for property taxes is usually prepaid during escrow for a period of time. Because escrow pays them at first, some buyers are surprised when their first property tax bill arrives.

Sorry to say, property taxes are due each and every year, based on a percentage of the purchase price. Some buyers don't realize that the tax is based on the purchase price before they make an offer, but that's the price you'll be reminded of each year when the tax bill arrives.

It's best to put aside a bit every month to cover the sum. While some lenders will deduct for property tax as part of the loan, it's better to pay it yourself and avoid any lender processing fees.

**Insurance.** Required by all lenders, property insurance is obviously a good idea. Before securing a loan, your lender will require proof of insurance. What type of insurance? As recent news events depict, insurance coverage can vary from basic to deluxe. Basic includes fire, theft and liability coverage. Extra insurance can be purchased to cover specified valuables, such as jewelry, antiques or silver. Special hazards are also extra, such as flood coverage. In Arizona, the good news is there are no hurricanes, earthquakes or tornadoes to buy extra insurance for.

Now that you have an idea of the fixed costs of property ownership, don't think "that's all folks." Money should be set aside for variable costs, including repairs, utilities and maintenance costs.

## What Can You Really Afford?

Most buyers have an idea of what they can afford then fall in love with a property that's out of their price range. Sometimes real estate agents try to nudge clients upward by showing higher-priced homes. Get real — you could be paying that mortgage for as long as 30 years or 360 checks.

To help you stay grounded while you're looking at beautiful homes, organize a list of all monthly income, compiling a realistic annual income total. Be sure to hang onto your last three pay stubs, which will be needed for proof of income. Self employed? No problem, just keep handy your tax returns from the past three years and be ready to provide a list of income and expenses.

Why expenses? Because they are just like calories: they add up quickly. Keeping a written log will help you organize costs, and keep you from unexpectedly dipping into savings to cover everyday expenses. Annual or semi-annual premiums, such as car insurance, tuition or memberships should be noted as well. They all add up, and will be needed to draw a complete financial picture for your lender.

## Qualifying For A Mortgage

Lenders will review your income, tabulate your spending, and check how much you have saved to estimate your net worth. As a rule of thumb, lenders will allow about 29 percent of your gross monthly income to be used for the mortgage payment.

So how much would you need to earn to afford $250,000 worth of mortgage? While the interest rate is part of the equation, for simplicity sake we'll use six percent as the rate. On a 30-year loan, the monthly payment would be $1,499.05, which means the borrower has to earn about $62,000 annually to qualify.

On a $350,000 loan, the annual income needed jumps to $86,838.90 on a six percent rate loan. On a $150,000 loan, about $37,220.00 annual income is needed to cover the $900 monthly payment.

## Loans & Points

Loans come in five basic varieties:

1. Conventional

2. Federal Housing (FHA)

3. Veteran Administration (VA)

4. Assumption

5. Seller Carryback

The first three usually are considered the "cleanest," since the seller is no longer financially involved.

You need to know about discount points when selecting a loan, too. "Discount points" are just that — a way to discount a loan up front by paying extra money for a better loan rate. Usually paid by the buyer, after all, they're the one getting the loan. A single "point" is a fancy way of saying one percent. Surprisingly, choice of buyer

or seller can be checked on the offer form. If the seller box is checked and they accept the offer, you're ahead by one percent of the loan amount.

The last two loan types, Assumption and Seller Carryback, are more complex and have different tax and credit implications (good and bad). Either option should be thoroughly discussed with a financial professional, such as an accountant.

## Conditional Loan Approval

A fairly recent invention, the Conditional Loan Approval Letter is a handy item to have in hand before making the offer. Some purchase offers require the letter be provided within a few days of the acceptance. Why take a chance? Once you've picked your loan, get a letter.

## Get Down

The other vital part of the "how much can we purchase?" equation involves the down payment. Be realistic, since proof of down payment will be asked for within days of a purchase offer being submitted. I've seen buyers fool themselves into thinking they can borrow the extra money at the last minute from friends and family, only to lose the property when they fell short.

Even if someone is gifting or giving you the money for the down payment, a letter indicating that the money is indeed a gift — and not a loan — may be required by the mortgage holder. Proof of savings of the amount down, going back three months prior is sometimes required, too. Surprised? Better be safe than sorry, and secure a realistic down payment before you start shopping.

## Ultimate Shopping

Before your search begins for a specific property, decide on your priorities of wants and needs. Start with your needs, of course, such as location in relation to schools, family, shopping and work. Get yourself a detailed map of the area you are considering and make several copies. Sharpen your pencil, and get a highlighter ready, since properties in Phoenix can be sizzling.

## What Makes Phoenix Unique?

The heat, for one. The average daytime temperature from May through September usually exceeds 90 degrees Fahrenheit. In June, July and August temperatures are nearly guaranteed to top 100 degrees. As a result, seasoned buyers know that "walking distance" in some cities simply isn't easy to walk to in Phoenix, especially for small children. As a result, don't depend on "nearby" in an ad — check out for yourself the distance to parks and schools.

Transportation. Like it or not, Phoenix is not a great town for public transportation, especially in the summer heat. Buses are a rare sight, and subways non-existent. A light-rail system that will serve downtown Phoenix and Tempe is under construction. It will take several years to complete. As a result, buyers need to look for a location that is close to their hub of needs, including work, schools and shopping.

For commuters, access to the freeway network is vital, and can easily be researched online or with a detailed local map. Be realistic about the length of the route and the time it will take. A long commute can easily overheat your credit cards with car repairs and gas bills.

Map copy in hand; start highlighting areas you think would cover your list. The map's scale, (such as 1/4 inch equals 1 mile) is always provided somewhere on the face and is handy for checking exact distances.

For example, if a school is just a few blocks away, the walk may be realistic. If it's more than a mile, better buy a camel. For students, check if the school district provides transportation or if there's convenient bus service.

Trim down your choice to between three to five specific areas or neighborhoods. Rank in order of preference, keeping a list that matches the maps for reference.

## Trade-Offs

Now that you've got a handle on what you can afford and where you prefer to live, it's time to make some decisions. Let's say a buyer can afford a property costing $500,000. For some buyers, space is the final (and most important) frontier, and they insist a large property to call home. They are willing to face hours behind the wheel and purchase on city fringe areas.

Other buyers insist on a specific location, and are willing to go with a condominium instead of a house. For example, when a couple was "priced out" of a single family home, they went for a duplex in the neighborhood they wanted. They would have preferred a single family home, but the duplex was the next best choice. The extra income from the second unit meant they could live in their desired neighborhood.

New condominiums are going up in many areas in the Valley of the Sun, many in choice locations. The option is clear — location or price may be the tradeoff.

## The Wading Game

You've done your homework, selected where you want to live, how much you have

to spend, and gotten pre-qualified. You've even checked around to comparison shop insurance rates. Now it's time to wade into the market.

Start by looking at open houses in the selected areas, talking to real estate agents and getting to know the range of prices for what you're looking for.

Having a good buyer's agent is important. Online ads and newspapers only go so far — they are not as time sensitive as actual real estate listings the professionals can access. Work with an agent who knows the area and lives in the area or nearby. They are often aware of listings that aren't yet public.

The agent should intimately know prices for the area, and hopefully advise you if a place is a fair deal or not. Some agents may pressure you into signing an exclusive contract. Keep in mind buyers agent agreements are rare, since the seller, not the buyer, pays the commission to both sides. If it's offered, don't agree to it.

## Make Me An Offer

Sometimes a good deal presents itself and you have to move fast. Often done in a flurry of excitement, purchase offers are often hurriedly written and without attention to detail. It's not hard to overlook something — there are pages upon pages of fine print to read over, and most make no sense at all the first time through.

Your agent should patiently explain the details. Here are a few to watch for:

Sale price. Seems self-explanatory, but it does have a catch — what if the property doesn't appraise for the full value? Be sure there's an appraisal contingency to cover any doubt. Bidding war? Jumping the gun and going for a too-high sales price

may leave you shooting yourself in the foot — and leaving a hole in your wallet. Ask the real estate agent for "comps" or comparison sales (not just listing prices) for the same type of property, including size and features in the same area.

Down payment. Usually divided in the contract into the "earnest money" amount (usually about 3 percent of the sales price) that opens escrow, the balance of down payment is due at closing. Be sure both numbers add up to what you have available as a total down payment.

Loan. Check that a maximum loan interest rate and point payable is listed on the contract to cover any unexpected jumps in rate — and your payments — before the deal closes.

Inspection contingencies. As a buyer, you have the right to inspect the property within limits — time limits, that is. Be sure there's enough inspection time filled in on the offer to give you ample time for scheduling inspections. Follow-up inspections are sometimes required to focus on a specific problem, such as mold, asbestos or termites. For Arizona, be sure to check the air conditioning system and know what you're getting into. Never waive the initial inspection or rely solely on a seller's disclosure report for inspection facts.

Escrow period. Too short? You may be rushed into buying the property. Too long? You may lose a good loan rate. Try to coordinate an escrow time that works for both parties. Forty-five to 90 days is the average range for escrows.

Once your purchase offer is submitted to the selling agent, one of three things may happen.

1. The seller does not respond or rejects your offer and the time limit expires.

2. The seller counters your offer with altered terms and conditions, such as price, length of escrow or even fixtures or appliances they want to keep — leaving you to accept or counter their counter offer (sounds complicated and it is!).

3. The seller accepts your price and terms.

Once you've worked out a deal, the escrow should begin without delay. Suddenly you're in a race against time to perform a list of items within the time limits detailed in the purchase contract.

## Ducks In A Row

Since you've done your homework and lined up your loan, insurance and inspectors, you're ready to plunge into escrow. The escrow company should provide you with a timetable which highlights the "drop dead" dates. As a buyer, you have a limited time to inspect and decide firmly on the price, terms and condition of the property. Some contracts deem "silence as approval" so watch out. Speak up (and put in writing) any requests or changes before the due dates in the contract or get ready to be shot down.

## Final Walk-Through And Closing

By the last week of escrow, you've jumped through almost all the hoops escrow has presented. Still to do? Check out the property one more time before closing, always a good exercise, since the property should be vacant at this point. Sometimes a walk-through reveals missing fixtures or items included with the property, such as appliances or light fixtures not excluded. Bringing a copy of the final purchase offer document for reference may be a good idea.

Signing off the documents is your last step in the closing process. Actually it's your hand that will be numb after this exercise, since it involves signing tons of paperwork, including loan documents. Since a notary needs to be available for some documents, most final sign-offs take place at the escrow office. Don't feel rushed — this could take several hours.

## Moving In

Sometime on the day of closing, you should get a phone call from your agent or escrow company letting you know the property has been officially recorded and transferred to your name. You're the new owner! Keys should be available to you right away, so get moving!

RESOURCES
www.annualcreditreport.com

## FREE GIFT from "Where to Live in Phoenix & the Valley of the Sun"

May we ask you a few questions? In return we have a gift for you.

We will send you the next two issues of Personal Real Estate Investor Magazine for FREE.

We will also send you updates on the next edition of Where to Live in Phoenix & the Valley of the Sun.

We will not share your specific information with anyone else.

1. Name _____

    Address _____

    City _____ State _____ ZIP_____

    Phone _____ E-mail _____

2. Please check one:  Male ☐        Female ☐

3. Marital status:  Married ☐    Single ☐

4. How many people live in your household?  1 ☐  2 ☐  3 ☐  4 ☐  5+ ☐

5. What is your age?  23-35 ☐  36-45 ☐  46-55 ☐  56-64 ☐  65+ ☐

6. What is your annual household income?

    ☐ Less than $29,000          ☐ $30,000-$49,000

    ☐ $50,000-$69,000            ☐ $70,000-$99,000

    ☐ $100,000-$199,000          ☐ $200,000+

7. What is your educational level?

Completed High School ☐     Completed College ☐  Completed Graduate School ☐

- - - - - - - - - - - - - - - - - - - - - - - - - - - - - - - - - - - - - - - - - - - - -

8. Do you rent or own?        Rent ☐   Own ☐

9. What is the value of your current home?

    ☐ Less than $249,000      ☐ $250,000-$349,000      ☐ $350,000-$449,000

    ☐ $450,000-$599,000       ☐ $600,000–$799,000      ☐ $800,000-$999,000

    ☐ more than $1,000,000     ☐                         ☐

10. What will be the price range of your next home purchase?

    ☐ Less than $249,000      ☐ $250,000-$349,000      ☐ $350,000-$449,000

    ☐ $450,000-$599,000       ☐ $600,000–$799,000      ☐ $800,000-$999,000

    ☐ more than $1,000,000

11. Where is your principle residence?  Arizona ☐  Other state/country: ☐

12. How many homes/properties do you own? Total number _____

13. Where did you purchase this book? _____

14. How could we make this book more useful? Your comments are welcomed.

_____

_____

_____

Thank you for buying this book and helping us improve the next edition.

For additional or bulk copies of Where to Live in Phoenix & the Valley of the Sun, go to www.WhereToLiveBooks.com.

To subscribe to Personal Real Estate Investor Magazine, go to www.PersonalRealEstateInvestorMag.com.

# FREE GIFT for Buying
## "Where to Live in Phoenix & the Valley of the Sun"

Just answer a few questions?
In return we have a gift for you. We will send you the next two issues
of Personal Real Estate Investor Magazine for FREE.
We will also send you updates on the next edition of
Where to Live in Phoenix & the Valley of the Sun.

**WHERE TO LIVE BOOKS**

Please fold here, tape or staple closed and mail.  No postage necessary

**WHERE TO LIVE BOOKS**

# Demystifying the Loan Process & Products

Alpine Mortgage has not provided the content of this section. It was independently researched and written by the editors of *Where to Live in Phoenix and the Valley of the Sun.*

## Finance First — Get Pre-Approved

Buying a house is all about how much you can afford, or are willing to spend on a property. Most of us calmly and rationally set a budget — then end up spending more for the home of our dreams.

Knowing how much you can or want to spend is the basis all of purchase decisions, especially your next home. It determines how big the house can be, what condition it will be in and where it will be located. Is it new, resale of a recent build or a refurb? Your ability to buy will normally consist of a deposit — money you have saved — and the credit necessary to obtain a mortgage.

## Get Pre-approved Financing For A Fast Start

In the Valley's fast-paced market, having a pre-approved loan is practically a necessity before a seller will consider your offer seriously. Loan pre-approval will reduce the chance of disappointment. It will enable you to make an offer for a house that is free of any "subject to finance approval" clause. If it is an auction you can be comfortable knowing how much you have to bid with.

There are three possible loan pre-approval states:

**A. Pre-qualified** — Lender has discussed your income, assets and your debt commitments. They now understand your ability to qualify for a specific loan amount. You do not have the money yet.

**B. Pre-approved** — Credit application and documentation has been submitted to the lender to meet very specific loan guidelines for the specific loan package. You still don't have the money to buy the house but you are closer.

**C. Approved** — A and B have occurred and lender has submitted the package into the loan underwriting process. The lender's underwriting officer has approved the loan subject to the borrower finding and entering into a contract for an approved property. This can shorten the time from contract to close from months to weeks. Now you are a credible buyer whose offers will be taken more seriously than someone in the earlier stages of this process.

Your ability to meet loan payments is only one factor in the underwriting and approval process. The bank needs to be satisfied that the property being offered for security is satisfactory. Depending on loan, they may need an appraisal by a certified appraiser, accepted by the lender.

So, once you know how much you can spend, you can go house hunting. Check our neighborhood information for house prices, to find out what areas or types of houses are best suited to your budget.

## Which Loan Product Best Suits You?

Loans come in a bewildering array of flavors. The difference in a loan offer is the based on the amount of risk the lender perceives. Risk is about three things:

1. Your credit score (plus income and assets).

2. The security offered by the property to be loaned against.

3. The amount of risk a banker/lender is willing to take against the fees to be earned in the deal.

This becomes the basis of what you and your house qualify for. This affects the nature of the loan and the offer a lender will finally make to you.

Most conventional lenders will lend up to 95 percent of a house's appraised value, sometimes more if conditions and fees merit this.

## The Loan To Value Ratio

The loan to value ratio (LTV) is the loan you and your property qualify for compared with the appraised value of the home you wish to buy. Every residential loan has a specific LTV limit. For example: With a 95 percent LTV loan on a home priced at

$150,000, you could borrow up to $142,500 (95 percent of $150,000.) The required down payment is $7,500. The LTV reflects the amount of equity the borrower has in a home. The higher the loan LTV the less the homebuyer has to pay as a deposit. So, to protect lenders against potential loss in case of default, higher LTV loans (80 percent or more) usually require mortgage insurance policies. If you are borrowing more than 75 percent of the purchase price, the lender will require mortgage protection insurance (PMI) in the event of you losing your income for some reason — injury, death or job loss.

## Visiting The Lender

Today there are many lending institutions that want to sell you a mortgage. Note — "sell you a mortgage." You are not going hat in hand to ask a favor. You are a customer. You are a valuable commodity. Expect to be treated like one. Lenders are always advertising special rates or conditions in the hope of netting new mortgage customers. Chances are you can obtain a mortgage from a traditional bank, a specialized mortgage bank and lender or through a mortgage broker. If you do business with a bank, you may take your day-to-day banking needs with you.

Check out the home loans your own bank has to offer then research the rest. Don't just compare interest rates and types of loans available but also charges for origination and processing a home loan. What are the other conditions? For example, can you make lump sum payments on a fixed interest loan without incurring pre-payment penalties? To top it off, consider which lender you feel best about — which one has given you good service and good advice.

Your lender will ask you to complete a credit application showing income and expenses, to determine how much money they think you can comfortably afford to repay.

## Types Of Loans

Consider which type of loan class suits your ability to pay and your lifestyle.

**15 or 30 Year Fixed Loans:** This is the most common type of loan that spreads regular payments over the term of the loan. Initially, a bigger portion of the payment is made up of interest and a smaller portion of the principal, but this reverses over time. The benefit of this type of loan is that it lets you budget well in advance with a set payment amount each month. These loans must meet specific requirements, as they are mortgage-backed securities underwritten by the federal loan guarantee plans that buy these mortgages. (Fannie Mae, etc.) The term differences are:

30-year loan — each monthly payment adjusts the ratio of interest to principal. For the first 23 years of the loan, more interest is paid than principal is paid down, meaning larger tax deductions. As inflation and costs of living increase, mortgage payments become a smaller part of overall household expenses.

15-year loan – the loan is usually made at a lower interest rate and equity is built faster because early payments pay more principal.

**Adjustable Rate Mortgages:** An adjustable rate mortgage (ARM) is a home loan that the interest rate is fixed for an initial time period (say three years) but can adjust according to the market rates in specified intervals. The advantages of an ARM loan is that payments increase or decrease on a regular schedule with changes in interest rates; increases subject to limits for the life of the loan. ARMs are linked to a specific index or margin. They are generally offered at a lower initial interest rate so monthly payments can be lower thus may allow the borrower to qualify for a larger loan therefore house purchase. An ARM makes sense if you are confident that your income will increase in the future or if you anticipate a move and are not concerned about potential increases in interest rates. Clearly an appreciating residential real estate market makes an ARM even more palatable.

**Interest Only:** Some lending institutions will allow you to pay just the interest and none of the principal, but usually only for a short period. These are typical of investor, construction or bridge loans. A bank or

lender typically makes these types of loans from their internal assets. This is called a portfolio loan. It is not sold on to Fannie Mae or other secondary market buyers.

**Composite Loan Products:** Some lenders offer essentially tailor-made loans that suit your particular circumstances, made up of a mix of different types of loan and interest. Check with your bank about this option.

**Hard Money Loan:** This is typically a very short-term loan lent at a interest rate as high as 18 percent for difficult projects or interim financing for investment properties.

The loan variety looks like this with the most popular in the center of the diagram:

## The Loan Sweet Spot

A single-family homeowner wants to be as near as possible to the center of this diagram to get the best terms and rates. If you decide to buy a duplex or triplex and live in one of the units as a buyer you begin to move away from the sweet spot where most homeowners are eligible for a Conventional, FHA or VA loan. (1, 2, & 3) If you are self-employed as so many individuals are, income documentation becomes more critical to getting the best terms and interest rates (4 & 5). Thereafter these loans become more security and risk-based and come with higher fees and interest rates to reflect the increased risk the lender perceives this loan and borrower appear to offer. Alpine Mortgage offers loan programs to suit nearly every home and borrower circumstance.

Chart 1

> The further a borrower is from the center box, the higher FICO score needs to be and the higher the down payment and interest rate can be. It serves the borrower or investor to be close to the center box as possible.
>
> *Thanks to Susie Mallory (602-290-9097) who inspired us to create this chart.*

Chart 1

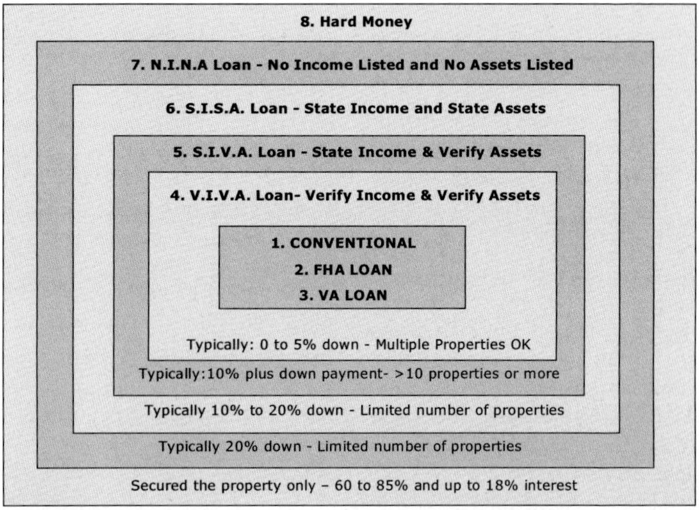

```
8. Hard Money
  7. N.I.N.A Loan - No Income Listed and No Assets Listed
    6. S.I.S.A. Loan - State Income and State Assets
      5. S.I.V.A. Loan - State Income & Verify Assets
        4. V.I.V.A. Loan- Verify Income & Verify Assets
            1. CONVENTIONAL
            2. FHA LOAN
            3. VA LOAN
          Typically: 0 to 5% down - Multiple Properties OK
        Typically:10% plus down payment- >10 properties or more
      Typically 10% to 20% down - Limited number of properties
    Typically 20% down - Limited number of properties
  Secured the property only – 60 to 85% and up to 18% interest
```

# ALPINE LENDING
## HOME LOANS

# HIGH RIS
## LOW PAYMENTS...

ALPINE LENDING SPECIALIZES IN HIGH RISE CONDOMINIUM PROGRAMS—CUSTOMIZED TO YOUR NEEDS, YOUR LIFESTYLE, AND YOUR BUDGET. WE PROVIDE YOU WITH A SIMPLER, FASTER, AND A MORE REWARDING MORTGAGE EXPERIENCE. PLUS, BY OFFERING OUR CLIENTS THE FULL SPECTRUM OF LENDING SERVICES, WE PROVIDE PURCHASING POWER THAT EXCEEDS OUR COMPETITORS AND AN ENTIRE STAFF DEDICATED TO EVERY DETAIL OF YOUR HIGH RISE MORTGAGE. ALPINE LENDING WILL SAVE YOU MONEY!

FAST, EASY, NO-HASSLE HIGH RISE CONDOMINIUM LOANS

- FULL AND STATED INCOME PROGRAMS
- FIXED & VARIABLE RATES AVAILABLE
- INTEREST ONLY LOANS AVAILABLE
- LOW FICO SCORE REQUIREMENTS

WE'RE IN THE BUSINESS OF BUILDING LIFELONG RELATIONSHIPS, SO WHEN WE SAY ALPINE LENDING PROVIDES THE BEST MORTGAGE EXPERIENCE; WE'RE WILLING TO PROVE IT.

## CALL TODAY FOR
# FREE
### CONSULTATION & LOAN ANALYSIS

# CALL ALPINE TODAY OR VISIT ALPINELENDING.COM
## PHOENIX, AZ 602.977.3926 • EAST VALLEY 480.214.0660 • WEST VALLEY 623. 487.1078

SPECIALIZING IN ARIZONA'S HIGH RISE LIFESTYLE LOCATIONS AND PHONE NUMBERS ALPINELENDING.COM

AZ BK# 904748          *All Programs are Subject to Credit Approval Interest Rates Subject to Change

# ellar Service
## FROM STELLAR TITLE!

Stellar Title is your complete solution for all your home financing settlement needs. Whether you are purchasing or refinancing your home, a realtor or lender, we can take care of it all.

Stellar Title will help you with purchases, sales, refinances of first or second mortgages, as well as judgments and liens.

Stellar Title is a national company with highly experienced people. We can produce your title commitments in 24 to 48 hours. Our closers and title staff are the best in the industry. We provide world class service, from the time we receive your order to our extremely quick title search and examination, through clearing the title and conducting the signing, receiving and disbursing funds, and the recording of documents, following the issuance of a title policy.

**GREAT CUSTOMER SERVICE, BILINGUAL CLOSERS, COMPETITIVE RATES**

- CLOSING AND ESCROW SERVICES
- PRELIMINARY TITLE REPORTS
- RECORDING SERVICE
- DOCUMENT PREPARATION
- NAME SEARCHES
- TAX SEARCHES
- ASSESSMENT SEARCHES
- OWNERS AND ENCUMBRANCES REPORTS
- ABSTRACTING
- TRACT SEARCHES
- LENDER'S TITLE INSURANCE
- OWNER'S TITLE INSURANCE
- COMMERCIAL AND RESIDENTIAL
- BILINGUAL ESCROW TEAM

**STELLAR TITLE**
ESCROW & TITLE SERVICES

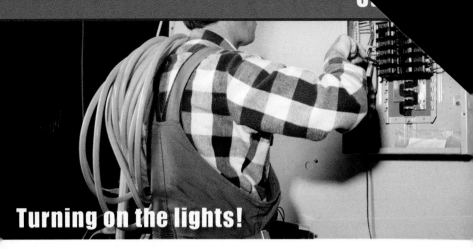

# Turning on the lights!

Welcome to Phoenix and the Valley of the Sun. If you are a normal resident you are going to want:

- Electricity
- Gas
- Phone (if you choose landline versus wireless)
- High-speed Internet
- Cable TV services
- Residential flood irrigation, and
- Water and other city services.

Unfortunately this is easy to say and just a little harder to do as no one vendor provides all of these services. The City of Mesa is an exception with electricity, gas, water, trash and sewer services delivered by one entity. Here is a list to help you get water, power and your utilities connected faster.

## Electricity

Phoenix and The Valley of The Sun is served by no fewer than three electrical utilities: One state, one federally chartered and one municipal service.

Most of the Valley is provided electrical services by the Salt River Project, (SRP). Arizona Public Service (APS) serves the major city centers, Central Phoenix, Central Scottsdale, Tempe, Glendale and Peoria, Chandler and Gilbert and western parts of the Valley. This is a legacy of a dated view municipal versus rural service. Now SRP has the lion's share of the geographic market, as

formerly rural areas have become the fastest growing communities in The Valley of The Sun. The City of Mesa is an exception as they provide electrical and gas services within a 5.5 square mile part of their municipal boundaries.

*Salt River Project – Residential Electric Service – 602-236-8888*
*www.srpnet.com*

*Arizona Public Service – 602-371-7171*
*www.aps.com*

*City of Mesa – Electric Service*
*480-644-2265*
*www.ci.mesa.az.us/utilities/electric*

## Gas

Luxury homebuyers prefer gas and will often pay to have their new or recently purchased homes equipped with gas. New build luxury and high-rise homes gourmet kitchens assume gas appliances. Electric doesn't provide the same cooking control or romance. If it is within a gas service area this is as easy as calling the local gas utility. The alternative, absent an existing gas utility, is installing a closed domestic gas system to heat the pool, the spa and cook steaks, all based on locally stored natural gas.

*Southwest Gas – 602-861-1999*
*www.SWGas.com*

*City of Mesa – Gas Service 480-644-2221 – www.ci.mesa.az.us/utilities/gas*

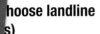

## ...hoose landline ...s)

...s ago this choice was ...trialists like Henry Ford: you could have a black phone or if you were very lucky, a white phone. You paid Ma Bell through the nose and were treated to rotten service. Today, choices are about more choices and more reasonable rates than our parents had. First are you choosing a landline or cell phone? If you choose a landline the predominant supplier of telephone service is Qwest, but you can buy phone service as part of your cable TV bundle. Long distance costs have dropped to a tenth of what our parents paid.

*Qwest – 800-491-0118*
*www.qwest.com/residential/newservice*

*Cox Cable – Phone Service*
*623-594-1000*
*www.cox.com/Support/Phoenix*

## High-speed Internet

When Internet connection is added to the mix, choices expand based on two technology types. DSL (Digital Services Line) or a cable modem from the cable TV company. Both are fine technologies but perform better in different environments. If you are close to the local telephone exchange, DSL works as well as cable Internet, but it is distance dependent. If you are out of DSL range, you may have no choice but cable for high speed Internet. If you can stand the pain, there is always dial-up!

**DSL – Internet**
*Qwest – 800-491-0118*
*www.qwest.com/residential/newservice*

**Cable Internet**
*Cox Cable – 623-594-1000*
*www.cox.com/HighSpeedInternet/*

Voice over the Internet (VoIP) is growing as an alternative to traditional (analog or digital) telephone services. VoIP is a high-speed Internet application. It is cheap or free and the voice quality is acceptable. Conversations cannot be asynchronous, where both parties to a call can talk at once and be heard. There is also limited or no 911 emergency service location ability.

## Cable TV

Cable TV has morphed from a necessity in areas with bad TV broadcast reception, to a luxury service and now to a necessity, all based on content and lifestyle inflation. The current trend is to buy bundled TV, high-speed Internet and telephone service all from one vendor. The cable companies have a huge advantage based on the cable media they use to distribute services. The phone companies are spending billions to upgrade, hold and expand their service. You choose the service, content and price benefits. The dominant supplier is Cox Cable with Cable America in Mesa, Queen Creek and other small parts of Maricopa County.

*Cox Cable – 623-594-1000*
*www.cox.com/HighSpeedInternet*

*Cable America – Mesa & Queen Creek*
*480-558-7260*
*www.cableamerica.com*

## Flood Irrigation

Flood irrigation is the ability to flood your yard with water provided by SRP Irrigation Services. You'll notice berms around your yard designed to contain the flood. If you are lucky enough to live in an older neighborhood with this feature, this irrigation process is more effective and cheaper than plumbing the yard for sprinklers.

*Salt River Project – 602-236-3333*
*www.srpnet.com*

## Water and other City Services

This is provided as part of a package of city services that includes water, trash pick-up and sewer services. This is dependent on your specific city.

# Best Condominium Locations in the Valley.

## ST★RPOINTE
### LUXURY CONDOMINIUM COMMUNITIES

COTTSDALE   NORTH & CENTRAL PHOENIX   CHANDLER   BILTMORE

## www.StarpointeProperties.com

*Building Homes, Building Values.*

*Phoenix*

# Phoenix

At its lowest ebb, about 25 years ago, Phoenix was a sea of decay dotted with manicured islands like Encanto-Palmcroft and the Phoenix Country Club. Homebuyers fled for the clean suburbs, fueling growth in the East Valley and Scottsdale. Good neighborhoods yellowed. Bad neighborhoods became modern Tombstones.

In the mid-1980s Phoenix died and came back stronger than before. The heart of the city was pierced when hundreds of historic homes were demolished to make way for Interstate 10. A belated but significant public outcry arose. Brave investors bought historic homes and renovated them. (People who bought places in Willo for $60,000 probably laugh themselves to sleep nowadays.)

Home tours and magazine features attracted attention. Prices began to tick upward. The America West Arena was built downtown, with the intention of reviving the city.

Art spaces like the Ice House poked their way downtown into large, cheap spaces. In the early 1990s, an alternative art foray meant having a cup of wine with a transient while you both watched a naked man roll around the floor wrapped in a bloody cow skin as a Goth chick sat on a stool reading aloud from "The Wreck of the Hesperus."

Now 10,000 people go to First Fridays and tour galleries at night, many of them fresh-faced teenagers from the suburbs.

## Home prices are climbing as people realize the convenience of living in the middle of the Valley

Arizona State University is building a downtown campus which will eventually enroll 15,000 students, many of them living downtown.

Downtown Phoenix now has chic wine bars, cafes, and restaurants. Advertising and public relations agencies moved offices to central Phoenix. A high rise living frenzy has seized the Central Corridor. Many neighborhoods are under renovation. Home prices are climbing as people realize the convenience of living in the middle of the Valley.

Some of the Valley's finest restaurants are in Phoenix. The city has massive mountain parks where you can climb a peak and sit in silence. It's a vast city, bigger than Los Angeles at 514 square miles, with 1.4 million people.

This also means anyone can find a house in Phoenix to suit any taste or budget. From mansions to golf course villas to Cotswold cottages to ranches, it's all here. Some people don't like Phoenix precisely because it's not a cookie-cutter subdivision with a homeowners association to govern aesthetics. Even though all the houses in Chandler are brown, at least none of them are purple.

In Phoenix, your neighbor can paint his house purple, and there's nothing you can do about it. The same goes for people who enjoy Christmas all year round, and decorate their homes accordingly. Find an agent who knows Phoenix, because there are thousands of fantastic homes, some tucked away on some not-so-fantastic streets. There are still scores of good buys in undervalued areas.

# Downtown Phoenix ★★★★★

B ack in 1990 tumbleweeds blew down Adams Street. Sixteen years later, those tumbleweeds have to wait 20 minutes in construction traffic.

Downtown Phoenix is the most vibrant area of a dynamic metropolis. More is happening here, more quickly, than anywhere else in the Valley. It will literally look completely different in two years.

Twenty-four high rises are planned or under construction. There are sleek glass-and-stainless lofts looking out over mountains and clouds, vast urban mansions with personal elevators, flats, multilevel layouts, tiny boutique projects with ten or eleven units which wouldn't look out of place in a Prada ad. The new lustrous spires join five existing towers, all of which offer great living.

ASU is building a downtown campus which will open in fall 2006 and eventually enroll 15,000 students. Downtown is the hub of the light rail system opening in 2008. Biotech labs and medical schools are clustering there. Thousands of people have already moved into the completed buildings, but the area's transformation is far from over.

Total Population: 19,500 approx.
Median Age: 36 years
Median Household Income: $31,000 p.a.

## Who Lives There?

Sophisticated, empty-nester, Baby Boomers who don't want to mow yards. Newlyweds. Hotshot bachelors. Gay singles and couples. Third-home owners who commute around the country. Baseball players. Medical and government workers. Kids whose parents bought them a loft. Gen Xers who want everything at their fingertips. City officials do not expect many students to live downtown, outside of the dorms. "They won't be able to afford it," one says.

## Homes

Everyone's definition of what constitutes a "loft" is different; not all are true urban lofts. There are flats, mid rises, and loft-style layouts, some multilevel. Buildings have concierges, rooftop gardens and swimming pools, maid's quarters, 22-foot ceilings, brick walls, private elevators, private gyms, gourmet kitchens, on-site chefs – there are buildings with amenities to pamper needs even the most demanding urbanites didn't know they had. Prices range from the low $200,000s well into the millions.

Bear in mind most of this isn't built yet. It's under construction. There are existing small pockets of historic houses, older condo complexes, and the luxurious five original towers like Crystal Point and Phoenix Towers.

## Amenities

### Schools ★★★

Public schools in Downtown Phoenix have improved dramatically in recent years, but standardized test results remain below average in the Phoenix Elementary and Phoenix Union High School Districts. A better option — if you can afford it — is one of the many outstanding private schools in the area.

Arizona School for the Arts is an "excelling" school for sixth through 12th students offering college preparatory and performing arts classes. Graduates have been accepted at Stanford, NYU, Vanderbilt and the Boston Conservatory.

Brophy College Preparatory is a Jesuit, all-boy high school. Ninety-nine percent

of the school's graduates pursue higher education, 97 percent at four-year universities. Next door is its sister school, Xavier College Preparatory. An all-girls Catholic high school, Xavier also excels academically. In the past 10 years, the school has had 82 National Merit Finalists.

### Shopping & Dining ★★★★

Pizzeria Bianco serves the best pizza in the United States, by decree of the New York Times. James Beard Award-winning Chef, Chris Bianco bakes pies in a wood-burning oven in a charming converted brick house off Washington and 7th Street. There's an

excellent wine bar next door while you wait for a table.

Seamus McCaffrey's is a rip-roaring old-fashioned Irish pub dubbed Shameless McCaffrey's by the cops, reporters, attorneys, and government workers who line the bar. It has a great nightlife on weekends, too.

Durant's is a Phoenix classic, opened by a shady character named Jack Durant more than 50 years ago. Walk in through the kitchen, sit at the long deep bar, sip a frigid martini, then have steak, stone crab and oysters. Not cheap, but unfailingly top-notch booze and food, and the best place in the city to spend a searing summer afternoon.

Shopping has yet to really appear downtown. The Arizona Center has a sorry array of stores, mostly selling Southwestern kitsch even a tourist from East Podunk wouldn't buy. The art galleries scattered around are great, but books, groceries and hardware haven't yet made their downtown debut. With millionaires and 15,000 students bearing down, it'll all come without fail. The nearest grocery store is a well-kept and well-stocked Safeway at 7th Street and McDowell.

## Leisure ★★★★

This is the sports and cultural mecca of Phoenix. From opera to baseball to concerts, it's downtown. And, if you're living there, you can walk to every last bit of it. The biggest stars are the America West Arena, Chase Field, the Herberger Theater, the Arizona Science Center, the Phoenix Museum of History, and the Heard Museum.

There are a few little-visited attractions downtown. The Japanese garden at Hance Park is fantastic. It's only open on Saturdays, for a $1 entrance fee. The state capitol is worth a quick look; go in and check out the massive ceremonial silver service from the USS Arizona engraved with the state's flora, fauna, and scenery. It was packed up before the war, thereby surviving the ship's destruction at Pearl Harbor.

The Heard Museum is world-renowned for its collection of art and artefacts from the native tribes of the American Southwest. The museum takes an integral look at Native American culture, incorporating the contemporary with historic perspectives. As a new Arizonan, start learning about your forebears here before visiting Cochise County or Monument Valley.

# Real Estate

## Trends

High rise lofts, apartments, and penthouses have been known to sell out within 18 hours. Some people have bought three $175,000 units and combined them to make a million-dollar home. The premium units are in highest demand. One development company redesigned their existing tower because premium units were coveted so highly by buyers. "The amount of people who want to be downtown is off the charts," one agent says. Existing places like the Artisan Lofts on Central are fully occupied. At last count about 3,000 people were on the waiting list for the Summit at Copper Square.

If you want to buy now, that's the bad news. However, announcements of new downtown buildings appear in the papers every day. How many of them will actually materialize remains to be seen. Consulting an agent who specializes in urban living and downtown is crucial. Some of them register with developers to be guaranteed units for their clients before public sales commence. They'll know the latest state of the marketplace and what's available.

## Rental & Investment

Investment in the new towers was capped at around 20 or 30 percent, so few rentals will be available when the new buildings are completed. If you want to rent and can find a loft or a condo in the existing high rises, expect to pay around $1,200 to $1,400 per month.

**Local Hero: Chris Bianco**

When New York Times food critic Ed Levine said if he could have just one pizza before dying it would be from Pizzeria Bianco (Heritage Square – Downtown) in Phoenix, a wailing and gnashing of teeth arose throughout the boroughs as Big Apple pie slingers cried foul.

Owner-chef, Chris Bianco, says the accolades also put the restaurant under closer scrutiny. "Every night is like a Broadway show," he says. "Yesterday's review is old news." He continues sweating the details and doing what feels right to him.

Chris and his partner Susan Pool opened Pane Bianco (Mid Central Village, at Campbell) two years ago to serve the lunchtime takeout crowd.

Chris visited the Valley for a vacation from New York 20 years ago. Something about Phoenix made an instant impression on him. The fact that he wasn't shovelling snow probably helped. "On that delusional January day, I had no idea how hot a dry heat really is," he says. He moved to Arizona two weeks later.

## Local Hero: Orpheum Theatre

The Orpheum Theatre is a local landmark which rose from the ashes. Built in 1929, the 1,364-seat Spanish Baroque Revival went from being the city's most glamorous night out to a crumbling vaudeville dump, to a Mexican movie theater, to an eyesore.

Then-Mayor Terry Goddard and the Junior League of Phoenix spearheaded a community effort to retain the architectural and historical integrity of the theater and helped place it on the National Register of Historic Places.

When Phoenix real estate tanked during the late 1980s, the flow of city as well as private money slowed to a trickle. The Orpheum's construction, as well as other cultural projects, was put on hold.

In 1990, then-Mayor Paul Johnson and the Phoenix City Council decided to incorporate the Orpheum into the construction plans for the new city hall to be built south of the theater.

Local business couple Delbert and Jewell Lewis headed fundraising activities which completed restoration of the elaborate interior. The Orpheum re-opened in January 1997 and now stages acts ranging from Dame Edna to Jethro Tull.

## At a Glance...

## House Prices

### Townhouses
| Bedrooms | |
| --- | --- |
| Price | $200,000 - $500,000 |

### Family home
| Bedrooms | |
| --- | --- |
| Price | $200,000 - $300,000 |

### Family home
| Bedrooms | |
| --- | --- |
| Price | $250,000 - $400,000 |

### Family home
| Bedrooms | |
| --- | --- |
| Price | $350,000 - $400,000+ |

### Executive home
| Area | Min. 4,000 sq. ft. |
| --- | --- |
| Price | $700,000 - $1,000,000 |

### The Summit at Copper Square
| Bedrooms | |
| --- | --- |
| Price | $379,000 - $539,000 |

### Stadium Lofts
| Bedrooms | |
| --- | --- |
| Price | $275,000 - $475,000 |

## Rentals

### Apartment
| Bedrooms | |
| --- | --- |
| Price | $900 - $1,300 month |

### Townhouse
| Bedrooms | |
| --- | --- |
| Price | $800 - $1,000 month |

### House
| Bedrooms | |
| --- | --- |
| Price | $900 - $1,200 month |

## Travel Times

Travel time to the airport
Peak: 10 – 15 minutes
Off Peak: 7 minutes

The Valley isn't all desert and mountains. Within the cores of the original cities lie neat green oases with lush lawns, elegant mansions with Mediterranean and Spanish roots, charming cottages from the English countryside, and roomy rambling ranches with 1960s Arizona cool. Four cities have designated historic neighborhoods. More – mostly post-war ranch and modernist areas – are under consideration.

Phoenix has 36 historic neighborhoods, Mesa has five, Scottsdale has two, and Glendale has one. Most of the historic districts are close to culture, nightlife, and sports venues. They're also close to the major employment centers, hence gloriously short commutes.

Most of these areas have annual home tours (pay a fee to spend an afternoon experiencing envy, guilt, and hopelessness). People have done some amazing restoration and renovation jobs. Not all historic homes have been completely renovated and priced accordingly. If you drive around Willo in Phoenix, you'll find few bargains, but Mesa and Glendale still have plenty of homes ready for creative drive and potential for capital gains. There are also plenty of areas within Phoenix which haven't yet been designated historic where attractive homes with good bones are waiting patiently behind layers

### Coronado
*Total Population: 6,300 approx.*
*Median Age: 31 years*
*Median Household Income: $35,000 p.a.*

### Encanto – Palmcroft
*Total Population: 1,000 approx.*
*Median Age: 38 years*
*Median Household Income: $77,000 p.a.*

### F. Q. Story
*Total Population: 2,800 approx.*
*Median Age: 32 years*
*Median Household Income: $31,000 p.a.*

### Willo
*Total Population: 2,000 approx.*
*Median Age: 40 years*
*Median Household Income: $58,000 p.a.*

of dead landscaping and wallpaper. If you're serious about renovating an historic home, look in areas adjacent to those already designated historic.

In many ways buying an historic house means investing in a very well-built old home which will always be in demand. Older homes were built with double brick walls, sound-resistant lathe and plaster, and raised wood floors which help heating and cooling. Many have high, curved ceilings, fireplaces, and gracious rooms. Most of the homes were custom-built; a street may be all Spanish Colonial Revival, but one home may have a turret entryway and another a stairway leading to a rooftop patio.

There are downsides. Kitchens weren't the focal point of life as they are now, so they're smaller, cozier. (This does not deter modern dinner guests from crowding in, however.) There aren't any walk-in closets – even wealthy people had less stuff than we have now – but clotheshorses find ways to surmount the problem. Rooms are smaller and swimming pools non-existent unless you build one yourself.

The tradeoffs are beauty, charm, individuality, quality construction, lush neighborhoods, and the feeling of being

## Smart Buy ✓

Agents recommend Garfield, Woodland, and Oakland/University Park to brave investors. The three areas are already designated historic, but they're also rough neighborhoods. Woodland and Oakland both have serious problems with homelessness, drugs, and crime. However, given the downtown renaissance, it's likely the market will drive the cleanup and restoration. Twenty years ago most of the restored historic areas looked like these three do today. It's well worth getting in there now.

in an oasis in the desert. Styles vary from Victorian to Bungalow, to Period Revival, to ranch across the Valley.

Phoenix led the charge to historic preservation in the 1980s when Interstate 10 was rammed through the heart of the city and hundreds of old homes were destroyed. Under then-Mayor Terry Goddard, the city established an historic preservation office in 1985. Roosevelt was the first area to earn the designation. They've become wildly popular across the Valley with everyone from artists, who want a Pueblo Revival with a sculpture garden, to antiquarians hunting for a Tudor Revival with built-in bookcases, to Scottsdale hipsters looking for a ranch to match that kidney-shaped coffee table. The following is a look at the four biggest historic districts in the Valley.

## Historic District Schools ★★★

The elementary schools of the historic neighborhoods tend to be some of the better schools in the Phoenix Elementary and Phoenix Union High School Districts. The Kenilworth primary school is "performing." Emerson and Lowell schools are "performing plus." The majority of teachers at these schools have more than 10 years of experience.

Many students in the historic neighborhoods attend North High School, a public school and International Baccalaureate (IB) magnet. Highly motivated students can participate in the IB program by taking an intense, pre-university course of study. In 2004, North had 62 National Merit Finalists, and two students have earned perfect scores on the SAT in recent years.

St. Mary's High School is another option. This co-ed Catholic school was founded in 1917 and has been at its present location at 3rd and Sheridan Streets since 1988. A three-story education center is scheduled for completion on campus in Spring 2007.

Coronado is the least expensive but most eclectic historic neighborhood. Built from 1900 to the 1930s, it has wide streets, small neighborhood markets, a large Sikh temple, and a funky tiny racquet club for tennis lessons. It's also unique in having more desert landscaping than any other historic district. A lot of artists live in Coronado. Many homes have accents like wall mosaics of colored glass and pottery or a motorcycle chopped and welded into a mailbox. The annual homes tour is well worth attending.

Some Coronado residents counter-commute to the East Valley or Scottsdale. The neighborhood association is active, organizing annual street fairs as well as the homes tour.

## Who Lives There?

East Coronado is predominantly Hispanic. The neighborhood has a large gay population. Occupations range from painters, editors, and set designers to hospital employees from Good Samaritan or the Grunow Clinic, to city and state employees who want to live close to work downtown, but not in a condo.

## Homes

Coronado has three architectural styles: Bungalow, Period Revival, and Ranch. Bungalows, the oldest, lie to the south where the neighborhood originated. Ranches are found near Thomas Road. House conditions range from gems to gems in the rough. Some blocks are universally charming, while others are spotty. Homes here tend to be smaller than Willo or Encanto because they were originally built for blue-collar families.

Renovated homes are usually in the $250,000 to $400,000 range, depending on size and features.

There are quite a few homes left for those with a yen to renovate. Expect to pay in the $150,000s for an unliveable bungalow ready for drywall and vision. Like Willo, some Coronado sellers milk the historic designation, asking $350,000 for a dumpy three-and-two 1,631 square foot ranch built in 1955.

# Real Estate

## Trends

Coronado has demonstrated excellent appreciation because people who can't afford Willo or Encanto buy there instead. Market forces will unquestionably complete Coronado's rejuvenation, but for the moment it's not as "done" as Willo.

Hunt around on the east and south sides of the neighborhood for lower-priced homes. Even homes in good condition are less expensive here than inferior homes in west Coronado.

# Encanto – Palmcroft  *Central Phoenix*

$S$ ome of the earliest fine homes in Phoenix were built – and still stand – in Encanto-Palmcroft. They remain some of the most stately homes in the country, rivalling anything in Southampton, Greenwich, or Charleston. Tall rows of palms stand at attention along the curving streets. Walkways lead across manicured lawns to carved stone door surrounds beneath wrought iron balconies. Encanto-Palmcroft is exclusive, romantic, and elegant.

The surrounding area's chic factor is soaring with antique shops and restaurants like My Florist, but not flashy enough to attract the Hummer-and-trophy-wife crowd. Residents couldn't care less about that sort of attention. Time stands still in Encanto-Palmcroft. This area has a quality no golf course or celebrity architect can ever bestow, no matter what the price tag.

## Who Lives There?

Encanto-Palmcroft residents tend to be in their 50s or 60s and at the top of their earning capacities. CEOs, doctors, and successful business owners live here, but the personalities are more eclectic than Arcadia. Your neighbor might be a wealthy Republican, as in Arcadia, but he enjoys collecting rare maps instead of golfing. Supreme Court Justice William Rehnquist was one prominent Palmcroft resident. Many residents have private security patrols watching over their precious homes.

## Homes

Design philosophy in the 1920s and 1930s integrated landscape with building in Encanto-Palmcroft. Curving streets slow traffic and create huge pie-shaped lots with interesting layouts. If it wasn't for the odd cactus, you'd never know you were living in the middle of a merciless desert.

Many Encanto-Palmcroft homes are two-story. Spanish Colonial Revival and Mediterranean Revival mansions dominate the area. Think Hollywood or the Petit Corniche in the 1930s: wrought iron railings and grilles, hand-forged hardware, trees in pots, Moorish tilework, demi-lune doors and windows. This is how silent film stars lived 70 years ago. You'll also find the odd ranch in there. Prices start in the high $600,000s and make deep forays into the millions

# Real Estate

## Trends

Buying in Encanto-Palmcroft is like buying in the Biltmore or Arcadia. The value of your home will never go down. These homes have set a standard since they were built. The really grand homes here rarely come up for sale, although there are smaller, single-story homes just as gracious towards the south end of the neighborhood which change hands more frequently.

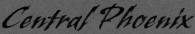

# Central Phoenix

# F.Q. Story

**F**.Q. Story is one of Phoenix's most manicured historic districts. Streets are lined with towering palms and canvas awnings top windows. What sets Story apart from other historic neighborhoods is its sense of whimsy. Large elegant homes often sport arty touches like custom chimney caps and window frames or driveways inlaid with plate fragments and license plates. Metal sculptures by Pete Deise are popular with Story residents. Artist John Peirce's Tudor Revival house is a neighborhood point of pride due to the five-foot winged copper dragon curling across the front porch, eyes glowing red at night.

## Who Lives There?

When Story was built it was popular with prominent Phoenicians (including a representative of the Anti-Saloon League). Now you'll find artists, antique dealers, architects, Realtors, and dentists in Story. It's also a family neighborhood with dogs and kids playing in yards. It's a tight neighborhood: there's a strong preservation association which stages the annual home tour, bestows a monthly visual award, and even has a welcoming committee.

## Homes

Story's 602 homes date to the late 1920s. When it was built it was marketed as a streetcar suburb close to the Grand Avenue and Kenilworth lines, the same way high rises tout proximity to the coming light rail system. Homes were laid out on deep, narrow lots to cut walking distance to streetcar lines. As the neighborhood spread west, cars became more common and homes started to feature detached garages and porte cocheres.

Architectural styles include Spanish Colonial Revival, English Tudor Revival, Craftsman bungalows and transitional ranch. Other Revival styles like English Cottage, Norman Cottage, Mediterranean, Pueblo, Mission, Neoclassical, Colonial and Art Moderne are all over the neighborhood.

Swimming pools are not unusual in Story.

## Real Estate Trends

When Story was built, there was a $5,000 minimum to build a home. Now, needless to say, you will pay much more dearly to live here. Low-end is $250,000 for a 1,200 square foot two-bedroom one bath. Typical prices are about $530,000 for a 1,900 square-foot four and two or $640,000 for a 2,231 square foot three and two.

Willo is one of the most spectacular historic neighborhoods. The lavish, spacious, and manicured homes are a bit more genteel than Coronado's blue-collar desert bungalows, lined along narrow streets shaded by arching trees. Interiors tend to match exteriors in terms of elegance. Historic code restrictions stop at the doorway and Willo's talented homeowners have often created jaw-dropping interiors. The firehouse blends right in, too.

An annual homes tour (for "those who do not have the privilege of living in our neighborhood," according to the noblesse-oblige-minded association) draws thousands every year. If you only go on one home tour, make it Willo's because it has excellent examples of the three major local residential architectural styles: Bungalow, Period Revival, and Ranch. Many homes have guest quarters.

## Who Lives There?

Some of the original owners from the 1920s and 1930s still live in Willo. There's a significant gay population. Other residents include sophisticated young couples, without children or with a baby, and finance and law professionals working on Central Avenue or downtown. The Willo staff car is a BMW sedan. Your neighbors are guaranteed not to park a truck on the lawn.

## Homes

Homes are smaller than Encanto-Palmcroft's, but larger than Coronado's. The earliest homes – Craftsman and California bungalows – are around McDowell Road. Heading north towards Thomas Road, Period Revivals – Spanish Colonial with grilles and arched doorways, Cotswold with wavy roofs, and Tudor with leaded glass windows and massive chimneys – dominate. Up by Thomas you'll find Art Moderne and International Ranches.

## Real Estate

### Trends

The fact that Willo home tours routinely get massive coverage in the newspaper does not help buyers. Willo sellers milk every inch of historic cachet mileage in their pricing. A nondescript three-and-two ranch towards the Thomas Road end of the neighborhood with a dead lawn goes for $200,000 more than it would in an ordinary neighborhood in North Phoenix.

A renovated home will cost considerably more. Here's a sample of what you might pay and what you might live in: mid to high $600,000s for a 1930s 1,700 square foot red brick, four bedrooms, one and three-quarter baths, formal living room, fireplace, 13 foot ceilings, fluted crown moldings, wood floors, and a big lot with a ramada in the backyard.

ZIP code 85003 has been first in appreciation in the entire metro Phoenix area. (Those numbers take into reckoning all the blight south of Interstate 10.)

## Coronado
## At a Glance...
### House Prices
**Family home**
Bedrooms
Price     $200,000 - $300,000

**Family home**
Bedrooms
Price     $200,000 - $350,000

**Family home**
Bedrooms
Price     $200,000 - $400,000

### Rentals
**House**
Bedrooms
Price     $800 - $1,200 month

## Willo
## At a Glance...
### House Prices
**Family home**
Bedrooms
Price     $250,000 - $400,000

**Family home**
Bedrooms
Price     $300,000 - $500,000

**Family home**
Bedrooms
Price     $300,000 - $650,000+

### Rentals
**House**
Bedrooms
Price     $1,000 - $1,500 month

## Encanto – Palmcroft
## At a Glance...
### House Prices
**Family home**
Bedrooms
Price     $200,000 - $400,000

**Family home**
Bedrooms
Price     $300,000 - $600,000

**Family home**
Bedrooms
Price     $500,000 - $900,000

**Executive home**
Area     Min. 4,000 sq. ft.
Price     $800,000 - $900,000

### Rentals
**House**
Bedrooms
Price     $1,000 - $1,500 month

## F.Q.Story
## At a Glance...
### House Prices
**Family home**
Bedrooms
Price     $250,000 - $350,000

**Family home**
Bedrooms
Price     $350,000 - $450,000

**Family home**
Bedrooms
Price     $400,000 - $500,000

### Rentals
**House**
Bedrooms
Price     $900 - $1,100 month

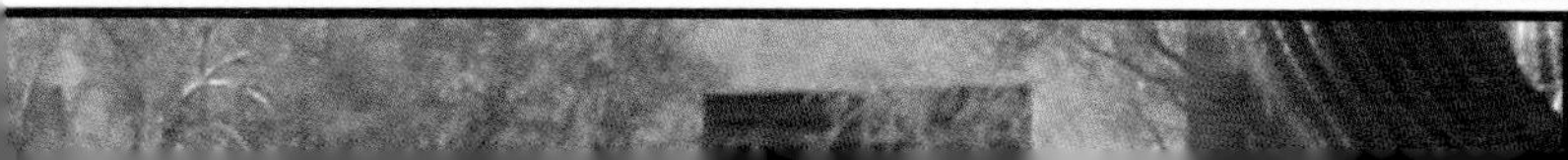

Nagaorth Central Avenue rivals any fine neighborhood in Paris or Vienna. Rows and rows of ash trees tower over canals and the gates of some of Arizona's most distinguished homes. A riding trail established when Wyatt Earp was Tombstone's sheriff, is used by women in jodhpurs today. The area doesn't look much different in historic photos than it does today. North Central isn't the Phoenix of the Wild West; this is the Phoenix of Model Ts, houses with striped awnings, swimming in the canals, and picnicking on the banks.

It's a two and a half mile-long historic streetscape running along Central Avenue from Bethany Home Road to the Arizona Canal. The city council recently placed the area on the city's historic property register, citing its 110 years of history and protecting it from "inappropriate" development. When a Cabinet member and the United States Senate's most powerful member live in your neighborhood, there's not a lot of danger of a check-cashing place or a tire store opening.

*Total Population: 13,000 approx.*
*Median Age: 42 years*
*Median Household Income: $66,000 p.a.*

## Who Lives There?

North Central is an old money bastion. People who grew up there – and who can blame them? – return and raise their own families in the big beautiful homes, sending them down the street to Xavier or Brophy.

Attorneys like the proximity to downtown. Former Arizona Governor, Secretary of the Interior, Grand Canyon champion, and northern Arizona rancher Bruce Babbitt lived off 2nd Avenue and Bethany Home Road for years. United States Senator John McCain and his wife Cindy have lived for years in her family mansion on North Central (although the couple are selling and ostensibly considering the Biltmore Estates). Those heavy hitters have made up the area's celebrity contingent. It's a low-key place, not like Paradise Valley, where you and Stevie Nicks pick up the morning paper in your bathrobes together.

"Unlike a lot of other areas like Arcadia and Paradise Valley, the people in North Central are older families," a resident says. "You see the same faces over the years."

The shady Murphy Bridle Path with its beautiful trees and century-old irrigation lateral serves walkers, joggers, strollers, and socializers as well as riders these days. The city of Phoenix owns and controls the right of way along the stretch. With the designation, the path on the east side of Central Avenue will not be paved over and the irrigation lateral on the west side of the road cannot be blocked. The ash trees are also protected. The North Central Phoenix Homeowners Association fought for the designation and won. The National Register of Historic Places also recognized North Central Avenue.

is all about private schools— and some of the Valley's best private schools at that.

Arizona School for the Arts is an "excelling" school for 6th through 12th grade students offering college preparatory and performing arts classes. Graduates have been accepted at Stanford, NYU, Vanderbilt and the Boston Conservatory.

Brophy College Preparatory is a Jesuit, all-boy high school. Ninety-nine percent of the school's graduates pursue higher education, 97 percent at four-year universities. Next door is its sister school, Xavier College Preparatory. An all-girls Catholic high school, Xavier also excels academically. In the past 10 years, the school has had 82 National Merit Finalists.

## Amenities

### Schools ★★★★

Although the Phoenix Elementary and Phoenix Union High School Districts have decent (at least "performing") schools in the neighborhood, North Central Avenue

## Real Estate

### Trends

Arizona Republican Sen. John McCain and his wife Cindy are selling their central Phoenix estate. The 11,000-square-foot home at Glendale and Central is listed for $4.25 million. Mrs. McCain grew up in the mansion. The home has been expanded and renovated. The gated estate sits on two acres, with a large guesthouse, nine bedrooms, eight bathrooms and plenty of security cameras. "The land alone is worth at least $2 million," the listing agent says.

## Smart Buy ✓

If you've got a lot of money and want to live in palatial splendor, North Central is a great buy. You can get twice the grandeur here as in Paradise Valley. No mountain views, but European-quality urban beauty is not a bad swap at all. Prices are climbing over $300 per square foot, but it's still a bargain luxury area.

## At a Glance...

### House Prices

**Townhouse**

| Bedrooms | 🛏 🛏 |
|---|---|
| Price | $200,000 - $300,000 |

**Family home**

Very few 2 bedrooms homes available in North Central Avenue

**Family home**

| Bedrooms | 🛏 🛏 🛏 |
|---|---|
| Price | $300,000 - $500,000 |

**Family home**

| Bedrooms | 🛏 🛏 🛏 🛏 |
|---|---|
| Price | $750,000 - $850,000+ |

**Executive home**

| Area | Min. 4,000 sq. ft. |
|---|---|
| Price | $750,000 - $4,000,000+ |

### Rentals

**Apartment**

| Bedrooms | 🛏 🛏 |
|---|---|
| Price | $1,100 - $1,400 month |

**Townhouse**

| Bedrooms | 🛏 🛏 |
|---|---|
| Price | $1,000 - $1,300 month |

**House**

| Bedrooms | 🛏 🛏 🛏 |
|---|---|
| Price | $1,200 - $1,400 month |

### Travel Times

Distance to downtown Phoenix: 8 miles

To downtown Phoenix:
Peak 15 minutes
Off-peak 10 minutes

To the airport:
Peak 30 minutes
Off-peak 20 minutes

East Phoenix is the land of hidden treasures. Even if you've lived there for decades, you'll still run across charming houses you've never seen before. Grand executive golf course homes on Lincoln Drive, luxurious estates tucked back along the Camelback corridor, 1920s bungalows, English Tudors, Spanish Colonial Revival mansions, chic and sleek new condos and rambling ranches.

It's a verdant area because it's so strongly established. Trees are tall, lawns are lush, and oleander hedges top 15 feet. Desert landscaping is mature, too; shady mesquites and palo verde trees, big stands of organ pipe and Mexican fence post cacti.

For these reasons and many more, East Phoenix has become much more popular in the past decade. The area becomes less expensive from north to south. Camelback Road prices are rocketing up on Thomas Road. Gentrification is hitting southwest east Phoenix and other areas. The downtown high rise boom, light rail's debut in two years, and the city's commitment to building a downtown ASU campus are all expected to increase demand to live in the heart of the Valley.

Total Population: 78,000 approx.
Median Age: 33 years
Median Household Income: $36,000 p.a.

## Who Lives There?

The bright lights of the Camelback corridor are drawing a hip crowd away from the new cool of Scottsdale towards the original cool of Phoenix. There are sun-spotted, bolo tie-wearing old Phoenicians who don't know what to make of their new black-clad neighbors who come home at four a.m. There is a significant Hispanic population: piñata makers, taco shops, carnicerias, and tire shops line some streets. They're surprised to see young white couples wearing Abercrombie & Fitch at the Ranch Market. East Phoenix has the Valley's largest gay population, mainly in the Roosevelt, Coronado, and Willo historic neighborhoods. North of Camelback Road is quiet, old money.

# East Phoenix

## Homes

At Squaw Peak latitude, homes are large, beautiful, and expensive. From there to Camelback Road, golf course estates and 3,000 square-foot plus showplaces sit on desert ridges and astride horse properties. From Camelback to Indian School Road you'll find luxurious and well-landscaped town home and patio home complexes. To the east, large ranches and custom homes characterize the streets. From 32nd Street to 16th Street, ranches and a few Spanish Colonial Revival homes are the norm.

Ranches built in the 1950s, 60s, and 70s run from Indian School Road to Roosevelt Street and between State Route 51 and Central Avenue. In the southeast section of east Phoenix you'll see bungalows and territorial homes mixed in with older, smaller ranches. Southeast around McDowell Road is largely Hispanic. Older block and brick ranch homes on large lots here are good starters, but are not undervalued.

Most of East Phoenix's historic neighborhoods lie between 16th Street and Central Avenue. They tend to be pretty well picked over and renovated by now (east Coronado off 16th Street has some opportunities left, however).

## Amenities

### Schools ★★★★

Two school districts serve East Phoenix. The first is the Balsz School District, which has three of its five campuses in East Phoenix — Brunson-Lee, Griffith, and Orangedale Elementary Schools for kids from pre-kindergarten through eighth grade.

The remaining schools belong to the Scottsdale Unified District. Hopi Elementary School is an "excelling" school that prides itself on integrating technology into its core curriculum areas. Like Hopi, Tavan Elementary students attend through fifth grade when they move on to Ingleside Middle School for sixth through eighth grade. Ingleside is also an "excelling" school, was awarded the National Blue Ribbon of Excellence in 2002, and has had finalists in both the Arizona Spelling Bee and Arizona National Geography Bee.

High school students attend Arcadia High School, also an "excelling" school. In addition to academics, the school has a good athletics program. More than 50 percent of the student body participates in athletics on some level. Arcadia is noted for its communication and broadcasting program, with a TV studio and film editing rooms. Arcadia is also known for its unique, wheel-shaped classroom building. In 2005

it underwent extensive remodelling and upgrading.

## Shopping & Dining ★★★★

Camelback Colonnade mall has a Best Buy, Marshall's, and a great discount designer shoe store. Town and Country across the street has a gym, Trader Joe's grocery store, Kinko's, Bookstar, and a home store. Junkers love the second-hand stores all over east Phoenix. Some good, rare and second-hand bookstores are in strip malls.

Great restaurants rule this side of town. Everyone's got a favorite place they've been going to since before air conditioning was invented. Here are a few:

Red Devil Pizza on McDowell has been loved for decades. La Grande Orange on Campbell is a chic neighborhood grocery with wood fired pizza, salads, and beautiful cakes. Go to Stanley's Polish Deli at 22nd Street and McDowell for an amazing sub and Eastern Bloc customer service. Delhi Palace, also on McDowell is the Valley's best Indian restaurant. Finally, we can't resist singing the praises of Richardson's at 16th Street and Bethany Home Road: stunning, authentic and consistent Southwestern food - and $20 for any bottle from their excellent cellar during happy hour.

## Leisure ★★★★★

Phoenix's original subdivision is at 46th Street and Washington in East Phoenix. Pueblo Grande is the ruins of a 1,500 year-old Hohokam village. A trail leads around

an enormous platform mound possibly used for ceremonies, along an excavated ballcourt (the Hohokam were vehement sports fans), alongside the last intact prehistoric canals, and by reproductions of prehistoric homes. No word on whether canal views started in the three macaws.

The intersection of 24th Street & Camelback has a great night life. There aren't any dance clubs, but chic watering holes like the Merc Bar have a fun, attractive crowd and a paucity of bratty 20 year-olds. Retreating to the blue-collar bars on Indian School can be a good night out too.

Papago Park is a natural Stonehenge of massive lumpy orange buttes sitting on a ridge with horizon-to-horizon views – a romantic picnic spot. If romance isn't happening, bring a hundred feet of static line and rappel instead. The city erased the road out to the buttes a few years ago, improving the park's experience. There's also fishing lagoons, bike paths, the Phoenix Zoo, the Desert Botanical Garden and a nicely priced public golf course.

The newest hit for kids is the Stuffington Bear Factory on Thomas Road, rather

severely described in company literature as an "education-oriented stuffed animal factory." Kids learn about the teddy bear's invention and habits of Arizona black bears, then get to make their own bears.

# Real Estate

## Trends

Buying teardowns has been the biggest trend in recent times. Pre-1970 lots tend to be big – 20 times more yard than you'll get in Chandler or Gilbert. Razing debilitated vintage homes and building larger custom homes has been particularly popular around north Central Avenue and North East Phoenix areas like Camelback Road to Northern around 16th Street. Agents recommend buying homes on those large lots even if you plan to renovate instead of tear down because the value of the land will stay strong.

## Rental & Investment

Properties of any type in this area are likely to be good investments because of light rail, ASU, and increasing density plans. Condos and townhomes for rent are rare. Rents range between $650 to $1,200 a month. Homes are more plentiful, ranging from about $750 for a two-bedroom cottage to $1,300 for a three-bedroom. The best way to find a rental house here is to drive around neighborhoods you'd like to live in and look for the signs. Apartment complexes are plentiful; take your pick of historic duplex or rat-maze with swimming pool and volleyball court.

## Smart Buy ⊘

East Phoenix seems a great buy in general for anyone. The schools are good and neighborhoods are diverse in types and prices. Plus it's got the added bonus of being close to Scottsdale fun.

## At a Glance...

### House Prices

**Townhouse**

| Bedrooms | 🛏 🛏 |
|---|---|
| Price | $150,000 - $300,000 |

**Family home**

| Bedrooms | 🛏 🛏 |
|---|---|
| Price | $150,000 - $250,000 |

**Family home**

| Bedrooms | 🛏 🛏 🛏 |
|---|---|
| Price | $400,000 - $500,000 |

**Family home**

| Bedrooms | 🛏 🛏 🛏 🛏 |
|---|---|
| Price | $400,000 - $600,000 |

**Executive home**

| Area | Min. 4,000 sq. ft. |
|---|---|
| Price | $1,000,000 - $1,500,000 |

### Rentals

**Apartment**

| Bedrooms | 🛏 🛏 |
|---|---|
| Price | $900 - $1,100 month |

**Townhouse**

| Bedrooms | 🛏 🛏 |
|---|---|
| Price | $650 - $1,800 month |

**House**

| Bedrooms | 🛏 🛏 🛏 |
|---|---|
| Price | $1,300 - $1,800 month |

### Travel Times

Distance to downtown Phoenix (from Indian School Road & 40th Street):

7.5 miles

To downtown Phoenix:

Peak: 16 – 20 minutes
Off-peak: 12 minutes

To the airport:

Peak: 10 – 15 minutes
Off-peak: 8 minutes

"Fair Arcadia, beneath the slopes of steep Kyllene," Homer wrote in the Iliad's catalog of ships. He may well have been writing about Arcadia beneath Camelback.

This is a breathtaking neighborhood. Oleander hedges and chorus lines of manicured palms tower over lush emerald lawns. Orange blossoms perfume the air in spring, beneath Camelback Mountain's jagged hump towering above.

Everyone living in Arcadia (and quite a few who don't) argue about its boundaries. At our own risk, we'll call it from 44th Street to 64th Street and from Camelback Mountain's southern slopes to Indian School Road.

Sprawling old postwar ranches with lavish yards are Arcadia's trademark. A trend in recent years has been to buy the 1950s and 1960s ranches, tear them down, and build something more contemporary. Arcadia is the best in classic Phoenix living. Sitting out by the pool under an orange tree, gazing at the mountain in moonlight, Arcadia casts a spell like no other neighborhood in the Valley of the Sun.

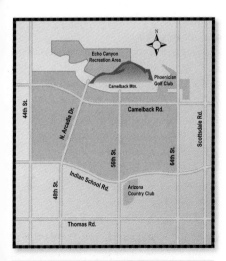

Total Population: 9,000 approx.
Median Age: 40 years
Median Household Income: $76,000 p.a.

## Who Lives There?

Arcadia has always been one of the bastions of old Phoenix money. That's changed a bit in the past decade or so, but it's still quiet money. Judges, doctors, law partners, and corporate chieftains all call Arcadia home. The difference between Arcadia and Paradise Valley is that Paradise Valley tends to have more wealthy people who are retired. Arcadia people get up in the morning and go run things. Arcadia wives go to Pilates at The Village sports club, then run the canal.

World's most famous Arcadian? Blockbuster Hollywood director Stephen Spielberg grew up at 3443 North 49th Street.

## Homes

The traditional Arcadia home is a four or five bedroom 1950s or 1960s ranch surrounded

by citrus trees. Swimming pools, old-growth landscaping, and enormous lots are the norm. Many homes have guest houses. Almost no one has desert landscaping in Arcadia. The neighborhood began as orange groves; tearing out citrus won't win friends with neighbors. Trees and greenery keep the neighborhood noticeably cooler in summer.

Although Arcadia is almost all single-family homes, there are a few beautiful townhouse complexes along Camelback Road and along the Arizona Canal by Indian School Road.

# Amenities

### Schools ★★★★

Arcadia schools score highly on the state's five-tier rating system. Arcadia parents

frequently hold fundraisers for the district, and the schools are well-equipped. The kindergarten through eighth grade Arcadia Neighborhood Learning Center, with advanced studies, comes in next to the top as "highly performing." Tavan Elementary and Ingleside Middle School are rated "highly performing."

### Shopping & Dining ★★★★★

Arcadia is almost entirely residential, so the only places to dine in the neighborhood proper are restaurants at The Phoenician and the Royal Palms Resort & Spa. Both are rated among the top 100 hotels in North America. Think triple figures for dinner for two with wine.

There is nowhere within Arcadia to pop in for a blue plate special. The closest place for that is the Original Pancake House on Camelback Road in Scottsdale. Great pancakes and crepes, but also lots of rules forbidding almost any behavior except eating quietly. Break them at your risk; the staff could send Seinfeld's soup Nazi yelping out the door.

For groceries, AJ's Fine Foods anchors a nice old shopping center at 44th Street and Camelback Road. There's also a Blockbuster, a tailor, hair salon, charming bakery/bistro, and a sports bar with $50 Scotches. Cork & Cleaver is an old favorite beef and booze place in the same

complex, favored by people having affairs and old men in pressed Oxford cloth shirts who drink expensive liquor and eye the gorgeous waitresses.

## Leisure ★★★★

Arizona Falls is a natural 20-foot drop along the Arizona Canal and Indian School Road between 56th and 58th Streets. Back in the 1890s, the falls were a big local gathering point for dances and picnics. The falls were covered for decades by a hydroelectric housing. Now they are the focal point of an amazing public art project.

Visitors can sit on large boulders enjoying the boom of the falls, surrounded by

Arizona Falls

### Why I live there

### Jenny and Jim Kurtzman

Jenny, a sales manager, is an Arcadia native. Jim, a construction executive, is from the Midwest. Homes in their area are low-slung comfortable roomy old Phoenix ranches, with views of Camelback Mountain from verdant backyards ringed with oleander hedges.

Jenny: "There's everything we need here. It's a nice residential area, but we have all the amenities of a big city. It just feels like a nice little area. Our neighbors Marge and Milo are 80, and they've lived here since 1959. In this neighborhood you have the older people who are still here and the younger couples who are moving in. There are more kids than there were five years ago. I really like that we can jump on the freeway and go anywhere.

Jim: "These houses have character. There's a history here. Most of the people who are remodeling them are keeping that ranch-style flavor: modernizing a little bit, but keeping that same feel."

water on three walls in the water room. Sheets of water fall over antique gears used in the original hydroelectric plant. Two aqueducts frame the water room and create the feeling of being inside the historic waterfall.

Shemer Arts Center is one of the places that make Phoenix special. It's a big beautiful old house with galleries, a permanent collection, exhibits and music performances, and arts classes. On the corner of Arcadia Drive (50th Street) and Camelback Road, the city runs this family-oriented institution with traditional and non-traditional work.

# Real Estate

## Trends

Demand for Arcadia has always been high. Current conditions are no different, and the area remains a seller's market. Teardowns are the latest trend; buyers with deep pockets demolishing old ranches and building lavish new homes.

## Look Out! ⓘ

About five years ago a new crowd moved into Arcadia for the verdant greenery and lovely citrus: roof rats. They ate oranges and lemons, raised families in attics, and infested oleander hedges. The neighborhood banded together, cleaned up fallen fruit, laid bait, and manicured landscaping. (A satirical Save the Roof Rats campaign also sprang up.) While the rats have moved on to other areas, they've become inextricably associated with Arcadia. If you're thinking about buying there, give your agent a heart attack and ask about them.

## At a Glance...

## House Prices
### Townhouse
Bedrooms
Price $300,000 - $400,000
### Family home
Bedrooms
Price $300,000 - $500,000
### Family home
Bedrooms
Price $500,000 - $600,000
### Family home
Bedrooms
Price $1,000,000 - $2,000,000
### Executive home
Area Min. 4,000 sq. ft.
Price $2,000,000 - $4,000,000

## Rentals
### Apartment
Bedrooms
Price $900 - $2,200 month
### Townhouse
Bedrooms
Price $900 - $1,500 month
### House
Bedrooms
Price $1,500 - $2,000 month

## Travel Times
Distance to downtown Phoenix: 8 miles

To downtown Phoenix:
Peak: 15 minutes
Off-peak: 10 minutes

To the airport:
Peak: 15 minutes
Off-peak: 10 minutes

including Taliverde, Biltmore Greens, and Colony Biltmore

The relationship between the legendary Arizona Biltmore and its surrounding neighborhood is a bit like that between the Tower of London's ravens and Britain: the neighborhood has always maintained its status because the resort has thrived. Set on 39 acres at the foot of the Phoenix Mountain Preserve, the Biltmore accommodates 738 guests and boasts eight swimming pools, seven tennis courts, an 18-hole putting course, and a full service European spa.

The area does appear charmed, as if the endless lawns manicure themselves and dead leaves fly elsewhere to drop. A gilded mystique emanates from the hotel. "If the Cloisters were on the other side of 24th Street, they'd be just another apartment complex," one agent says. Probably, but they're in a neighborhood that every sitting President since 1929 has visited.

The neighborhood is the Grande Old Dame of Phoenix in a couple of other respects too: you're going to pay dearly to experience it, and it's going to be worth every penny.

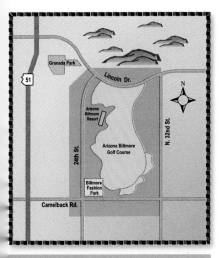

*Total Population: 2,500 approx.*
*Median Age: 54 years*
*Median Household Income: $87,000 p.a.*

## Who Lives There?

Local resident and radio personality Paul Harvey sometimes tells the end of his stories wearing pyjamas in his upstairs circle studio. Anaheim Angels owner Artie Moreno also lives on the circle estate surrounding the Adobe Golf Course. Doctors, professional athletes, powerful politicos, publishers, major real estate brokers, and similar movers-and-shakers all live in the Biltmore Estates. The rich and newly-separated wait out divorce proceedings in the Cloisters and the Meridian condos.

## Homes

Secluded, old world Spanish Colonial Revival estates, gracious golf course patio homes, and leafy condo complexes

with courtyard fountains are all typical Biltmore dwellings.

The neighborhood is bordered by Camelback Road to the south, Lincoln Drive to the north, 24th Street to the west, and 32nd Street to the east. The resort and the 18-hole Adobe Golf Course lie in the middle like a donut hole.

Estate homes on the old money circle start at around $3 million. A teardown on the circle, if you're lucky enough to find one, costs about $2 million. (If you're looking for 3,000 square feet anywhere in the Biltmore area, it's not available under $1 million.)

Homes in gated Taliverde on the eastern side cost from about $700,000 to $1.4 million, depending on size and how much remodelling has been done to the property.

In the northeast, a 1,700 square-foot fix-up home in the Biltmore Greens costs from $650,000 to $1.2 million. Two-bedroom patio homes run between $600,000 to $700,000.

Colony Biltmore patio homes are priced between $500,000 to $750,000, more if they look out on a golf course.

# Amenities

### Schools ★★★★★

Biltmore-area students begin their academic careers in the Madison School District. Of the seven schools in this district, five are ranked as either "highly performing" or "excelling" schools. In 2004, Madison School District eighth graders ranked fourth in reading, first in writing, and sixth in math on the AIMS test compared to eighth graders at other Maricopa County schools.

Students continue their education at Camelback High School, one of the 13 high schools in the Phoenix Union High School District. Camelback has a Junior ROTC program and an indoor shooting range. Students can take advanced placement, gifted and honors classes.

### Shopping & Dining ★★★★★

The outdoor Biltmore Fashion Park has always been a genteel place to shop. Brick walkways, tinkling fountains, and glossy people carrying glossy bags from Williams-Sonoma, Gucci, and Saks Fifth Avenue. There's also a Borders Books & Music, Macy's, and Polo Ralph Lauren. A massive makeover started in 2005 will give the retail buildings urban flair and restore the landscaping.

Wright's, the resort's signature restaurant, is rightfully celebrated. One Taliverde resident bought his house in the neighborhood just so he could walk to the hotel for dinner. Down in the Biltmore Fashion Park, Christopher's Fermier Brasserie serves excellent French food; great wine flights, too. Capital Grille is the new cool spot in the area for beef and booze; think oil paintings of men in wigs and mounted animal heads.

## Leisure ★★★

Needless to say, you won't find a go-cart track in the area. All activities here involve legwork: golf, hiking, and jogging.

Golf rules the Biltmore Estates, and the hotel has two 18-hole courses. The 50 year-old Adobe has stately fairways and a spacious layout. The Links is newer and more challenging.

Squaw Peak's jagged spire beckons hikers to the north. Runners can enjoy jogging beside the Arizona Canal's glassy waters.

# Real Estate

## Trends

Nothing here will ever go down in value according to the pundits. "It's bubble-proof, because it's so totally unique," one Realtor says. Prices here can be celestial. On the Circle, prices reach about $5.9 million for a five-bedroom estate with three fireplaces and $2.5 million for a six-bedroom with two guest houses.

## Rental & Investment

Del Prado, on the southeast side, rents run at about $970 per month for a two-bedroom apartment. It was built in the 1970s, but is very well-maintained. Residents say the best aspect is the quiet. Condos and single-family homes are available for rent, usually through brokers. Rental homes are scarce to non-existent.

## Local Hero – The Arizona Biltmore Hotel

The Biltmore opened in 1929 and was immediately crowned "The Jewel of the Desert." Frank Lloyd Wright inspired its unique design. In 1930 chewing gum magnate William Wrigley Jr. became its sole owner. For the next 43 years, the Wrigley family owned and operated the Biltmore.

It has always been popular with the rich and famous. In the early years well-to-do easterners spent the winter there, amusing themselves with parties and dances. Ronald and Nancy Reagan honeymooned here, Clark Gable golfed, Marilyn Monroe swam in the pools, and Irving Berlin penned "White Christmas" poolside. Other famous guests include Frank Sinatra, Dean Martin, Sammy Davis Jr., Liza Minelli, Bing Crosby, Spencer Tracy, Harpo Marx, Carole Lombard, Ava Gardner, and Tony Bennett.

For golfers, the adjacent Arizona Biltmore Country Club offers two 18-hole PGA golf courses. It has four restaurants, including Wright's, and serves afternoon tea.

You don't have to be rich or famous to enjoy the Biltmore. Many Phoenicians have special memories of celebrations of all kinds hosted at the Biltmore. It's a Phoenix original. It's aged, but looks and acts like a youngster.

## At a Glance...

### House Prices

**Townhouse**
Very few townhouses available in Biltmore Estates.

**Family home**
| | |
|---|---|
| Bedrooms | |
| Price | $500,000 - $600,000 |

**Family home**
| | |
|---|---|
| Bedrooms | |
| Price | $600,000 - $800,000 |

**Family home**
| | |
|---|---|
| Bedrooms | |
| Price | $700,000 - $1,300,000 |

**Executive home**
| | |
|---|---|
| Area | Min. 4,000 sq. ft. |
| Price | $3,000,000 - $8,000,000 |

### Rentals

**Apartment**
| | |
|---|---|
| Bedrooms | |
| Price | $1,000 - $1,500 month |

**Townhouse**
| | |
|---|---|
| Bedrooms | |
| Price | $1,500 - $2,500 month |

**House**
| | |
|---|---|
| Bedrooms | |
| Price | $2,000 - $3,000 month |

### Travel Times

Distance to downtown Phoenix: 7 miles

To downtown Phoenix (via State Route 51):
Peak: 25 minutes
Off-peak: 12 minutes

To the airport (via State Route 51 & the Loop 202 Freeway):
Peak: 25 minutes
Off-peak: 12 minutes

Welcome to west Phoenix, a real taste of the Old West. You're not in the Green Zone anymore. Every big city has bad areas. Statistically there may be more crime in East Phoenix, but anecdotally and visibly West Phoenix wins hands-down. Watch the evening news five nights in a row. The demented old lady living with 80 dogs, the biker cooking meth with 300 rifles and a human skull in his house – it all happens in the avenues.

That's the bad news. The good news is, it's not all bad. There are big chunks of West Phoenix which are showcase neighborhoods – like everything east of Interstate 17.

In the rest of the area, you can find some great houses and nice streets here and there. Overall though, bad-tempered single men who own large dogs, brave and childless couples, fearless investors, wannabe superheroes, or those who want to live cheaply and hone their combat skills should check it out.

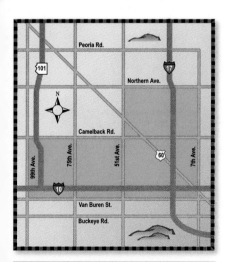

Total Population: 43,000 approx.
Median Age: 27 years
Median Household Income: $34,000 p.a.

## Who Lives There?

This is a blue-collar area. Those without blue collars have blue teardrops tattooed below their eyes. What the *%&# are you looking at?

## Homes

Everything east of Interstate 17 is excellent. Many historic neighborhoods like Willo, FQ Story, Encanto-Palmcroft are nearby. The neighborhoods which are not historic in this area are great as well. There are many lovely homes of different styles and it's a quiet area. Local people who ignore the west side stigma because they know better, and out- of-state people who just know they've found a superb house, buy here.

West of Interstate 17, from Northern Avenue south to Camelback Road, is also

a very nice area with well-kept, attractive homes. Big clean brick ranches with clipped lawns, oleander hedges, and swimming pools, Art Moderne bungalows and English Cottage styles.

South of Camelback the area goes medieval in a hurry. Junk stacked on porches, laundry hanging in carports, shopping carts in yards, BEWARE OF THE DOG signs – it gets even worse closer to Interstate 10, where the aforementioned features actually characterize the better areas. These neighborhoods can look a

little sleepy during the day. If somehow you've become convinced to buy here, drive to the property at 10 p.m. and have another look. Make sure you have 911 on speed dial and the phone in your hand.

## Amenities

### Schools ★★

Although several school districts lay claim to West Phoenix, Alhambra Elementary District, Phoenix Union High School District, Isaac Elementary District, and Cartwright Elementary District are the most prominent. The schools of West Phoenix may be in different districts, but most share common elements — low standardized test results, schools in and out of improvement and corrective statuses, and a high percentage (over 75 percent in most schools) of Hispanic students, many of whom speak English as a second language.

Schools in West Phoenix often do not follow the traditional grade level groupings. Depending on the district, there might be K-5, K-3, or K-8 schools. Cartwright Elementary District even has four separate sixth grade schools. Keep this in mind when considering neighborhoods

because the closest school may not have the appropriate grade level for your child.

One bright note in West Phoenix schools is the traditional school. Both Alhambra Traditional School and Magnet Traditional School are "excelling" schools that emphasize a back-to-basics approach. Although it doesn't have "traditional" in it's name, Palm Lane Elementary School is also a traditional school offering a back-to-basics approach. This school is "performing plus."

## Shopping, Dining & Leisure ★

Unlike North Scottsdale, the west side has a lot of bars which open at 8 a.m. The State Fair is held here every fall. It's a sociological wonderland that everyone should experience (maybe just once) because it challenges the conventional law of evolution. Finally, there's roller derby at the Castle Sports Club: punk rock, beer in plastic cups, and girls in miniskirts beating the hell out of each other.

Seventh Avenue has become an antique and junk enclave during the past decade. It joins Scottsdale and Glendale in the Second-Hand Triple Crown. In general, the furniture and knick-knacks here have a hipper edge than those other areas.

Fish and chip places, taquerias, pizza and wings – you make the call. This ain't the Ritz.

# Real Estate

## Trends

To the many West Phoenix residents who do care, we apologize in advance; your efforts and flowerbeds stand out. Eventually, years from now, sprawl will pressure land values here to the point that redevelopment is inevitable and these neighborhoods will see dramatic improvements. That time is not now.

## Rental & Investment

There are plenty of apartment complexes, enormous rat mazes off the Black Canyon Freeway lit by police helicopters at night. If the neighborhoods are bad, the apartment complexes are even worse,

rife with methamphetamine, shootouts, child abuse, and domestic violence. The latest trend is entire complexes being evacuated by hazmat and SWAT teams because a resident's hobby is do-it-yourself bioweapons or explosives. If you have to live here, a two-bedroom costs between $500 to $600 per month.

## Smart Buy ⊘

Homes in the good areas (see Homes above) have ridden the same wave of appreciation as similar quality neighborhoods in other areas. Don't write the entire area off; attractive streets are plentiful north of Camelback and east of Interstate 17. It's not like Scottsdale, East Phoenix, or Chandler, where you can throw a dart at the map and hit a desirable home. West Phoenix takes a bit of effort, but you'll be surprised at what's hidden away there. These homes will retain value.

## At a Glance...

### House Prices

#### Townhouse
| Bedrooms | 🛏 🛏 |
|---|---|
| Price | $300,000 - $400,000 |

#### Family home
| Bedrooms | 🛏 🛏 |
|---|---|
| Price | $150,000 - $300,000 |

#### Family home
| Bedrooms | 🛏 🛏 🛏 |
|---|---|
| Price | $200,000 - $350,000 |

#### Family home
| Bedrooms | 🛏 🛏 🛏 🛏 |
|---|---|
| Price | $250,000 - $350,000 |

#### Executive home
| Area | Min. 4,000 sq. ft. |
|---|---|
| Price | $800,000 - $1,000,000 |

### Rentals

#### Apartment
| Bedrooms | 🛏 🛏 |
|---|---|
| Price | $500 - $1,000 month |

#### Townhouse
| Bedrooms | 🛏 🛏 |
|---|---|
| Price | $600 - $1,000 month |

#### House
| Bedrooms | 🛏 🛏 🛏 |
|---|---|
| Price | $1,000 - $1,300 month |

### Travel Times

Distance to downtown Phoenix: 10.5 miles

To downtown (from 67th Avenue and Indian School Road via I-10):

Peak: 20 – 22 minutes
Off-peak: 16 minutes

To the airport (from 67th Avenue and Indian School Road via I-10):

Peak: 25 – 30 minutes
Off-peak: 21 minutes

including Deer Valley and Desert View

North Phoenix is a vast area of more than 242 square miles. What characterizes the area is business parks and corporate offices, small mountains and wide washes, and miles of single-family homes. It looks a lot like southern California. It's a solidly middle-class area; think Chandler or Gilbert without the drive.

North Phoenix's most distinct feature is its topography. It's hilly, with a few picturesque volcanic cone mountains poking their noses above the Valley floor. You can find homes with views costing much less than mountainside lots.

Deer Valley starts at about 16th Street and Greenway Road, covering everything northwest of that point. The northern half of the area has vast stretches of vacant land rapidly being developed with luxury homes in the mountainous north and starter family homes in the south. Master-planned communities sprawl adjacent to low-slung office parks lining the interstate, interspersed with big-box malls and chain restaurants.

Desert View is the area between Deer Valley and Scottsdale. About 25,000 people live in this lush desert neighborhood.

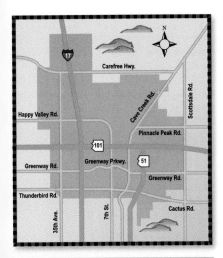

*Total Population: 494,000 approx.*
*Median Age: 34 years*
*Median Household Income: $53,000 p.a.*

## Who Lives There?

It's such a big area the whole spectrum of society is here. White-collar occupations dominate the population: teachers, insurance agents, senior vice presidents, and consultants. Cubicle cowboys like engineers and managers arise from their Crate & Barrel bunks and mosey on down the freeways in the morning. Aviation-related business is big due to the Deer Valley Airport. Scottsdale workers can live here with a third off the cost of a house.

## Homes

Housing here is all three decades old or newer. There are no historic areas. Homes are either custom, semi-custom, or production. There are horse properties; west of Interstate 17, the block between

Bell and Thunderbird Roads and 35th and 51st Avenues is a great horse area.

South of the Loop 101 Freeway, homes are older, built from the 1970s through the 1980s. A three-bedroom, two-bath 1,800 square foot home built in 1980 sells in the low $300,000s. East of Lookout Mountain there are enormous custom homes, including an Italianate mansion just built on 28th Street. Teardowns are taking over outdated homes on lots with views. Nearby, the Moon Valley Canyon subdivision is very attractive, perched on a series of hillsides and ravines. Obviously

any of the homes clinging to ridgelines and mountaintops are in high demand.

North of the Loop 101 Freeway homes are five years old or newer. Subdivisions up here are usually mid-sized: 1,000 to 1,200 acres, with 2,000 to 3,000 homes all starting in the $500,000-range. The new Tuscan styles of stucco-and-tile are prevalent in the north. The smaller subdivisions are marketed to specific demographics like empty-nesters or upscale retirees.

# Amenities

### Schools ★★

Four major districts account for the schools in North Phoenix. Washington Elementary School District, the State's largest elementary district, has most of its 32 schools in North Phoenix. These schools are almost all "performing" schools with only Lookout Mountain Elementary School in the Moon Valley neighborhood and Abraham Lincoln Traditional School ranked as "excelling."

Deer Valley Unified School District has ten schools in North Phoenix including one high school. While most of the district's schools are "excelling" or "highly performing," the schools in North Phoenix tend to be the district's worst schools. Barry Goldwater High School is the exception, though. The high school is "highly performing" and its teachers and

Barry Goldwater High School

coaches have received both district and regional recognition for their outstanding achievements.

Paradise Valley Unified District is arguably North Phoenix's best school district. Several elementary schools—Boulder Creek, Desert Trails, Larkspur, Quail Run, and Sunset Canyon—are "excelling" with many more ranked as "highly performing." Mountain Trails Middle School is another "excelling" school as is Pinnacle High School. Shea Middle School, North Canyon High School, and Shadow Mountain High School are all "highly performing."

Glendale Union High School District has five Phoenix high schools. All are "highly performing," including Greenway High School, which was a National Blue Ribbon Schools Award Winner in 2001.

## Shopping & Dining ★★★★

Paradise Valley Mall is the area's oldest mall, in southeast North Phoenix. Dillard's, Macy's, Sears, and other department stores are surrounded by a complex of smaller stores and restaurants.

Desert Ridge Marketplace on the Loop 101 Freeway is extremely popular for entertainment as well as shopping. More than 110 stores and restaurants fill 1.2 million square feet of retail space.

Happy Valley Town Center on Interstate 17 is the newest mega mall. It features more than 800,000 square feet anchored by a Wal-Mart Super Center, Lowe's, Barnes & Noble, Circuit City, Linens 'N Things, Cost Plus, and other stores.

The big malls of Desert Ridge and Paradise Valley Mall have upscale chain restaurants like Bamboo Club, Z Tejas, and California Pizza Kitchen. For more personal dining, there are little chef-owner places tucked away in small strip malls. The New Asia Kitchen, Attila's European Deli, and Romanelli's Italian Foods are three great places to check out.

## Leisure ★★★

At the Deer Valley Rock Art Center you can see more than 1,500 prehistoric petroglyphs. The Ben Avery Shooting Range is a beloved Phoenix landmark. Lake Pleasant is about ten to 15 minutes away, depending on where you live.

# Real Estate

## Trends

Big corporate employers like USAA Insurance and American Express love this area. (One reason is Deer Valley Airport, the second-busiest general aviation airport in the nation; corporate executives

can land their jets and be at their offices in ten minutes.) Engineering firms, industrial yards, and high-tech aircraft machining are some of the fastest-growing categories. Average household income in the area is high. Consequently, housing is racing to accommodate white-collar workers.

## Rental & Investment

North Phoenix has great views, good housing, jobs, and no crummy infrastructure. There are more than 41,000 planned new homes in the area, equating to more than 117,000 additional people. The area will be explosive for the next decade, making it an excellent investment.

The vast apartment complexes in the area can have as many as 1,400 units. With that many tenants, the potential for good service and quality of life goes south fast. Find a house or a small complex with 12 units, but avoid the rat mazes.

## Look Out! ⚠

Try to avoid the frontage neighborhoods surrounding State Route 51. Lots of tinfoil in the windows and trucks parked in yards.

## At a Glance...

### House Prices

**Townhouse**
| | |
|---|---|
| Bedrooms | 🛏 🛏 |
| Price | $110,000 - $150,000 |

**Family home**
| | |
|---|---|
| Bedrooms | 🛏 🛏 |
| Price | $110,000 - $200,000 |

**Family home**
| | |
|---|---|
| Bedrooms | 🛏 🛏 🛏 |
| Price | $200,000 - $350,000 |

**Family home**
| | |
|---|---|
| Bedrooms | 🛏 🛏 🛏 🛏 |
| Price | $300,000 - $500,000 |

**Executive home**
| | |
|---|---|
| Area | Min. 4,000 sq. ft. |
| Price | $300,000 - $500,000 |

### Rentals

**Apartment**
| | |
|---|---|
| Bedrooms | 🛏 🛏 |
| Price | $700 - $900 month |

**Townhouse**
| | |
|---|---|
| Bedrooms | 🛏 🛏 |
| Price | $800 - $900 month |

**House**
| | |
|---|---|
| Bedrooms | 🛏 🛏 🛏 |
| Price | $1,000 - $2,000 month |

### Travel Times

Distance to downtown Phoenix: 19 miles (from Union Hills Drive & 16th Street via State Route 51)

To downtown Phoenix:
Peak: 35 – 45 minutes
Off-peak: 25 minutes

To the airport:
Peak: 36 – 46 minutes
Off-peak: 26 minutes

including Parkside and Anthem Country Club

The most striking aspect of Anthem, Del Webb's every-age master-planned community, is it actually looks like its billboard ads: people smiling and jogging, baseball players on a manicured diamond, kids riding swings in parks. After a few miles of vainly hunting for a spiked-hair teen wearing chains or a vagrant trying to squeegee your windshield, you realize the new town is exactly what it's being touted as: peaceful existence free of big-city hassles.

What sets Anthem apart from all the other master-planned communities across the Valley is stuff to do. There are more activities here than on a fleet of cruise ships. That has sold a lot of residents – about 7,200 to date – on Anthem. Rock climbing, golf, baseball, swimming, a water park, hiking trails, a kiddie railroad. The homeowners' association publishes a quarterly activities guide which runs to 50 pages.

Homeowners' fees run about $75 monthly in Parkside. Country Club fees are about $130. Golf memberships in the Country Club are another $92.

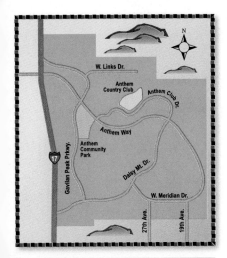

*Total Population: 7,200 approx.*
*Median Age: 37 years*
*Median Household Income: $67,000 p.a.*

## Who Lives There?

Anthem is a Del Webb community, but it's not age restricted. Young families, mid-career dual-income with no kids, retirees, and singles make up Anthem. Residents joke about not drinking the water up here because there are so many families. More than 10 percent of insurance behemoth USAA's employees live in Anthem, a five-minute drive from their Phoenix campus. A lot of residents work from their homes.

## Homes

"Everything is new here," crows a resident in the brochure. "It's like a new beginning." It's a new beginning, but not too new. The same homebuilders you find in Ahwatukee and Gilbert are here, and houses look the same as they do in those areas: tile roofs

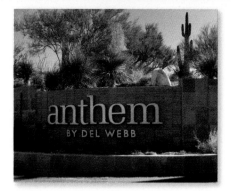

and garages facing streets. In the country club area, the houses look like North Scottsdale. Del Webb didn't reinvent the wheel out here; they just painted it brown to match the mountains.

Anthem is divided into two areas: Parkside and Anthem Country Club. Parkside is the family area: pools, basketball hoops, Big Wheels in the driveway. Country Club is retired golfers in the sun.

# Amenities

### Schools ★★★

Deer Valley Unified School District operates four elementary schools and a high school.

Anthem School, an 88,000-square-foot kindergarten through eighth grade school,

opened for classes in August 1999. Del Webb donated the land and paid for the design and construction.

The second kindergarten through eighth grade, Gavilan Peak Elementary, opened in fall 2002 and 50-acre Boulder Creek High School, a vo-tech school serving grades nine to 12, opened in 2005. It was designed with eight distinct "houses" or clusters so students can change classes in-house rather than walk across the large campus. Boulder Creek is also home to the North Valley Regional Library, a 40,000-book Maricopa County library that is intended for school and public use.

## Shopping & Dining ★★

If you want to eat higher up the food chain than burgers or pizza, you'd better be able to cook. There's a decent Italian place – Franco's Ristorante – but beyond that, it's big golden arches and buy eight, get your ninth smoothie/sub/juice/bagel free.

All the essentials are covered in two shopping centers with groceries, video rentals, hair and nails, insurance, dry cleaners, pet grooming, hardware, and so on. An outlet mall across I-17 features Polo, Bose, Gap, and 87 other stores.

Just north of the outlet mall is one of Arizona's best cactus nurseries, Old West Cactus Farm. Every cactus you ever

wanted, in 200 sizes, and way cheaper than in Phoenix.

## Leisure ★★★★

Activities drive Anthem. "When we first drove to our new home, my three-year-old thought we were in Disneyland," a resident says in marketing materials.

A catch-and-release lake is stocked with more than 40,000 fish. The Country Club has two 18-hole golf courses. A three-story rock climbing wall in the community center. A water park with a giant bucket that drops 40,000 gallons on screaming delighted children. Basketball courts. Sports fields. Fitness and aerobics centers and a skateboard park.

There are scads more activities too, and a 130-member staff to administer them. About 1,500 kids – ten percent of the local population - are enrolled in sports ranging from karate to Little League.

# Real Estate

## Trends

Anthem is so new there aren't any real trends, or fixer-uppers for that matter. The Anthem resale market has slowed slightly but appreciation remains comparatively high. The development was projected to have a sales lifespan of 20 years. Now it is projected to sell out by 2007.

## Rental & Investment

The rental market is flooded, so Anthem might be a good place to lease temporarily.

## Look Out! ⊘

A lawsuit alleging expansive soils caused cracks in walls and roof leaks in both Country Club and Parkside has been filed by a group of homeowners. Del Webb denies there are any community-wide systemic problems and will correct defective homes. Expansive soils can be fixed at a reasonable cost.

## At a Glance...

## House Prices

**Townhouse**
| Bedrooms | 🛏 🛏 |
|---|---|
| Price | $200,000 - $300,000 |

**Family home**
| Bedrooms | 🛏 🛏 |
|---|---|
| Price | $300,000 - $500,000 |

**Family home**
| Bedrooms | 🛏 🛏 🛏 |
|---|---|
| Price | $300,000 - $550,000 |

**Family home**
| Bedrooms | 🛏 🛏 🛏 🛏 |
|---|---|
| Price | $450,000 - $650,000 |

**Executive home**
| Area | Min. 4,000 sq. ft. |
|---|---|
| Price | $750,000 - $950,000 |

## Rentals

**Apartment**
| Bedrooms | 🛏 🛏 |
|---|---|
| Price | $900 - $1,100 month |

**Townhouse**
| Bedrooms | 🛏 🛏 |
|---|---|
| Price | $900 - $1,000 month |

**House**
| Bedrooms | 🛏 🛏 🛏 |
|---|---|
| Price | $1,000 - $2,000 month |

## Travel Times

Distance to downtown Phoenix: 33 miles

To downtown Phoenix:
Peak: 50 minutes – 1 hour 10 minutes
Off-peak: 39 minutes

To the airport:
Peak: 1 hour – 1.5 hours
Off-peak: 45 minutes

Anthem driving tip: Do not attempt to go into Phoenix on a Sunday afternoon. Half the Valley is coming back from Flagstaff and the I-17 is a parking lot.

Moon Valley is the jewel of north Phoenix. It was built as a rural country club in the early 1960s, with opulent homes centered around the golf course and a race track a mile up the road. If Frank Sinatra hadn't lived in Palm Springs, he might've chosen Moon Valley. Like Scottsdale and Paradise Valley, it was once a remote desert playground for the wealthy.

Now, of course, Moon Valley is right in the thick of things, but it's still a very desirable place to live. There's a gourmet grocery store to serve the million-dollar mountainside residences. Old-growth trees and lawns are tall and thick. At Christmas the streets are lined with luminarias. It's old Phoenix upper middle-class or gracious Western living a la *Sunset* magazine: homes with swimming pools and citrus on big lots.

The area is in a valley, so peak views are everywhere. Its location between Interstate 17 and State Route 51 makes access to downtown, Scottsdale, and regional malls a snap. Think of Moon Valley as North Phoenix's Arcadia at a slightly lower price, with more down-to-earth residents.

Total Population: 11,500 approx.
Median Age: 40 years
Median Household Income: $69,000 p.a.

## Who Lives There?

Traditionally, Moon Valley was populated by management from Honeywell and other large corporations; big families with country club memberships who went to church every Sunday. That's still the typical Moon Valley resident. While there are plenty of business owners and corporate middle managers, more and more professionals have moved into the area in the past decade.

## Homes

Because Moon Valley was built in the 1960s, the area's 29 subdivisions have a rural country club feel with tall trees and thick lawns. "It feels like you're driving through a nice neighborhood back East," one resident says. Desert landscaping

is not uncommon, however; it does have a rustic Paradise Valley-feel with creosote, mesquites, and palm rows. The original properties were ranch homes, Southwestern Period Revivals, and a few Federal and Colonial styles. Newer houses are stucco-and-tile, with desert landscaping and some greenery, like a grassy backyard. The average Moon Valley home is about 2,400 square feet. Most homes have pools. Lots tend to be large – about one-third of an acre.

## Amenities

### Schools ★★★★

The primary schools in Moon Valley are part of the Washington Elementary School District, the largest elementary district in Arizona, with 32 schools. Kindergartners through sixth grade students attend either Lookout Mountain Elementary School, a "excelling" school, or Moon Mountain Elementary School ("highly performing"). They then move on to Mountain Sky Junior High School. Mountain Sky is also a "highly performing" school with a strong music program and 10 consecutive wrestling titles.

Most students in Moon Valley attend Thunderbird High School, another "highly performing" school. Thunderbird has three computer labs and a photography lab. It is home to the most outstanding Navy League unit in the nation. The school's average standardized test scores for all tests including the ACT and SAT tests exceed district, county, and state averages.

### Shopping & Dining ★★★

Metrocenter on the Black Canyon Freeway has been purchased by the parent company of Westcor, which owns and operates the Valley's best malls. When Westcor is done, it will have beautiful landscaping, well-designed public spaces, and upscale tenants. Arrowhead Town Center isn't far away for entertainment and shopping. Desert Ridge Marketplace is five minutes away on the Loop 101 Freeway for wine tastings, movies, and a dazzling array of shops.

A meal at the Hilton Tapatio Cliffs resort's Pointe in Tyme is sublime.

There's an AJ's Fine Foods in Moon Valley – a status symbol in any neighborhood – so you can buy excellent deli food. Try Ammaccapane's Restaurant and Sports Bar, owned by Moon Valley girl and LPGA superstar Danielle Ammaccapane and her father Ralph. It has an all-day menu with burgers, subs, sandwiches, pastas and pizzas.

## Leisure ★★★

Turf Paradise opened in 1956. It's a great place to watch the ponies.

If you've got kids, Lake Pleasant is close, and the North Mountain Preserve is a fine hike. Moon Valley Park has a playground, basketball, tennis courts and soccer fields.

# Real Estate

## Trends

Most of the housing is older, high-end homes. Teardowns have begun in Moon Valley, although not to the same extent as Paradise Valley or Arcadia. Moon Valley Drive is a prestige street where teardowns have replaced outdated homes.

Up along the mountains (Moon Mountain, for instance), homes are gated, custom, and in the millions. There is a variety of housing, although on the whole it's more of a mid- to high-range. Moon Valley is a stable area and will continue to have long-term value.

Housing is diverse: territorial, ranch, Southwestern pueblo styles. Most of the stock is block, however, many people add rooms and change kitchen styles. Homes cost about $400,000 to $600,000. On top of Moon Mountain it's $2-3 million, down lower $800,000. You're getting a 3,000 square foot home on a mountainside, in a location that's convenient to everything.

Down on the valley floor, there are occasional good value buys, but in general, agents are only too aware of the demand to live here and that tends to be reflected in the prices.

## Rental & Investment

North Central's location makes any property here valuable, especially in an area like Moon Valley.

Houses rent for about $1,500 to $2,000 a month in the heart of Moon Valley. Apartment complexes are available on the north and east side.

## At a Glance...

## House Prices

### Townhouse
| Bedrooms | 🛏 🛏 |
|---|---|
| Price | $100,000 - $200,000 |

### Family home
| Bedrooms | 🛏 🛏 |
|---|---|
| Price | $175,000 - $300,000 |

### Family home
| Bedrooms | 🛏 🛏 🛏 |
|---|---|
| Price | $300,000 - $500,000 |

### Family home
| Bedrooms | 🛏 🛏 🛏 🛏 |
|---|---|
| Price | $400,000 - $700,000 |

### Executive home
| Area | Min. 4,000 sq. ft. |
|---|---|
| Price | $700,000 - $1,000,000 |

## Rentals

### Apartment
| Bedrooms | 🛏 🛏 |
|---|---|
| Price | $700 - $900 month |

### Townhouse
| Bedrooms | 🛏 🛏 |
|---|---|
| Price | $900 - $1,200 month |

### House
| Bedrooms | 🛏 🛏 🛏 |
|---|---|
| Price | $1,200 - $2,500 month |

## Travel Times

Distance to downtown Phoenix: 15 miles

To downtown Phoenix (via 7th Street):
Peak: 45 minutes
Off-peak: 36 minutes

To the airport (via State Route 51):
Peak: 45 – 50 minutes
Off-peak: 30 minutes

Sunnyslope is a 14-square-mile area at the northern end of Phoenix's central corridor. It has been one of the Valley's most-maligned areas for decades, because of history. Sunnyslope started off as a haven for "lungers," people who moved to the arid Arizona desert with tuberculosis and other lung ailments. They lived in tent houses and woke the world with their coughing.

Lungers in Arizona were treated like Okies in California. Sunnyslope was literally dumped on. People drove up to Sunnyslope to dump trash in washes. It long had a reputation as one of the city's more rundown areas.

That's changing. Local citizens groups and city officials have successfully partnered in recent years to have unsightly apartment complexes demolished. The local hospital – John C. Lincoln – has helped enormously by funding a nonprofit revitalization corporation which has won national awards for excellence in community service. It has brought in a new shopping center, bought and leveled eyesore homes, and built market-rate homes with affordable financing.

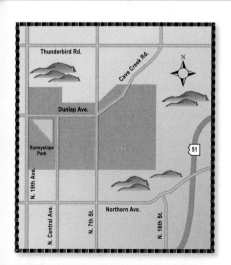

*Total Population: 49,500 approx.*
*Median Age: 31 years*
*Median Household Income: $34,000 p.a.*

## Who Lives There?

Sunnyslope residents match the housing stock, from attorneys and architects to welders and cashiers. The population of about 50,000 is mostly Anglo, with the next biggest population being Hispanic. There are sizeable populations of Afghan and Vietnamese refugees (the latter used to cast nets in the canals for white Russian carp). The Slope also has a large Mennonite community. About 26 languages are spoken at Sunnyslope High School. It's probably the most racially and economically diverse area in the Valley.

## Homes

Tucked in at the base of a narrow draw between two mountains in the North Mountain Preserve, Sunnyslope has a

# Sunnyslope

# Sunnyslope

*North Phoenix*

landscape prettier than many places in the Valley. Houses are all over the map in style and price. Real estate agents say the Slope is no longer the poor man's Paradise Valley. Ranches dominate close to both sides of Central Avenue.

Recently the rest of the world has looked in on Sunnyslope and found mountainside homes in the middle of the city at bargain prices. While that's less true today, you can still get a great price on a centrally-located home seven minutes from downtown that is rapidly cleaning up, with an amazing high school. Sunnyslope is becoming discovered.

# Amenities

### Schools ★★★★★

Facility improvements are the order of the day. Sunnyslope Elementary School is

being torn down and replaced, and a new middle school is being built. Currently, seventh and eighth graders attend Royal Palm Middle School. These schools have a year-round school calendar.

Sunnyslope High School is one of the State's top schools, with nationally recognized teachers. *Newsweek* listed the school as one of America's best high schools based on the number of Advanced Placement or International Baccalaureate tests taken by all students at the school in 2004 divided by the number of graduating seniors. Some people have actually moved to Sunnyslope just so their kids can attend the high school.

## Shopping & Dining ★★★

The slope has entirely acceptable Mexican restaurants. For one of the Valley's best fine dining experiences, try the Pointe in Tyme at the Pointe Hilton Tapatio Cliffs Resort. Executive Chef Ivan Flowers shines in the kitchen. He's the reason this section got three stars instead of two; this chef's a star in his own right.

There are some great decorative iron shops in Sunnyslope. Small businesses dominate the village. Both Wal-Mart and Home Depot made moves to open outlets in the village, but were fought off by local residents. A new shopping center at Central and Dunlap Avenues opened in 2000, anchored by a Food City. New

86

restaurants are also inching their way into the area, and businesses are starting to perk up their premises and facades.

For department stores and similar shopping, the Camelback Corridor is the nearest option.

# Real Estate

## Trends

Private contractors are coming in, tearing down, and building single-family homes in the area between Central Avenue and 7th Street and Dunlap Avenue to the Arizona Canal. At the eastern end of Dunlap Avenue $350,000 condos are perched on mountain slopes. New single-family homes are also being built at 17th Avenue and Shangri-La Road. Senior housing is also under construction at a few locations. A local community development corporation is building new homes in Sunnyslope for low-income families.

## Rental & Investment

Up towards the mountains there are some resort-style apartment and condo complexes in Sunnyslope with pools, volleyball, and workout rooms. Down on the Valley floor, apartments become less like resorts and more like Baghdad; don't move here without owning a bullet-proof vest. A three-bedroom remodeled mountainside home rents for about $1,100 a month.

## Smart Buy ⊘

Do-it-yourselfers and bargain hunters take heed: if you hunt around, you'll find salvageable 1,200-square-foot bungalows tucked away which need about $15,000 worth of renovation and yard work to turn into $150,000 homes.

## At a Glance...

## House Prices

### Townhouse
Bedrooms
Price        $150,000 - $300,000

### Family home
Bedrooms
Price        $150,000 - $200,000

### Family home
Bedrooms
Price        $200,000 - $400,000

### Family home
Bedrooms
Price        $250,000 - $600,000

### Executive home
Area         Min. 4,000 sq. ft.
Price        $600,000 - $700,000

## Rentals

### Apartment
Bedrooms
Price        $800 - $1,400 month

### Townhouse
Bedrooms
Price        $1,200 - $1,500 month

### House
Bedrooms
Price        $1,000 - $1,300 month

## Travel Times

Distance to downtown Phoenix: 8 miles

To downtown Phoenix:
Peak 15 minutes
Off-peak 10 minutes

To the airport:
Peak 30 minutes
Off-peak 20 minutes

The very name "South Phoenix" used to conjure up images of helicopters and mug shots on the 10 o'clock news. But South Phoenix's rough history is as far in the past as Tombstone's. Total crimes dropped by more than 1,500 cases between 1996 and 2001, according to the Phoenix police. Now South Phoenix is better known for its canals, golf courses, orange groves, a city park encompassing an entire mountain range, sweeping foothill views, flower farms and a hot real estate market.

South Phoenix ranges almost 40 square miles between the Salt River and South Mountain and between 44th Street to 19th Avenue. It's 10 minutes from the airport, downtown, Interstate-17 and Interstate-10.

Think about commute times, views, home prices, and construction quality. As the Valley grows, this area will only improve and become more desirable. Six hundred acres of the Salt River bed has been restored with a massive cleanup, replanting, and reforestation. Now there's 10 miles of trails, a 12-acre forest of 1,000 cottonwood trees, a 16-acre marsh, and a 140-acre mesquite woodland. It's emblematic of the whole neighborhood.

Total Population: 84,000 approx.
Median Age: 27 years
Median Household Income: $34,000 p.a.

## Who Lives There?

Former City Councilman Cody Williams saw the area's potential and took busloads of developers to see the city views and rolling fields. In 1995 he convinced two bold businessmen to build a pair of luxury golf resorts. They started a stampede. Now about 30 residential developments are being built, as well as two high-end retail projects and an enormous river park.

One developer built 41 single-family homes at 32nd Street and Baseline Road and marketed the $415,000 to $650,000 houses successfully to young professional Scottsdale and Ahwatukee residents.

People moving to South Phoenix now are coming from all over the map. Easterners buy investment homes for children. Californians snap up golf course patio homes. Ahwatukee refugees flee traffic. Shoppers glassy-eyed from Scottsdale sticker shock are finding the same home they did in Grayhawk, but for $80,000 less. Airline pilots play golf 10 minutes from where they work. ASU students – and their parents – find far more house than they could afford in Tempe. The mountains and golf courses are waking up everyone to the area's charm.

## Homes

While the buzz is all about the new stucco-and-tile communities, there is variety in South Phoenix if you want to play fix-up, take a bit of risk, and look hard. Drive down lanes that pop up behind canals and you'll run into funky adobes half-hidden behind citrus and palms. Equestrians will like the sprawling horse properties along streets like Vineyard Avenue at the base of the mountain. Not all the subdivisions are stucco-and-tile; a few elegant Santa Fe contemporary designs lay along the foothills.

# Amenities

## Schools ★

Roosevelt School District has not enjoyed a good reputation. Infighting between ethnic groups on the school board traditionally results in split 4-3 votes. As a result, many of the schools languish, but several are showing improved test results as well as increased parental and community involvement.

Cesar Chavez and South Mountain are the local high schools, part of the Phoenix Union High School District. These schools, too, are showing improvement, both are rated "performing." South Mountain campus includes television, radio, and music recording studios as well as flight simulators.

For families wishing to avoid South Phoenix's public schools, there are two ways to get around the situation. The first

is the state's open enrollment system, which allows parents to send their children to the excellent Kyrene School District in Tempe. The second option is to enroll their children in a quality charter school.

## Shopping & Dining ★★★

Produce stands along Baseline Road have always been one of the pleasures of living in South Phoenix. Chilies, citrus, vegetables, and pumpkins fill bins in earthy, swamp-cooled stands on the edges of the groves. However, if you wanted paper towels and pork chops, there were two options: drive to Tempe or endure the dismal markets on Central Avenue. Not any more.

The Pederson Group – builders of the most exclusive retail developments in the Valley – opened the 335,000-square-foot Legacy Village with a 124,000-square-foot Target, a Fry's grocery store, Ace Hardware, and a Bank of America branch at 24th Street and Baseline.

Down the road at 32nd Street, a mixed-use development at South Mountain Village Center offers 90,000 square feet of boutique office space, five restaurants along the lines of Chipotle Grill, and residential lofts.

South Phoenix residents have to travel further than most for shopping. The closest major shopping area is at I-10 and U.S. 60. Arizona Mills is a huge, enclosed outlet mall with a food court and movie theatre.

South Phoenix lays claim to the best Mexican restaurants in the Valley: enchiladas at Pancho's, seafood cocktails and grilled fish at Mariscos Las Glorias, and Los Dos Molinos in Tom Mix's old house on Central south of Baseline.

## Leisure ★★★

Golfers can head out to the renovated Thunderbirds Golf Club at Seventh Street and South Mountain, or the area's three new courses, vaunted to be the best in metro Phoenix. The Legacy Golf Resort hosted an LPGA Tour event in 2000 on its 18-hole championship course. Nearby the Raven at South Mountain also offers an 18-hole course. Still no tee times available? Farther out on 35th Avenue the municipal Aguila Golf Course has an 18-hole course spread over 210 acres.

Hikers have plenty of room to wander too. South Mountain Park is the world's largest city park. More than 16,000 acres lead to hidden valleys where the city vanishes and prehistoric petroglyphs are tucked in shady spots.

For a shady walk on the banks of a cool river, check out the Rio Salado project that opened in 2005. Ten miles of paved trails lead through a 580-acre restored wetlands habitat of cottonwood and willow forests

### Local Hero: Los Dos Molinos

Tom Mix was a 1930s cowboy movie star. In California he lived in a mansion with 40 rooms (including billiards), an indoor pool, croquet and lawn tennis courts, kitchens running day and night, and a six-car garage plus staff. He liked parties, pretty girls and driving fast. In Phoenix he owned a hacienda at the rocky foot of South Mountain.

That hacienda is now Los Dos Molinos, one of Phoenix's most beloved Mexican restaurants. Mix's spirit lives on, especially after a few giant margaritas amid the bougainvillaea blossoming in the courtyard.

The Dos serves New Mexican-style food. Owner/chef Victoria Chavez cooks with chillies from Hatch, New Mexico so hot they induce visions. Mouth-watering green chilli enchiladas, savory beef tacos, chunky handmade guacamole's, blue corn tamales, slow-cooked adobada ribs - there are good reasons Saturday night waits can top two hours.

*Gourmet* magazine and the *New York Times* have both given the Dos rave reviews. It's one of Phoenix's few culinary exports to Manhattan; one of Chavez's daughters runs a location near Times Square, and Chavez herself flies in to cook.

---

along the Salt River between 19th Avenue to where I–10 crosses 32nd Street. There are public swimming pools at El Prado, Roosevelt and Hermoso city parks, along with lit soccer, baseball, tennis and volleyball play areas.

# Real Estate

## Trends

Despite the clatter of graders along Baseline, city officials predict slow growth for South Phoenix. The area is projected to add only 10,000 more households by 2020.

Until five years ago this was an undesirable part of town, but it's changing. It's a great place for folks who want an affordable area with an easy commute and are willing to live through the transition. Those who can't wait and want everything clean and well-ordered now, are better off in higher-priced Ahwatukee. Minivans from Ahwatukee and BMWs from Scottsdale now venture in to South Phoenix to buy homes 10 minutes from downtown offices. South Mountain is being called the new Camelback, with $600,000-plus custom homes ascending its flanks. And new starter homes are being snapped up by young couples as fast as they can be built.

# Look Out! ⊘

South Phoenix is shedding its rough and tumble past, but it's still in transition. Residents still hear the odd gun shot. Families with small children have to travel several miles to find schools with safe and secure learning environments. Shopping is inconvenient. These drawbacks will be offset for those who have a pioneer spirit. While waiting to reap the benefits of getting in early on an area destined to grow and appreciate, focus on the natural beauty and easy commutes.

## At a Glance...

### House Prices

**Townhouse**

| Bedrooms | |
|---|---|
| Price | $300,000 - $400,000 |

**Family home**

| Bedrooms | |
|---|---|
| Price | $150,000 - $300,000 |

**Family home**

| Bedrooms | |
|---|---|
| Price | $200,000 - $350,000 |

**Family home**

| Bedrooms | |
|---|---|
| Price | $250,000 - $400,000 |

**Executive home**

| Area | Min. 4,000 sq. ft. |
|---|---|
| Price | $800,000 - $1,000,000 |

### Rentals

**Apartment**

| Bedrooms | |
|---|---|
| Price | $1,000 - $1,500 month |

**Townhouse**

| Bedrooms | |
|---|---|
| Price | $1,300 - $1,400 month |

**House**

| Bedrooms | |
|---|---|
| Price | $1,000 - $1,300 month |

### Travel Times

Distance to downtown Phoenix: 5 miles

To downtown Phoenix:
Peak: 12 minutes
Off peak: 12 minutes

To the airport:
Peak: 12 minutes
Off-peak: 12 minutes

# Ahwatukee ★★★★★ *South Phoenix*

including Mountain Park Ranch, The Foothills and Lakewood

Ahwatukee is the world's largest cul-de-sac. It's outside the Valley, south of South Mountain, with no freeway outlet from the western end. All downtown-bound traffic has to use Interstate 10. There's constant talk about running a freeway through South Mountain Park, but Ahwatukee residents oppose it. They like their cul-de-sac and the mountain wall separating them from the rest of Phoenix.

The name was chosen by Helen Brinton in 1935 when she bought Ahwatukee's first home, a 17-room mansion in the desert, built in 1922 for a wealthy dentist. She called it Ahwatukee, a Crow Indian word meaning "House of Dreams."

While Ahwatukee is officially part of Phoenix, its master-planned communities, golf courses, and lakes make it look more like the better areas of the East Valley. Palm trees and stucco walls line the streets. Trails for biking and jogging thread throughout the place. It's known as a family area with a small-town atmosphere. A school per year has opened for several years now to accommodate families.

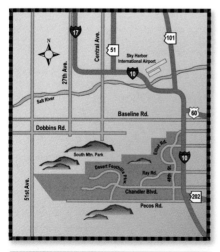

Total Population: 77,000 approx.
Median Age: 35 years
Median Household Income: $72,000 p.a.

## Who Lives There?

Ahwatukee people tend to be go-getters; they work hard and play hard. Bicycling – both road racing and mountain biking – are enormously popular. "Most everyone in Ahwatukee is in pretty good shape," a resident says. Entrepreneurs, chip cowboys, financial advisors, pilots, engineers, and other type-A personalities live in the foothills. Education is prized here, there are Montessori day care centers. "You don't see that everywhere," one agent says. Quite a few professional athletes enjoy the neighborhood's proximity to downtown and Tempe sports facilities. There are a lot of residents from New York, New Jersey, and Chicago. Young stay-at-home moms jogging and pushing strollers are common Ahwatukee morning sights.

## Homes

Ahwatukee has terrific mountain views and no blight anywhere. That's also why it's the most expensive place to buy in the southeast Valley. A $350,000 three-bedroom stucco-and-tile home in Ahwatukee will cost $300,000 in Gilbert or $260,000 in Tempe.

However stucco-and-tile is your only option in Ahwatukee. The area has several master-planned communities. There are four major subdivisions, each with a different advantage.

Ahwatukee is the original development with homes varying from $90,000 town homes to $2.5 million for custom Southwest contemporary homes.

Mountain Park Ranch is the most family-friendly. There are three community centers with swimming pools, tennis courts and picnic areas. Choices range from patio homes to large single family estate homes. Expect to pay between $170,000 to $450,000 here.

The Foothills is more upscale, with an 18-hole golf course designed by Tom Weiskopf attracting golfers. It's west, away from the freeway and closer to the mountain, boasting more than 40 miles of trails to stroll and eyeball the scenery, even if you're not chasing a white ball.

Lakewood is built around a chain of man-made lakes. Some homes have small docks with paddleboats moored at them.

For tycoon-caliber living, go to the foot of the mountain around 36th Street - saltwater pools, heated floors, jet tubs, cherrywood millwork, wine cellars, swim-up bars, and price tags to match. Some homes in this area top the $5 million mark.

There are a few Ahwatukee homes with a fantastic feature the MLS doesn't list. Some properties have boulders in the backyard covered in prehistoric petroglyphs carved about the same time as the fall of Rome. Suns, spirals, scorpions, snakes, and spirits are common. If you're looking at a home that backs up directly to South Mountain Park, wander out and check. Please don't, however, paint the boulder white like one uninformed couple did a few years ago.

## Amenities

### Schools ★★★★★

Schools in Ahwatukee are part of the Kyrene School District, one of the state's

most highly rated. Seven of the nine elementary schools are rated "excelling," two are "highly performing." The three middle schools are "excelling."

The schools have computers and Internet access in each classroom. Kyrene Altadena Middle School, Kyrene Akimel A-al Middle School, and Kyrene Centennial Middle School each have athletic, band, and chorus programs.

Students in Ahwatukee attend one of two Tempe Union high schools. Desert Vista High School has honors, gifted and work programs, and in 2004, 19 Desert Vista students received perfect math scores on their SATs.

Mountain Pointe High School has 21 varsity sports, more than 80 clubs, and was named by *Redbook* magazine as one of America's top 50 schools.

## Leisure ★★★★

The Sheraton Wild Horse Pass Resort and Spa on the adjacent Gila River Indian

Community has a 17,500-square-foot Native American-themed spa, two 18-hole golf courses, an equestrian center, and celebrity chef dining.

Mountain bikers and hikers enjoy easy access to the 16,000-acre South Mountain Park. Ahwatukee also has four public golf courses, scores of neighborhood parks, community centers, a public swimming pool, and a fairly active shopping and nightlife area near its center at 48th Street and Ray Road. There's also a very plush multiplex with reclining seats.

Motorsports fans have a short trip to Firebird International Raceway.

## Shopping & Dining ★★★

On the three main streets leading into Ahwatukee from Interstate 10, you'll find every chain and big-box store imaginable. Barnes & Noble, Home Depot, Target, Linens 'N Things, Pier One – it's all here. Expect quality stores for day-to-day needs, not rare books or Oriental rugs. Ahwatukee's East Coast natives arrived, took one bite of the local food, threw up their hands, and opened their own joints. You will find excellent trattorias, delis, and sports bars everywhere with Big Apple and Windy City-themes. The same chains you find everywhere else in the Valley have stores here, too: P.F. Chang's, Macaroni Grill, and Chili's, for instance. The neighborhood is in dire need of

restaurants; waits can top an hour at any of those eateries. "You just can't get into a restaurant," one resident wails.

# Real Estate

## Trends

Houses ripe for renovation are almost non-existent. Everything that could be fixed and flipped already has been. You rarely pick up anything undervalued.

Condos are becoming more expensive in Ahwatukee. That may change as a recent trend of converting high-end apartments into condos fills the market. A complex at Liberty Lane and 19th Avenue is being condo-converted.

## Rental & Investment

Single-family homes rent for a lot more here because they're in such good shape. Expect to pay about $1,200 for a three-bedroom. More luxurious homes rent for about $2,000. Apartments lease from $750 to about $1,000 for a two-bedroom. Ahwatukee apartment complexes look like resorts. Pools, cabanas, spas, gyms, golf course views, wood-burning fireplaces, tennis courts; all that, plus your neighbor is highly unlikely to steal cars for a living.

# Look Out! ⊘

Beware: if you have teenagers and are considering buying in west Ahwatukee, Kyrene School District ends at 19th Avenue. This means your children will have to enroll in the abysmal Roosevelt School District in south Phoenix. While open enrollment allows you to enroll your child in Kyrene, both Desert Vista and Mountain Pointe High Schools are at capacity.

# At a Glance...

## House Prices
### Townhouse
Bedrooms 🛏 🛏
Price $250,000 - $400,000
### Family home
Bedrooms 🛏 🛏
Price $150,000 - $250,000
### Family home
Bedrooms 🛏 🛏 🛏
Price $250,000 - $350,000
### Family home
Bedrooms 🛏 🛏 🛏 🛏
Price $400,000 - $500,000
### Executive home
Area Min. 4,000 sq. ft.
Price $1,000,000 - $2,000,000

## Rentals
### Apartment
Bedrooms 🛏 🛏
Price $750 - $1,100 month
### Townhouse
Bedrooms 🛏 🛏
Price $900 - $1,200 month
### House
Bedrooms 🛏 🛏 🛏
Price $1,800 - $2,200 month

## Travel Times
Distance to downtown Phoenix: 17.5 miles

To downtown Phoenix:
Peak: Up to 1 hour
Off peak: 25 minutes

To the airport:
Peak: 50 minutes
Off-peak: 17 minutes

Mesa

Mesa is the biggest city you never heard of. More people live in Mesa than Atlanta, St. Louis, or Miami. "We're a quiet city," an official chuckles. Mesa is so low-profile a downtown hotel changed its name to the Hilton Phoenix East / Mesa. Out-of-state visitors and meeting planners had no idea whether the hotel was on the Mexican border or the Navajo reservation. It is a quiet city, and it has conservative roots, founded by Mormon pioneers who toiled to turn some of the harshest terrain on the planet into green fields, groves, and streets.

Mesa lacks the Hummers, raucous blondes, and night clubs of Scottsdale and Tempe. However, it's one of the top places in the Valley if you want to live on a clean, quiet street where kids get a good education.

It also has the most diverse housing stock in the Valley after Phoenix and Fountain Hills. Mesa has a home for everyone: multimillion-dollar luxury showplaces near Red Mountain; horse properties abutting orange groves; wonderful historic areas of bungalows and period revivals; spacious contemporary stucco-and-tile neighborhoods with soccer fields and backyard pools. Mesa's pride is its neighborhoods.

Mesa doesn't have a property tax currently, which is a big draw for many homebuyers.

Northern Mesa used to be a long drive from the center of the Valley. Post-freeways, it's a half-hour drive, making it more desirable. Agents predict a

## it's one of the top places in the Valley if you want to live on a clean, quiet street where kids get a good education

wave of gentrification to hit Mesa's northwestern corner at the intersection of two freeways.

The city has more than 20 golf courses, 55 city parks, three libraries, 13 public pools, and more than 250 tennis, racquetball, and basketball courts. The Chicago Cubs have played spring training games at Hohokam Stadium for decades. Mesa's crown jewel is the brand-new $98 million Mesa Arts Center. The three-building complex covers 212,775 square feet on seven acres. Galleries and classes are year-round. It stages 600 to 800 performances annually. The biggest arts facility in Arizona, it's drawing talent away from smaller venues.

Upscale shopping is appearing in Mesa, stores you never would have seen 15 years ago. At the same time, neighborhoods south of the town center are becoming more Hispanic. People priced out of Scottsdale are choosing Mesa. Changes are dramatic and the city is shaping up to be something quite different from what it has been for decades.

City officials have tried for years to spice up Mesa's image, but nothing's really stuck. Bicycle around Lehi and North Mesa on a spring afternoon and smell the orange blossoms. Watch your kids play soccer at the vast Red Mountain sports complex park. Play a round of golf at Superstition Springs. Mesa's got a lot going for it.

# Central Mesa ★★★★☆

*Mesa*

The heart of Mesa is a green, peaceful Norman Rockwell-in-the-desert kind of place. In the late 1870s Mormon pioneers arrived to a desolate, windswept tabletop formed from sediment dumped by a rogue river. They rolled up their sleeves and turned a truly inhospitable landscape into an area that looks like Illinois with citrus and cactus. Central Mesa is tall, green trees over quiet streets. It has the most historic districts – five – of any other Valley city besides Phoenix. Eight more have been identified and await certification.

Downtown Mesa has always been a sleepy strip of collectibles stores and empty storefronts, but the new arts center is expected to have a positive effect on its surroundings. Meanwhile, residents simply enjoy living beneath shady trees in charming suburbs. Neighborhoods here are comparable to the historic Willo or F.Q. Story neighborhoods in Phoenix, with $100,000 off the price. If you need family space and a pool, spacious stucco-and-tile without headaches awaits at both ends of central Mesa.

Total Population: 91,000 approx.
Median Age: 28 years
Median Household Income: $40,000 p.a.

## Who Lives There?

In general Central Mesa decreases in cost and increases in density from north to south.

Original farming families still live in Lehi, an old citrus ranch area south of the 202 Freeway. (The freeway destroyed huge chunks of this old Arizona enclave.) Immediately south, beyond the orange groves, newer single-family homes on large lots have popped up. Homes become slightly smaller towards the city center, but there are still the same pleasant wide streets, big hedges, trees and lush lawns.

Central Mesa residents are a diverse mix. Young couples starting out, hip young couples renovating historics, Hispanic families getting by, Mesa natives in their senior years, and salt-of-the-earth farmers all live in Central Mesa.

## Homes

Housing is as diverse as the residents. There are late 1980s stucco-and-tile mid-level executive homes near Lehi. (Lehi itself is occupied by a few old families who are unlikely to ever relinquish their citrus fiefdoms.) Between the town center and the U.S. 60 Freeway are smaller brick and block homes from the 1940s, 50s, and 60s. This area appears in the news from time to time. Caveat emptor; Mesa police say this is the city's highest crime area. South of the freeway Central Mesa neighborhoods suddenly and startlingly morph into the executive/golf course/fake lake variety of homes, accompanied by income-appropriate shopping and chain restaurants.

## Amenities

### Schools ★★★★

Students in Central Mesa attend schools in the Mesa Unified District. Stanford 9 and AIMS test results are high for these schools, and on average, parents give these schools overwhelmingly high marks.

Three of the schools — Franklin Elementary, Franklin South Elementary, and Franklin West Elementary Schools

in North Mesa — emphasize a back-to-basics approach. Open to all Mesa students, the Franklin schools have high academic standards, a strict dress code, and mandatory homework. All three are rated "excelling."

Most of these students move on to one of the area's seven junior high schools. Stapley Junior High, rated "highly performing," won the state championship in the National Academic League competition.

Central Mesa's two high schools have strong academic credentials. Mesa High School is "highly performing." Mountain View High in North Mesa achieved "excelling" status. Mountain View students scored above state and national averages on the ACT/SAT tests. Mountain View also has a successful sports program with 11 regional championships and two state championship teams.

Hohokam Stadium

There are two alternative school options in Central Mesa. For students in the fifth through eighth grade who have not been successful in their neighborhood schools, McKellips Middle School offers small-group instruction, support groups, and behavior modification programs. Mesa Vista High School provides similar opportunities for older students.

## Leisure ★★★

The new Mesa Arts Center is the biggest in the state. The center also offers classes in lavish studios and exhibitions in lovely galleries. About a dozen antique and collectible shops line Main Street in downtown Mesa, where there's a farmer's market every Friday.

Mesa also has some great museums for kids (if they're at the dinosaur age, check out the Mesa Southwest Museum). Golf Land down on the freeway isn't as intellectually stimulating, but it has mini golf, a waterpark, bumper cars, and three million arcade games.

Canyon, Apache, and Roosevelt Lakes are just 20 minutes drive, and serious golf is never far away. The Chicago Cubs have held spring training in Mesa off and on since 1952; Hohokam Stadium tickets are some of the most popular in the Cactus League.

## Shopping ★★

Upscale shopping a la Scottsdale or Tempe has at last come to Mesa with the Village Square at Dana Park. It's a 70-acre shopping center at Val Vista and Baseline Roads, featuring date palms, cobblestone streets, fountains, and stores such as Coldwater Creek, AJ's Fine Foods, and Ann Taylor.

Superstition Springs Center at the corner of Power Road and the U.S. 60 Freeway has 1.3 million square feet of stores and restaurants including Bath & Body Works, Victoria's Secret, and Robinsons-May.

## Local Hero: The Mesa Easter Pageant

The Mesa Easter Pageant is an annual tradition. It started humbly in 1928 as a sunrise service with choral groups, and has grown to "the largest annual outdoor Easter pageant in the world," with more than 400 performers and live animals including sheep, donkeys, and horses.

Volunteers work year round on the 75-minute performance, titled "Jesus the Christ." About 25 people design, prepare and sew more than 100 Biblical costumes using fabric that is donated. Some of it comes from the Middle East.

Nearly 1,200 hopefuls audition each year for the 400 parts in the production — sometimes entire families audition. In addition, there are about 100 backstage workers who do the costuming, make-up, construction, lighting, sound, publicity and security.

More than 150,000 people attended the 2005 performance during its nine-day run.

Performances are free to the public. For more information call 480-964-7164 or visit the pageant's Web site at www.easterpageant.org.

# Real Estate

## Trends

Around the town center the historic areas have bungalows, period revivals, and ranches. They're not all perfectly redone as in Phoenix, leaving plenty of opportunity for remodelling. High-rise living hasn't come to downtown Mesa yet. The city's struggle to revive downtown's lethargic image didn't end with the arts center's creation. It's a $98 million attraction surrounded by sandwich shops and second-hand stores selling *Star Trek* mugs. However, the hot buzz about the arts center is causing restaurateurs and retailers to take hard looks at downtown Mesa. Even if white tablecloths make their area debut, there's not a grocery store near downtown. Nearby house prices haven't noticeably ticked up as yet, and it may be another couple of years before downtown Mesa living becomes in demand.

## Rental & Investment

Homes rent for about $800 a month for a three-bedroom. Single-family homes on nice streets are your best bet.

# Look Out! ⃠

Some apartment complexes in this area can be rough. One resident summed up his surroundings: "Drugs, trash, illegal aliens, prostitutes, two green swimming pools, and appliances that shock you. The cops don't bother to leave because they know they'll just have to turn around and come right back again. The head of maintenance is an alcoholic handyman with eighth grade shop-class skills. Run away; run far away."

## At a Glance...

## House Prices

### Townhouse
Bedrooms
Price        $100,000 - $150,000

### Family home
Bedrooms
Price        $100,000 - $140,000

### Family home
Bedrooms
Price        $120,000 - $150,000

### Family home
Bedrooms
Price        $260,000 - $300,000

### Executive home
Area         Min. 4,000 sq. ft.
Price        $500,000 - $700,000

## Rentals

### Apartment
Bedrooms
Price        $700 - $900 month

### Townhouse
Bedrooms
Price        $800 - $1,500 month

### House
Bedrooms
Price        $800 - $1,200 month

## Travel Times

Distance to downtown Phoenix:
17.5 miles

To downtown Phoenix (via the 202):
Peak: 35 - 40 minutes
Off-peak: 25 minutes

To the airport (via the 202):
Peak: 33 - 40 minutes
Off-peak: 23 minutes

including Red Mountain, Las Sendas, Alta Mesa, Leisure World, Parkwood Ranch & The Groves

North Mesa is where Scottsdale prestige meets East Valley family-friendly. Homes here can top the $3 million mark, 18 holes of golf can cost $150 in winter, and Diamondbacks players can pass you in their Hummers. The nearest night club or art gallery is far away, but the parks and schools are fantastic. Commutes are easy, too. "Scottsdale has nicer restaurants, and that's it," one resident says.

With increasingly sophisticated residents moving in, North Mesa is shaking off some of the God-fearing conservatism for which the city has long had a reputation. Only recently, a wine bar opened in the same area as a video store that was sued by Hollywood studios for editing sex and violence out of rentals. Thankfully, it's now possible to go home with both a nice bottle of pinot and "Kill Bill 2."

The Salt River Pima and Maricopa Indians believe their tribes will thrive as long as they live in sight of Red Mountain. Your tribe could thrive there too.

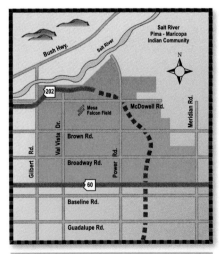

Total Population: 198,000 approx.
Median Age: 40 years
Median Household Income: $45,000 p.a.

## Who Lives There?

In the Las Sendas luxury area, you'll find executives, lawyers, doctors, and professionals of every stripe, plus pro athletes here and there. Families like Red Mountain's consistent look, excellent schools, and hillside and city lights views. The area is seeing an influx of retiring Midwesterners who have written off Florida.

## Homes

Realtors generally compare northeast Mesa's quality with Scottsdale's, at $100,000 less for any size of home. Stucco-and-tile is the order of the day, with some Santa Fe contemporary custom homes sprinkled around the top-drawer developments. This is not an area to go looking for a bargain buy. Most homeowners and agents are only too aware of property values.

Both Red Mountain and Las Sendas have patio homes and townhouses, but not small single-family homes. Three bedrooms start at around $300,000 and go well into the millions. Low end in Las Sendas is around $400,000.

Drive across north Mesa in spring and the air is perfumed with orange blossoms. Some of the groves are left, but many were bulldozed for housing. The Groves is an older subdivision along the Eastern Canal near Brown Road and Val Vista Drive named after the citrus it replaced. Alta Mesa is a well-kept neighborhood in the same area with great value and tall trees.

## Amenities

### Schools ★★★

North Mesa schools are academically solid schools in the Mesa Unified School District and provide many outstanding learning opportunities. One example of this is Salk Elementary School, which partners with Boeing for its Junior Achievement program and has a Boeing flight center with child-sized simulators on campus.

Both of the area's junior high schools—Fremont and Smith—have been rated

as "excelling" and have high marks on the AIMS and Stanford 9 tests, especially in math.

Red Mountain and Skyline are the two North Mesa high schools.

For students who have difficulty in their neighborhood schools, North Mesa has two alternative public schools. Power Middle School provides smaller classes and daily parent contact for seventh through ninth graders. Boulder Canyon High School offers 10th through 12th graders a similar program with focus on career development.

North Mesa is also home to School-Home Adjustment Reinforcement Program (SHARP) for special education students who require a more comprehensive program than neighborhood schools can offer.

## Shopping & Dining ★★★

It was quite awhile before decent restaurants appeared, leaving people in million-plus homes in the curious position of weighing a drive to Scottsdale versus takeout chile rellenos. Much to their relief, that has now changed. The Village at Las Sendas at McDowell and Power Roads features the D-vine Wine Bar & Bistro, a handmade bread bakery, and a Spanish fusion restaurant. North Mesa's first tennis shop also opened in the Village. Anzio Landing at Falcon Field is a good Italian place (popular with Mesa veterans who were actually at Anzio).

For a big mall, you need to drive to Fiesta Mall down on the 60. There are strip malls with discount clothing outlets and dry cleaners, but for Tiffany's, $300 jeans, and Williams-Sonoma, head to Scottsdale.

## Leisure ★★★

Red Mountain Park is one of the best city parks in the Valley. At 1,146 acres, it's also one of the biggest. Ballfields, playgrounds, walking trails, volleyball courts, picnic armadas, and a lake stocked with rainbow trout, bluegill, and largemouth bass are a few of its features. There's also a multigenerational (as opposed to senior) center with a gym, climbing wall, dance and sports classes, and a club for kids up to age eight.

Las Sendas has a Robert Trent Jones-designed golf course.

# Real Estate

## Trends

Remodels in older northeast Mesa neighborhoods are popular. Buyers like the larger lots older homes were built on. Prices run from $200,000 to $300,000 for a 40- to 50-year-old home. There's very little below that price. There are no single-family homes below $100,000 available any more.

Mesa orange grove homes, many of them custom-built on acre-and-a-half lots, are more affordable than similar properties in Chandler or Tempe. Those homes and high gas prices are heating up the north and east Mesa markets.

This area may well skyrocket even more. High tech businesses are moving into industrial parks surrounding Falcon Field because they've got both eye-blink freeway access to the Loop 202 and an airfield at their front door. Only half of Falcon Field's land is developed. Land prices at the Scottsdale Airpark are soaring. With 200 vacant acres of cheaper land, expect companies with corporate aviation needs to move here. Fast-movers who run those businesses will want to live close to work. They won't want to move to the east side of town with green gravel lawns and ceramic Dalmations in the yard. That leaves Red Mountain and Las Sendas.

## Rental & Investment

Investment has put some quality homes on the rental market. Expect to pay about $950 per month for a three-bedroom two-bath built in 2002. Vacation rentals are plentiful, but snowbird rates ($800 per week, in some cases) make them untenable for year-round residents.

For retirees, Leisure World is considered an undervalued development which will appreciate quickly due to the upcoming wave of Baby Boomers joining the Metamucil generation.

## Local Hero: Canyon Lake

Canyon Lake is the prettiest and most interesting of the Valley's seven lakes. Forty-five miles northeast of Phoenix, the 950-acre lake's 28-mile shoreline is interspersed by red rock cliffs soaring from the water. Bighorn sheep scamper over ledges. It's a wild place; a few years ago a mountain lion tried to pull a small boy from a rowboat. Teenagers go cliff jumping in spring.

Fishermen cast for bass, bluegill, walleye, and rainbow trout. Jet skiing and water skiing are popular. If you're looking for peace and quiet, go to the east end of the lake where the canyon narrows. Boat camping is allowed at designated spots. If you don't have a boat, take a dinner cruise on the Dolly Steamboat and watch the canyon walls turn gold at sunset. You can also rent boats at the marina.

Tortilla Flat is an old stage stop and saloon at the end of the lake favored by bikers and European tourists. The barstools are saddles. Snakeskins are nailed on the walls. The food guarantees an authentic territorial Arizona experience; the cook apparently learned his trade in a cow camp. The place stays in business for three reasons: no one can ruin beer, the Germans won't be back anyway, and bikers don't care what they eat.

## At a Glance...

## House Prices

### Townhouse
| | |
|---|---|
| Bedrooms | 🛏 🛏 |
| Price | $150,000+ |

### Family home
| | |
|---|---|
| Bedrooms | 🛏 🛏 |
| Price | $200,000 - $300,000 |

### Family home
| | |
|---|---|
| Bedrooms | 🛏 🛏 🛏 |
| Price | $200,000 - $300,000+ |

### Family home
| | |
|---|---|
| Bedrooms | 🛏 🛏 🛏 🛏 |
| Price | $400,000 - $900,000 |

### Executive home
| | |
|---|---|
| Area | Min. 4,000 sq. ft. |
| Price | $800,000 - $2,000,000 |

## Rentals

### Apartment
| | |
|---|---|
| Bedrooms | 🛏 🛏 |
| Price | $800 - $1,000 month |

### Townhouse
| | |
|---|---|
| Bedrooms | 🛏 🛏 |
| Price | $1,000 - $1,500 month |

### House
| | |
|---|---|
| Bedrooms | 🛏 🛏 🛏 |
| Price | $900 - $1,200 month |

## Travel Times

Distance to downtown Phoenix (from McDowell & Power Roads via the 202):

27 miles

To downtown Phoenix (from McDowell & Power Roads via the 202):

Peak: 40 minutes
Off-peak: 30 minutes

To the airport (from McDowell & Power Roads via the 202):

Peak: 35 minutes
Off-peak: 25 minutes

*Mesa*

South Mesa is all new: new homes, new schools, new shopping centers. Gleaming golf courses, mountain views in select spots, professional neighbors, and uncongested streets are a few reasons why south Mesa turns heads. There are two main draws which make the 85212 ZIP code Mesa's hottest: it's in the excellent Gilbert school district, but it's taxed by the city of Mesa, meaning there are no property taxes.

New malls have poured into South Mesa in recent years, with more to come. "One corner has three Starbuck's," one agent says. "At five bucks for a cup of coffee, it's a pretty good indicator there is money here."

Almost all the neighborhoods in this area of Mesa are clustered just south of the U.S. 60 Freeway. The southern end is occupied by Williams Gateway Airport and the massive 5,000-acre General Motors Proving Grounds. The city has tried to make Williams another Scottsdale Airpark or a regional cargo hub, but nothing has really taken hold since the Air Force pulled out in 1993.

Total Population: 20,000 approx.
Median Age: 36 years
Median Household Income: $54,000 p.a.

## Who Lives There?

With Falcon Field and Williams Gateway nearby, and Sky Harbor a short drive away, aviation workers like Boeing engineers, commercial pilots, and flight training instructors form a large slice of the population. General Motors and TRW workers also enjoy South Mesa.

Young families, naturally, are the largest demographic. Retirees who don't want to live in a geriatric ghetto like the golf course patio homes. "You've never seen so many older couples living next door to families with four kids," according to one agent. "Younger, single people who want to be at the Scottsdale and Tempe bars, it's not for them."

## Homes

Homes here are typical of the south East Valley: stucco-and-tile houses, condos, and patio homes. Residents are quick to point out they have mountain views, which Chandler does not; actually this depends more on the individual home than the area. Everything's new or nearly new. This area was desert, not farmland, before development, meaning there won't be any problems with walls or foundations cracking because of expansive soils.

# Amenities

### Schools ★★★★

South Mesa schools are some of the newest schools in the Valley. Although located within the City of Mesa, these schools fall within the Gilbert Unified School District.

There are five elementary schools in the area. Superstition Springs and Boulder Creek Elementary Schools both have earned Reading Renaissance Master School status, meaning that less than 15 percent of the students are at risk in reading.

A new school, Desert Ridge, was awarded numerous band and orchestra awards during its first year. With its high Stanford 9 scores, Highland is an academic force to be reckoned with and its teachers have received many awards to prove it.

Equally as strong are the two high schools. Desert Ridge High School is a new high school that has recently received an Intel grant for a pre-engineering program. Highland High School also has strong athletic and musical programs. The boys volleyball team won the 5A State championship in 2004, and Highland High marching band was selected to perform in the 2004 Macy's Parade.

### Shopping & Dining ★★★

Retail is rapidly following residential into South Mesa. There are eight neighborhood shopping centers, centered around either Baseline or Ellsworth Roads. They're all nearly new, with well-appointed grocery stores and necessities like hair, nails, tanning, pizza, and bars.

Superstition Springs Center

The Superstition Gateway mall, on Baseline Road near Signal Butte Road and U.S. 60, will feature 700,000 square feet of retail when it opens in 2006. Tenants include Wal-Mart, Kohl's, Staples, Bed, Bath & Beyond and a multiplex.

Superstitions Springs Center is the area's power mall. More than 150 stores include Gap, Victoria's Secret, Dillard's, and Robinson's-May.

A yet-to-be-named mall will open in 2007 at Signal Butte Road and U.S. 60. The $125 million project, anchored by a 16-screen multiplex, will also feature big box stores, restaurants and smaller retailers. Tenants had not been announced at press time.

Beyond locally-owned pizza and Chinese places, dining is limited to chains like Olive Garden and Chili's.

## Leisure ★ ★ ★ ★ ★

One of the most exciting ways to shoot down an afternoon is at Fighter Combat International at Williams Gateway Airport. You fly up with military fighter pilots in an aerobatic plane, they then hand over the controls, and you fight it out in the desert skies. No flight experience is required, believe it or not.

A motorcycle track and a shooting range are about ten minutes away. Both Gilbert and Mesa have plenty of sports leagues for kids and adults.

For a more idyllic afternoon, Payson, snow, and the cool pines are an hour away. Canyon and Saguaro Lakes are within a 20 minute drive, including a stop to fill the ice chest.

Augusta Ranch Golf Course gets great reviews, and residents of neighboring master-plans receive 20 percent off greens fees.

# Real Estate

## Trends

Despite the family majority, the most sought-after housing in South Mesa is geared towards singles. Single-level two-car garage patio homes, especially those on golf course lots, are in high demand. Single parents, snowbirds wanting second homes, widowers, nurses and medical techs from nearby Banner Baywood hospital all hunt for patio homes.

Two new hospitals are expected to create even more demand for condos and patio homes. The Mountain Vista Medical Center is under construction at Southern Avenue and Crismon Road and Banner Gateway Medical Center is being built in Gilbert at Higley and Baseline roads.

## Rental & Investment

South Mesa is full of families who rent because they want the good schools and quiet neighborhoods, but can't afford homes. House rentals are abundant, and don't cost much more than renting an apartment. A four-bedroom will rent for about $1,100 a month and a three-bedroom for about $900. Townhouses are in demand, but you may find one for about $750 to $850 a month for a two-bedroom.

### Why I live there

### Uffelman family

Clean, family-friendly neighborhoods attracted the Uffelman family to their South Mesa home where Brent, Katrina, and their two children, Jacob and Colleen, have lived since moving from Apache Junction.

"We chose to live in Mesa because of the variety of restaurants and the stores," Katrina said. "We're close to Power Road here and all that area has to offer."

Superstition Springs Mall anchors the Power Road and Interstate 60 megastores where the family shops and dines at nearby restaurants. For entertainment, they venture to Harkins Superstition Springs Luxury 25 movie theater.

## At a Glance...
## House Prices

### Townhouse
| Bedrooms | |
| --- | --- |
| Price | $170,000 - $210,000 |

### Family home
| Bedrooms | |
| --- | --- |
| Price | $250,000 - $300,000 |

### Family home
| Bedrooms | |
| --- | --- |
| Price | $250,000 - $350,000 |

### Family home
| Bedrooms | |
| --- | --- |
| Price | $300,000 - $400,000 |

### Executive home
| Area | Min. 4,000 sq. ft. |
| --- | --- |
| Price | $350,000 - $550,000 |

### Patio Home on a golf course
| Bedrooms | |
| --- | --- |
| Price | $250,000 - $450,000 |

## Rentals

### Apartment
Very few apartments available for rent. You may find one for about $700 to $800 a month.

### Townhouse
Very few townhouses available for monthly rental.

### House
| Bedrooms | |
| --- | --- |
| Price | $900 - $1,200 month |

## Travel Times
Distance to downtown Phoenix:
30 miles

To downtown Phoenix:
Peak: 45 minutes – 1 hour
Off-peak: 35 minutes

To the airport:
Peak: 52 minutes – 1 hour 5 minutes
Off-peak: 28 minutes

North West Mesa, called Mesa Grande, may be one of the best value suburbs in the Valley. Real estate agents call the area a sleeper. Freeway location southeast of the intersection of the Loops 101 and 202 is unbeatable for getting anywhere quickly. A massive regional mall and office complex being built is expected to catalyze neighborhood improvements.

When Riverview at Dobson opens by summer 2007 at the Loop 101 and Dobson Road, it will feature a 16-screen movie theater, a Wal-Mart Supercenter, a Home Depot, a Bass Pro Shops store, an auto mall, and a five-building office complex. (Developers estimate about 6,000 jobs will be created.) Like South Scottsdale with ASU's upcoming thinktank, home values and competition to buy is heating up before the project is even built.

Towards the Mesa Country Club, east of Country Club Drive, the quality of homes and streets jumps dramatically. All of West Mesa south of the U.S. 60 Freeway looks like a country club. Dobson Ranch, a 30 year-old master-planned community of 5,000 homes, dominates this corner of the city. It has established landscaping, winding streets, three schools, six churches, seven lakes, a golf course and a strong homeowners' association.

*Total Population: 112,000 approx.*
*Median Age: 28 years*
*Median Household Income: $38,000 p.a.*

## Who Lives There?

Mesa Grande has always been a working class area. There is a sizeable population of Hispanics for whom Spanish is their first language. Dobson Ranch residents are attorneys, business owners, and white-collar chip jockeys. Many of them have lived in the community since it was built in the early 1970s.

## Homes

Mesa Grande homes and townhouses range from the early 1950s to the 1970s. Solidly-built post-war ranches with mature landscaping are great value. A 40 year-old three bedroom home will cost around $300,000. The same home will cost $450,000 in Tempe or $550,000 in Scottsdale. Lots are big, too.

Realtors recommend hunting in the quadrant between Main Street and McKellips Road and Dobson Road and Mesa Drive. Anything in that area under $300,000 will have positive appreciation and resale value.

Townhouses run from $105,000 for a small 1980s two-bedroom, two-bath to the high $190,000s for a large early 1990s two-bedroom two-bath with a fireplace, microwave, community pool, and attractive landscaping. Five bedroom family homes range from the mid to high $400,000s.

Farther east, around the Mesa Country Club, 2,200 square-foot executive patio homes in the $300,000s look out over the golf course.

Dobson Ranch homes were built from the 1970s through the early 1980s. They range from thick stucco with shake roofs to creamy white 1980s stucco with tile roofs. Homes with golf course or lakefront views, or within school walking distance, are the most sought after. Housing includes single-family homes, patio homes, condominiums and townhouses.

# Amenities

### Schools ★★★

West Mesa is home to some of the Valley's best school enrichment and

extracurricular programs. All schools in this area are part of the Mesa Unified District, all but one are rated "performing" or higher. There are 13 elementary schools, four junior high schools and three high schools.

Washington Elementary has an accelerated reader program. Hendrix Junior High in Chandler has a weather station/agricultural project lab. At Rhodes Junior High 42 percent of students make the honor roll. These three school are rated "highly performing."

Westwood and Dobson high schools provide a traditional high school experience. More than 90 percent of Dobson's graduating class plan on continuing their education.

East Valley Academy is the area's third high school. Located on the East Valley

Institute of Technology (EVIT) campus, nearly all students attend classes at the Academy in the morning and technical programs at the Institute in the afternoon. Some of the technical programs available are firefighting, cosmetology, nursing, and graphic design.

Also on the EVIT campus is the Teenage Parent Program (TAPP). This is an all-girls school that helps students complete the academic requirements for graduation while learning parenting skills.

Another option is the Eagleridge Enrichment Program. This campus brings together home-schooled students for classroom experience one to two times a week.

The East Valley Institute of Technology is a public, regional, technical education district that serves students from ten East Valley school districts. Students spend a half-day in a technology programs like computer technology and health sciences and the other half-day at their home high school. All 10th, 11th and 12th grade

students can attend free if they meet class prerequisites. Free bus services are provided by the student's home school district.

## Shopping & Dining ★★

Fiesta Mall, a long-time Mesa shopping staple at the U.S. 60 and Alma School Road, has more than 135 stores including Macy's, Robinson's-May, and Sears.

Larada's Army Surplus and Outdoor Store is a Mesa institution at 764 W. Main. Ammo cans for whitewater rafting, sleeping bags, knives, camouflage netting, bungee cords, gold pans – it's an adventure superstore. Merchandise is a lot cheaper than the chain outdoor goods stores.

The Landmark Restaurant on Main Street plates well-done American food like prime rib, chicken Marsala, salmon, and roast lamb. Beyond that, if you have a palate, flee the area.

## Leisure ★★

Dobson Ranch residents have privileges at four swimming pools, three recreation centers, several tennis courts, racket ball and basketball courts, picnic grounds with ramadas, and a public park, as well as the lakes and golf course.

Mesa Grande has the advantage of proximity to Riverview Park, a city park with a stocked fishing lake, a golf course, athletic fields, and picnic areas. With expansive mountain and Valley views it's

*Mesa*

# West Mesa

a perfect place to watch Fourth of July fireworks.

The private Mesa Country Club welcomes applications for golf, tennis, clubhouse, and social memberships.

# Real Estate

## Trends

Realtors call Mesa Grande one of the best value areas in the entire Valley because of price, location, and promise. They compare it to South Scottsdale five or six years ago: an underpriced area with a great location, homes with good bones, and revitalization projects in the wings. For a good investment, find a rough house on a well-manicured street. (Agents rave about the neighborhood northeast of Main Street and Alma School Road.)

## At a Glance...

### House Prices

**Townhouse**

| Bedrooms | |
|---|---|
| Price | $100,000 - $200,000 |

**Family home**

| Bedrooms | |
|---|---|
| Price | $250,000 - $300,000 |

**Family home**

| Bedrooms | |
|---|---|
| Price | $300,000 - $350,000 |

**Family home**

| Bedrooms | |
|---|---|
| Price | $300,000 - $400,000 |

**Executive home**

| Area | Min. 4,000 sq. ft. |
|---|---|
| Price | $400,000 - $500,000+ |

### Rentals

**Apartment**

Very few apartments available for rent. If you find one it will run about $600 to $800 a month for a two-bedroom.

**Townhouse**

| Bedrooms | |
|---|---|
| Price | $600 - $800 month |

**House**

| Bedrooms | |
|---|---|
| Price | $900 - $1,100 month |

### Travel Times

Distance to downtown Phoenix: 42 miles

To downtown Phoenix:
Peak: 35 – 45 min
Off-peak: 25 minutes

To the airport:
Peak: 25 – 35 minutes
Off-peak: 18 minutes

Scottsdale

A local headline a few years back read "Scottsdale Couple Insists They Own Road." The headline was in reference to a zoning right-of-way dispute, but managed to simultaneously convey a not-inaccurate stereotype.

No other city in the Valley has an Arabian horse show, the world's most famous collector car auction, professional golf tournaments, resorts Nebuchadnezzar would've been spoiled by, and Hollywood stars flying in to party at their night clubs. Celebrities love Scottsdale because clubs like AXIS / Radius, the Cateye Lounge, the James Hotel, and AZ88 are lavish and paparazzi nonexistent. Sushi bars are everywhere, outnumbered only by the Beautiful People.

Scottsdale's national image, however, has been blue-rinsed matrons playing

golf. That's history. Retirees are rapidly being replaced by a young, hip crowd. As the older generation passes away or moves into assisted living, twenty- and thirtysomethings are buying old Sun Belt condos and ranch homes. They want to live where they party, so they're replacing the snowbird flocks. The younger generation is gutting the 40 and 50 year-old vacation properties and pouring tens of thousands of dollars into renovations.

Demand is also increasing as the city approaches buildout. Home values in the once-maligned south have skyrocketed with the announcement of ASU's intention to build a tech thinktank. Freeway access for both North and South Scottsdale via

## Sushi bars are everywhere, outnumbered only by the Beautiful People.

the Loop 101 has also driven convenience and pricing.

Conscientious and dedicated oversight by the city and citizens groups have guided quality development. Traffic islands in Scottsdale are landscaped; if there's room, you might find a sculpture plonked down as well. Scottsdale was the first city in the Valley to have its freeways decorated with public art. It's also the only city to demand one of five approved colors for North Scottsdale homes, so they blend into the desert from a distance (it works, too; try picking out McDowell Mountain Ranch from the freeway). The city came up with a design idea book for the old south Scottsdale ranch homes, complete with blueprints.

Scottsdale has long cultivated its image of Western gentility, but there's substance behind the veneer.

Art is a huge part of Scottsdale life. James Turrell, Allen Ginsberg, Louise Nevelson, and Fritz Scholder have all contributed to Scottsdale's national reputation as an arts town.

Dining reigns supreme alongside art in Scottsdale. James Beard Award winners and celebrity chefs outnumber golf courses. In most cities, only tourists eat and drink at hotels. In the Valley, locals celebrate special occasions and romantic weekends at Scottsdale's glittering resorts.

Not all of Scottsdale's charms are so rarefied. Scottsdale Stadium hosts Cactus League spring training baseball and is the winter home of the San Francisco Giants. The Parada del Sol, a Scottsdale institution, is the longest equestrian parade in the world.

Beautiful mountains, excellent schools, wonderful amenities — there are a lot of reasons Scottsdale deserves its enviable reputation.

# Central Scottsdale ★★★★ *Scottsdale*

including Gainey Ranch, McCormick Ranch, Scottsdale Ranch

South Scottsdale is for art, partying and shopping. North Scottsdale is for events and golf. But Central Scottsdale is the place for living. The area between Chaparral Road and the Central Arizona Project Canal certainly has its fair share of golf courses, shopping, and resorts, but it's dominated by housing of all stripes. Golf course and lakefront executive homes, horse properties, retro Sun Belt condos and patio homes ripe for rehabbing, all of them replete with swimming pools, palm trees, and sunshine. This is the Scottsdale from the ads. This is the good life.

There are also plenty of single family ranch homes built in the 1960s and 1970s, some of them move-in ready, some just waiting for vision and paint. Look west between Scottsdale Road and the Phoenix border for lower-priced (but hardly bargain) resale homes if you want to save, remodel, and still live in the West's Most Western Town.

The Scottsdale Airpark is the area's economic driver. The executive airport is surrounded by an industrial park, home to dozens of young, hip companies: China Mist iced tea, JDA Software, a controversial stun gun maker and exotic sports car importers. Slews of software designers start work early and leave work late on their way to the American IPO dream.

Total Population: 87,000 approx.
Median Age: 43 years
Median Household Income: $63,000 p.a.

## Who Lives There?

Central Scottsdale is undeniably upper middle-class. Here you'll find grand mothers in tennis whites, real estate power women, developers who have built the rest of the Valley, and moms who wouldn' be caught dead wearing sweatpants to the grocery store.

There is a sizeable Muslim population working in the airpark tech industry and living in the area; Arizona's largest mosque is in central Scottsdale. Retirees still flock to south central Scottsdale to live in townhome complexes, although fewer and fewer every year.

Horse people are holding on by their hooves to their traditional properties despite almost total buildout and East Coast newcomers complaining about dust and flies.

## Homes

Central Scottsdale is dominated by three master-planned communities built in the 1970s and 1980s.

McCormick Ranch, a former cattle and horse ranch, was the city's first master-planned community. It's very green with mature trees, lawns, and tropical palms and sports 130 acres of man-made lakes for sailing and fishing, together with two 18-hole golf courses.

Scottsdale Ranch, east on Shea, has a 42-acre lake and homes ranging from one-bedroom condominiums to multi-million dollar luxury homes. It's impeccably maintained and landscaped.

Gainey Ranch is an exclusive gated golf community. More than a few Arizona power brokers from industry and government live here. Homes range from genteel condominiums to executive showplaces.

Central Scottsdale features quite a few horse properties, especially around Cactus and Sweetwater, and in the arm of Scottsdale heading east to Fountain Hills. There are two horse parks with arenas, round pens, and other facilities; Mescal Park and Stonegate Equestrian Park.

## Amenities

### Schools ★★★★★

The Scottsdale Unified School District educates most of Scottsdale's students, including those in Central Scottsdale. Most of the schools in the district are either "excelling" or "highly performing" schools.

One of the better schools is Cochise Elementary School, which consistently scores high on both state and national tests. The school was recently awarded an Exxon Mobile Educational Alliance Program grant to use in its science lab. Pueblo Elementary School also has a strong academic program. Most students in the area move on to Mohave Middle School.

Both of Central Scottsdale's high schools are "excelling." Ninety percent of Saguaro High School's graduates pursue higher education, and Chaparral High School seems to always have a high number of National Merit semi-finalists.

### Shopping & Dining ★★★★★

The Shops at Gainey Village is a shopping and gathering spot with upscale boutiques

# Central Scottsdale

and restaurants a mile or so from the Scottsdale Hyatt Regency.

Kierland Commons, located on the Phoenix side of Scottsdale Road, has attracted national attention for its main street-style outdoor shopping. Buildings of varying heights surround a central plaza, mixing offices and lofts with about 70 high-end stores like Gauthier, Lucky Brand Dungarees, and Anthropologie. (42 Saint – considered by the dapper set to be the Valley's coolest clothing store – is here). It's a happening place, prowled during the day by ladies who lunch and at night by the young and the beautiful.

Frank Lloyd Wright Boulevard from Scottsdale Road to the 101 Freeway is wall-to-wall big box stores and auto dealerships. Washing machines, stereos, kids clothes, BMWs – it's consumption junction.

You won't find a dining establishment which has been beloved by all for decades in Central Scottsdale, but you will find world-class food at the resorts and beyond. Zinc Bistro is a European-style treasure with truly great food.

Robert McGrath of Roaring Fork is a national star, winner of the James Beard Award in 2001. If you don't have hundreds for dinner, go in to the Fork down on

Chaparral, have the best burger you ever had in your life, and thank Robert for giving the working man a chance to taste Beard-caliber food.

## Leisure ★★★

Golf, naturally, is the dominant pastime in Central Scottsdale. It's not the only activity, however.

Architecture and design junkies can visit Taliesin West, Frank Lloyd Wright's winter home and studio. Central Scottsdale is home to 30-acre McCormick-Stillman Park which has a carousel and a miniature train that winds along a one-mile track. The 42-acre Scottsdale Ranch Park features lighted ball courts of all kinds, including 14 tennis courts. There are miles of paved pathways that connect all the parks. Bikers, joggers, walkers and skaters can go from park to park without having to cross a street.

The Cattletrack artists colony is a 13-acre collection of historic homes and artists studios built in the 1930s alongside a canal. Cattletrack is creative, elegantly rustic, and laid-back; it's the best of Scottsdale.

# Real Estate

## Trends

The Chaparral Road area is surrounded by townhome complexes. For decades, they catered to snowbirds. As retirees have fled Scottsdale's hubbub, people in their late twenties and thirties have bought south central townhomes, gutted them, and remodeled. The $200,000 to high $300,000 prices they paid are fantastic value, especially when it's three minutes from Fashion Square, five minutes from downtown clubs, and two minutes from the 101 Freeway.

## Rental & Investment

The savvy renter can do well in Central Scottsdale. For instance, a two-bedroom two-bath gated condo in McCormick Ranch, with a garage, fireplace, and a wet bar, rents for about $1,200 a month. A two-bedroom two-bath in a rat-maze apartment complex (with a pool, volleyball court, workout room, and BBQ pits) rents for about $900 and change. Living like a human is worth another $10 a day.

## Local Hero: Mighty Mud Mania

You'd think the preferred children's activity in Scottsdale would be recognizing Dolce & Gabbana jeans from 100 feet away, perfecting the backhand smash or introductory dressage, but in fact it's playing in mud.

Eleven thousand children. One hundred tons of mud. This is Mighty Mud Mania, and Valley kids have loved this more than Christmas for two decades.

Mighty Mud Mania began 20 years ago as a promotional schtick for a pre-wash spray. The sponsoring company handed out 300 white T-shirts. The pre-wash couldn't get out that Arizona mud, so the company dropped the event. However, it was so wildly popular the parks department incorporated it into their summer recreation program. Some of the first kids to go to Mighty Mud Mania now bring their own little ones. Last year four women in their thirties drove down from Prescott to go through wearing old prom dresses.

Bring garbage bags for the car seats and wear clothes you plan to throw away.

## At a Glance...

## House Prices
### Townhouse
Bedrooms 🛏 🛏
Price $350,000 - $450,000
### Family home
Bedrooms 🛏 🛏
Price $400,000 - $650,000
### Family home
Bedrooms 🛏 🛏 🛏
Price $500,000 - $700,000
### Family home
Bedrooms 🛏 🛏 🛏 🛏
Price $600,000 - $900,000
### Executive home
Area Min. 4,000 sq. ft.
Price $1,500,000 - $2,500,000

## Rentals
### Apartment
Bedrooms 🛏 🛏
Price $1,100 - $2,000 month
### Townhouse
Bedrooms 🛏 🛏
Price $2,000 - $2,500 month
### House
Bedrooms 🛏 🛏 🛏
Price $1,700 - $2,000 month

## Travel Times
Distance to downtown Phoenix: 17 miles

To downtown Phoenix:
Peak: 35 minutes
Off-peak: 25 minutes

To the airport:
Peak: 33 minutes
Off-peak: 23 minutes

# North Scottsdale ★★★★★ *Scottsdale*

### including Grayhawk, DC Ranch, McDowell Mountain Ranch, Estancia and Desert Mountain

North Scottsdale is one of the nation's 12 most expensive second-home markets. The median home price in 2004 was $528,000. Only in Paradise Valley and the Biltmore Estate are homes pricier. You don't see builders' signs reading "Jackalope Trails – From the Low $1,000,000s" anywhere else in the Valley.

No exact boundaries exist, but North Scottsdale is generally defined as the area north of the Central Arizona Project Canal. It's a Bel Air of the desert, an enclave of retired CEOs and tycoons of one sort or another. North Scottsdale is all about status: European SUVs, polo matches, golf tournaments, and $38 steaks.

Many of the state's most up-market communities are here, with private golf courses, country clubs, custom homes and 24-hour guard-gates. Many of the communities, such as Estancia, Desert Highlands and Troon, and a Four Seasons resort, nestle around the base of Pinnacle Peak, North Scottsdale's most distinctive and coveted landmark.

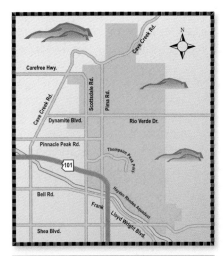

Total Population: 45,000 approx.
Median Age: 43 years
Median Household Income: $99,000 p.a.

## Who Lives There?

North Scottsdale is overwhelmingly white and rich. The North Scottsdale stereotype is a blonde trophy wife racing to Pilates class in a Mercedes-Benz Roadster (red, convertible) barking orders at her interior designer on her cell.

There are also the Jaguar-and-golf retirees, many from the Midwest and East Coast. New money has a substantial foothold in North Scottsdale; afternoon day-care pickup can look like Playboy tryouts.

Residents in North Scottsdale's three big master-planned communities tend to be younger and more middle class. A typical Grayhawk resident is a young couple with a baby; he works in finance and she's a homemaker. White-collar, dual-income couples with children gravitate towards DC Ranch and McDowell Mountain Ranch.

There are also horse people who live on a few acres in the desert and want nothing to do with planned communities. Old timers who until recently lived in rustic, isolated splendor and remember when real cowboys tied up their horses at Reata Pass; and a few other folks who are neither rich nor retired, but just want to live in a pretty place.

## Homes

Homes are mostly newer; ten years and less. They're large and lavish. Some of them have guesthouses bigger than most central Phoenix homes. North Scottsdale has hundreds of really beautiful homes, built and designed with exquisite taste. Santa Fe contemporary is a popular architectural style, with its clean, timeless desert lines. There are unbelievable homes tucked away in Estancia and Desert Mountain; places which look like some Spanish lord built them 700 years ago.

Homes in Estancia start at around $2 million. For anything affordable, say less than the $400,000, expect town and patio homes, condominiums, old homes that need rejuvenation and older houses sitting out in the desert.

Building and aesthetics regulations here are strictly controlled by the city. Powerful local citizens groups have kept the area from turning into a fast-food and big-box carnival. Architecture is mandated to blend into the desert, no neon or bright lights. Houses must be painted one of the city-approved beige hues.

## Amenities

### Schools ★★★★★

The schools of North Scottsdale tend to be newer and almost universally "excelling." Students are motivated, and parents are involved. Although there are a few Cave Creek Unified District schools in the area, most students attend Scottsdale Unified District schools.

Desert Mountain High School epitomizes the schools of this area. New and well-funded, this school has an excellent academic program and is an International Baccalaureate (IB) World School, offering students the chance to complete rigorous pre-college coursework. Apparently, the IB program and emphasis on academic success is paying off — in 2004, Desert Mountain students earned over $6.4 million in scholarships!

### Shopping & Dining ★★★★

Neighborhood shopping is mostly boutiques offering high-end clothing, home accessories, custom kitchens, fine art and crafts. You can also buy a hammer at Ace Hardware, aspirin at Osco or Walgreen's and groceries at nearby Safeway and Bashas'. AJ's Fine Foods is a neighborhood magnet that draws folks for morning coffee, weekend BBQs and fancy take-home dinners.

Drive about 20 minutes and all your shopping fantasies are fulfilled. Costco is in the Scottsdale Airpark, along with several remodelling and decorating stores, some at near-wholesale prices. Shopping behemoths Desert Ridge, Kierland Commons, the Promenade and 101 North are within a 15 minute drive.

Need more horsepower? The Scottsdale 101 Auto Collection includes all the fantasy-for-most brands: Aston-Martin, BMW, Mercedes, Porsche and others. Ironically, these plush showrooms sit on the former Chauncey Ranch where champion Arabian horses once grazed.

Mastro's steakhouse sits on the northeast corner of Pinnacle Peak and Pima Roads. On weekends it's a meet/meat market where steaks and patrons both have sizzle to spare. You'll also occasionally find a neckless retired mobster in a tracksuit peacefully smoking a cigar. For a more casual meal, dine at Nick's, Thai Pan or Café Ted – small and intimate privately-owned cafes.

## Leisure ★★★★

If golf is your game, prepare to break open the piggy bank. At local public course Troon North, you will pay up to $295 for 18 holes on a weekend during the winter season. The Tournament Players Club (TPC) at the Princess Resort, also public, is slightly less: $228.50 for the Stadium Course, peak season. The TPC's Desert Course comes in at a very modest $57. Private golf clubs usually have residency requirements; membership fees start around $95,000.

The McDowell Mountains provide an elegant backdrop for many of winter's big events. The Thunderbird Classic balloon festival, Barrett-Jackson car auction and Arabian Horse Show at WestWorld. The FBR (formerly Phoenix) Open golf tournament at the TPC; fine art and arts and crafts shows, polo matches, and horse and dog shows.

# Real Estate

## Trends

In May 2004, Scottsdale voters approved an additional sales tax to purchase 16,600 acres to add to the McDowell Sonoran Land Trust's current 11,250 acres. That vote essentially put a cap on growth and sent prices soaring into the stratosphere.

The era has ended for large, planned communities like DC Ranch and Grayhawk; there are no more big chunks of land. Two smaller developments are in the pipeline: 80 acres on the northeast corner of Pima and Happy Valley Roads, and 160 acres at the southeast corner of Pinnacle Peak and Scottsdale Roads (where Rawhide was located).

## Rental & Investment

There are some very posh luxury apartment/condo complexes in Grayhawk. Beyond that, renting condos and homes can cost $3,000 per month and more during the winter. The great summer rental deals of a decade ago are gone forever; too many people now live in the Valley year-round.

## Local Hero: Greasewood Flat

Greasewood Flat was built in the late 1880s and used as a bunkhouse for cowboys working the local ranches. In the 1950s, Doc Cavalliere bought Greasewood, along with Reata Pass and 50 acres of surrounding land. Over the years, Greasewood has become an institution that packs in locals, regulars and tourists.

Greasewood patrons ride up in Harleys, BMWs and pick-up trucks to sip long-neck beers and do the two-step to the live country-western music. The floor is dirt and the ceiling is the sky. On chilly evenings, mesquite-wood fires crackle and glow.

Greasewood is one of the few spots where you can soak up some Old West atmosphere, dance the night away and forget it's 2006. For more, go to www.greasewoodflat.net.

# Smart Buy ✓

The best buy for investors now is raw land. A 10-acre, unimproved lot listed at $2.5 million can be split into four 2.5-acre lots for $1.35 million each . You can't go wrong buying land in North Scottsdale, even at today's prices. There isn't any more land and there aren't going to be any new projects.

## At a Glance...

## House Prices

### Townhouse
| | |
|---|---|
| Bedrooms | 🛏 🛏 |
| Price | $350,000 - $550,000 |

### Townhouse
| | |
|---|---|
| Bedrooms | 🛏 🛏 🛏 |
| Price | $400,000 - $700,000 |

### Family home
| | |
|---|---|
| Bedrooms | 🛏 🛏 |
| Price | $600,000 - $1,000,000 |

### Family home
| | |
|---|---|
| Bedrooms | 🛏 🛏 🛏 |
| Price | $700,000 - $1,000,000 |

### Family home
| | |
|---|---|
| Bedrooms | 🛏 🛏 🛏 🛏 |
| Price | $900,000 - $2,000,000 |

### Executive home
| | |
|---|---|
| Area | Min. 4,000 sq. ft. |
| Price | $1,500,000 - $3,000,000 |

## Rentals

### Apartment
| | |
|---|---|
| Bedrooms | 🛏 🛏 |
| Price | $1,500 - $3,000 month |

### Townhouse
| | |
|---|---|
| Bedrooms | 🛏 🛏 |
| Price | $1,500 - $3,000 month |

### House
| | |
|---|---|
| Bedrooms | 🛏 🛏 🛏 |
| Price | $2,500 - $4,000 month |

## Travel Times

Distance to downtown Phoenix: 28.5 miles

To downtown Phoenix:
Peak: 45 minutes – 1 hour
Off-peak: 30 – 45 minutes

To the airport:
Peak: 30 – 45 minutes
Off-peak: 30 minutes

South Scottsdale is where the legend began. Stately palms. Fragrant orange trees. Art galleries. Posh resorts. Affluent residents and visitors. Tennis. Genteel dude ranches. Martini-toting blondes in cowboy hats. Golf. Sunsets glowing on desert mountains.

That's the Scottsdale image formed (and fostered) when the city was incorporated more than 50 years ago. Back then the city didn't go much farther than Camelback Road, so geographical and social perceptions about "North Scottsdale" and "South Scottsdale" – the "Snobs & Slobs" – schism didn't exist.

As the city aged and grew, the original core deteriorated. It never became a slum, but lawns yellowed, shopping cheapened, and a tinge of seediness dulled the area's luster. Well-heeled residents migrated north to golf country.

Now the stigma is changing. Homebuyers realize they can have a $300,000 home for $200,000 close to two huge parks, seconds from the 101 and 202 Freeways, in one of the state's best school districts, and adjacent to the Valley's most happening downtown. Original Scottsdale is back on the horse. Yippie-kay-ay.

*Total Population: 66,000 approx.*
*Median Age: 40 years*
*Median Household Income: $41,000 p.a.*

## Who Lives There?

South Scottsdale is young; the median age is 40. Some of the original Motorola engineers still live there, chuckling over what they paid for their homes and what they're worth now. ASU faculty and staff enjoy proximity to the main Tempe campus, but without Tempe's perpetual carnival atmosphere. Entrepreneurs working slave hours in the Scottsdale Airpark come home late at night. Blue-collar workers tend to be more the type of guy who owns a custom body shop rather than someone who changes oil at a Jiffy Lube.

Generally, younger people are replacing the World War II generation. However those are young people with good salaries working in banking, finance, and high end retail. Now couples starting out are snapping up vintage ranch homes, gutting them, and plowing in another $50,000 in granite countertops and Jacuzzis.

Snowbirds still like South Scottsdale too. It remains a popular second home market.

## Homes

Almost all the homes are classic post-war ranch homes: California Ranch, Cowboy Ranch, and Swiss chalet Character Ranch are a few styles. Two South Scottsdale neighborhoods have been designated historic; more will follow.

Generally, Scottsdale prices drop from north to south. Starting uptown, the swanky twin 13-story Waterfront project towers on the corner of Camelback and Scottsdale Roads is projected to set you back from $400,000 to $3 million. Upscale retail, restaurants, and office space will occupy the first three floors. They'll be the city's tallest buildings, and mountain views should be jaw-droppers.

For those with kids, dogs, boats, and a penchant for gardening, the vintage ranches farther south are a good buy. They're well-built and are some of the best neighborhoods in the Valley.

# Amenities

## Schools ★★★

While not as new or, for the most part, as highly ranked as their North Scottsdale counterparts, South Scottsdale schools

are academically solid. One kindergarten through eighth grade school, Arcadia Neighborhood Learning Center, is nationally recognized for positive student behavior. Videos of the school's methods are distributed to educators throughout the country.

Ingleside Middle School is another nationally recognized area school. Designated a Blue Ribbon school by the US Department of Education in 2002, it is exceptional academically and has a strong band and orchestra program.

With its wheel-shaped school design, Arcadia High School is not to be outdone. This "excelling" school has a strong golf program and a television production studio.

## Shopping & Dining ★★★★★

More than 120 art galleries and studios are scattered across Scottsdale. Everything

from cutting-edge conceptual art, antique cavalry uniforms, gilt Spanish Colonial candelabra, 300-year-old armoires, Russian oil paintings – Scottsdale is a connoisseur's paradise. Marshall Way and West Main Street is where you'll find fine art, rugs, and antiques.

Old Town – on the east side of Scottsdale Road – is where you'll find rubber tomahawks, suspect turquoise jewelry, and three T-shirts for $10 depicting

desiccated skeletons and the legend "It's A Dry Heat."

Behemoth Scottsdale Fashion Square mall has Neiman Marcus and other upscale department stores, as well as boutiques like Louis Vuitton, and Tiffany & Co. When you're exhausted from shopping, relax with a movie in the multiplex or at one of the swanky bars and restaurants.

The Antique Center on Scottsdale Road north of McDowell is a great place to find Mexican antiques at a third of what you'll pay on West Main Street.

Dining is almost as daunting a choice in Scottsdale as shopping. From south to north; a few favorites:

De Falco's Italian Deli at 2334 N. Scottsdale Road has great subs and everything else Etruscan. AZ88, across from the Scottsdale Center for the Arts is the Valley's most elegant bar. Z Tejas in Scottsdale Fashion Square, serves lethal margaritas (they cut you off at three) and good food. Malee's On Main is a wonderful Thai place in the gallery district with gracious service.

## Leisure ★★★★★

Indian Bend Wash is a 7.5 mile-long greenbelt with parks, golf courses, bike

paths, picnic areas, small lakes for boating and fishing, ball fields, and tennis courts. The city also built the Wedge Skatepark, an excellent skateboarding facility, in Indian Bend Wash.

# Real Estate

## Trends

Some North Scottsdale residents are moving to South Scottsdale for more manageable sized homes and reduced traffic and travel time.

Along Granite Reef and Hayden Roads townhomes are being snapped up and renovated by Generation Y.

Brokers, planners, and pundits predict the strip of tribal land between the Loop 101 Freeway and Scottsdale's eastern border will be devoted to housing. Nothing is in the works just now, but ripples from the ASU tech center will spur the market to strike deals.

Home values are confidently expected to rise in the next five to eight years as more young people move in and revitalize the area. Also, development on the Salt River Pima-Maricopa Indian Community and the old Los Arcos site will speed up and add value to the area's homes.

## Rental & Investment

Enclose the carport on that 1950s ranch, agents say. You'll add another 400 or so liveable square feet for about $5,000 and boost the home's value another $15,000 to $20,000.

House rentals are plentiful in South Scottsdale, at around $900 to $1,200 a month.

New high-rise condominiums builds are priced by the foot and finished to your specifications. For example, Scottsdale Waterfront costs start at $333 a square foot, units range in size from 1,200 to 4,000 square feet.

## At a Glance...

## House Prices

### Townhouse
| | |
|---|---|
| Bedrooms | |
| Price | $200,000 - $300,000 |

### Townhouse
| | |
|---|---|
| Bedrooms | |
| Price | $250,000 - $350,000 |

### Family home
| | |
|---|---|
| Bedrooms | |
| Price | $250,000 - $350,000 |

### Family home
| | |
|---|---|
| Bedrooms | |
| Price | $300,000 - $400,000 |

### Family home
| | |
|---|---|
| Bedrooms | |
| Price | $350,000 - $550,000 |

### Executive home
| | |
|---|---|
| Area | Min. 4,000 sq. ft. |
| Price | $650,000 - $800,000 |

## Rentals

### Apartment
| | |
|---|---|
| Bedrooms | |
| Price | $1,000 - $1,500 month |

### Townhouse
| | |
|---|---|
| Bedrooms | |
| Price | $900 - $2,000 month |

### House
| | |
|---|---|
| Bedrooms | |
| Price | $900 - $1,500 month |

## Travel Times

To downtown Phoenix via 101 Freeway
Peak: 30 – 35 minutes
Off-peak: 25 – 30 minutes

To the airport via 101 Freeway:
Peak: 25 – 30 minutes

Off-peak: 20 – 25 minutes

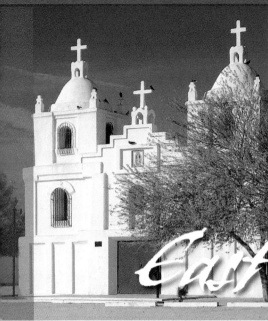
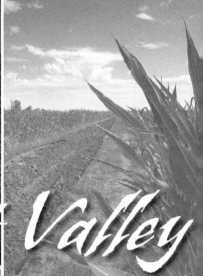

East Valley

Satellites and chips for most of the computers on the planet are made in the East Valley by some very smart people. Million-dollar plus homes are common. Upscale shopping is now the norm south of the U.S. 60 Freeway.

The area developed before the West Valley for two elemental reasons: sun and water. For a commute to Phoenix, the rising sun is at your back in the morning and the afternoon. The East Valley also has more canals than the West Valley, making it cheaper for developers to deliver water to their subdivisions.

Young families have turned to the East Valley for affordable homes since the 1970s. The stucco-and-tile homes surrounded by dirt yards they bought in the early 1990s are now surrounded by lush trees.

Homes are becoming less affordable across Chandler and Gilbert as areas mature, freeways add convenience, and high-paid tech workers put upward price pressure on homes adjacent to chip plants. The Chandler tech plants have also brought a significant number of Malaysians, Singaporeans, and Chinese into the area, fuelling demand still further.

Queen Creek is what these areas used to be, the place miles from anywhere where you can buy a lot of brand-new home for a little bit of money. However, if you hunt around Chandler or Gilbert, you can still find plenty of affordable resale homes. Apache Junction has the some of the best-priced mountainside homes in the Valley.

# Apache Junction has the some of the best-priced mountainside homes in the Valley

Production housing has always dominated the East Valley. The latest trend is diversification. South Chandler has seen an explosion of multi-million dollar homes. The two poshest ZIP codes are 85249, with a median value of $340,000, and 85248, where homes in the Ocotillo and Sun Lakes areas have a median price of about $335,000.

The East Valley isn't just about family homes and millionaire playgrounds amidst the citrus. Tempe has a couple of sophisticated condo/loft projects up and running, with more under construction. (Face it: if you live in any significant Valley city, construction is going to drive you mad for the next three years.) The Tempe towers are sited within summer walking distance of light rail and feature Generation Y amenities like downstairs grocery stores and video gaming rooms.

The new face of Tempe will be a 28 year-old software wizard sprawled in a $300,000 state of the art condo, playing Halo on his plasma. (The old face was an ageing hippy who sold weed out of a cinderblock bunker apartment and listened to the Gin Blossoms at Long Wongs on most nights.) Even Chandler will soon boast a 15-story high rise with lofts and luxury condos.

Expect the East Valley to become still more desirable as Pinal County's 200,000 population balloons to more than one million in the next two decades.

Not long ago, Apache Junction was where the pavement turned to sand. Bordering the foreboding western wall of the Superstition Mountains, it earned its name because it sits at the junction of the Apache Trail and the Phoenix-Superior highway.

Many Apache Junction roads are still dirt. North and east AJ has a funky Western atmosphere replete with floods, rattlesnakes, coyotes, and owls. If you blindfolded a Californian and dropped them out there, they wouldn't mistake the city being anywhere else but Arizona. To the south and west, snowbird RV parks outnumber horse properties, but both share the Valley's most spectacular mountain views.

Whatever you might be seeking, AJ is a great place to live. Homes are a bargain. A fabled wilderness area half the size of Los Angeles sits right out the back door. Two gorgeous lakes nestle in deep canyons. Off-peak rush hours, downtown Phoenix is only 40 minutes away. Dining is limited to the Dirtwater Springs Café and the Mining Camp restaurant, but the quail in your front yard are real, and so is that snake curled up on your welcome mat.

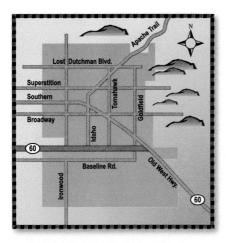

Total Population: 34,000 approx.
Median Age: 44 years
Median Household Income: $33,000 p.a.

## Who Lives There?

Eccentrics have always been a staple of Apache Junction life. Cowboys, bikers, militia, and other loners pop up all over the landscape. Gunfighters frequented the place as recently as the early 1960s during a war over the Lost Dutchman legend. A column in the local paper once referred to the city's neighbors as "the five evil cities to the West." Once spotted in AJ: an old man riding a bicycle, wearing cutoffs, flipflops and a tank top, with a holstered revolver flapping his skinny shanks. The Coen brothers filmed part of "Raising Arizona" here in 1986. It was an accurate depiction.

About 40,000 snowbirds pour in every winter. Demographic makeup is the same as the rest of the state: mostly white, followed by Hispanic. Recreation and retirement are the city's two main industries.

Retirees are still moving to AJ, though not in their traditional numbers. Families like the affordability. Californians are floored by low prices. Phoenicians wanting rabbits and quail instead of car thieves in their backyards are also moving to AJ.

## Homes

State officials have four ways of describing Apache Junction lifestyles. It helps to read between the lines:

• *Western rural acreage.* What you see out the window looks like a John Wayne movie location. Saguaros may grow in the middle of your street, which is dirt. Flooding is an issue for you, as in an issue of hours or possibly days before you can get to pavement during a real gullywasher. Learn to deal with it and other rural issues or move to Tempe. The wildlife in your yard is real. Most of your neighbors own horses or large machinery. Often both.

• *Urban single-family residential neighborhoods.* Pretty much what you see in the rest of the Valley — stucco-and-tile of varying ages and qualities, except in Apache Junction almost no one has trees or lawns. Lots are big and desert landscaping rules. Sidewalks are scarce to nonexistent. People have horses in these neighborhoods too.

• *Adult-only retirement clusters.* Enormous RV parks with activity halls and other commons. American and Canadian flags, Astroturf carpets, lawn chairs, carved wooden signs announcing names and hometowns, whirligigs, gnomes, and golf carts. Friendly neighbors who fought World War II and now enjoy the sun. No horses. No kids either.

• *Mixed age-group living areas.* Houses, duplexes, trailers, apartment complexes. You might get horses here. You might get a lot of things.

# Amenities

### Schools ★★★★

Apache Junction's Four Peaks Elementary and Thunder Mountain Middle schools are rated "performing." Apache Junction High School and five others achieved the "performing plus" rating. Apache Elementary School is "highly performing."

### Shopping & Dining ★

The basics: basic clothes, basic food, basic whatever. Sorry, princess, no Saks in these here parts. So you've got to drive to a Borders once a week. You'll survive.

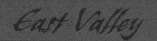
## Leisure ★★★★

Apache Junction is an outdoorsman's paradise. Boating, fishing, horseback riding, backpacking, golf – it's all here, and it's all top-notch. Crossing the vast and treacherous Superstition Wilderness on foot is a six-day world-class trek. Apache and Canyon Lakes go on for miles into serene coves where bighorn sheep descend to the water.

There is a city library, a senior center, a community swimming pool, and nine parks, some of which include ball fields and sports courts. There is a municipal rodeo arena and a 1,600-acre city park.

AJ Culture comes in the form of the Renaissance Faire in the winter and spring. A full-scale 30-acre permanent set of a medieval town sits out in the desert past Gold Canyon. Thousands throng the streets, gorging on turkey legs and $6 pints of Guinness. Stores hawk swords and other stuff you'll be sorry you bought when you get home out of the sun and away from the Guinness.

Lost Dutchman Days in February feature a rodeo, beauty pageant, burro and wild horse auction, carnival, and live music. The food's more reasonably-priced than at the Renaissance Faire, but don't drink too many Coors and come home with a burro instead of a sword.

Do not expect Scottsdale-caliber night life. Or any kind of night life besides the neighbors getting up to drink Metamucil in the middle of the night or a coyote eating a housecat.

## Real Estate

### Trends

The long-standing and unfair joke about Apache Junction has always been that it's a trailer town. The truth is, housing stock runs a wide gamut. It's true you can buy a big desert lot for $35,000 with two clapped-out RVs and some beautiful saguaros. You can also buy luxury homes well over the $300,000 mark rivaling anything in North Scottsdale, beneath Superstition murals of soaring rock and blue sky and cactus.

Apache Junction is still a bargain compared to the more popular Valley cities. You can find fixer-upper shacks on .22-acre lots for $60,000 or a three-bedroom three-bath on an acre for $320,000. Block, wood frame, stucco-and-tile – architecture varies from lot to lot.

People like the open spaces, the spectacular mountain views, and close access to the best lakes in the metro area. Obviously the Superstition foothills are the best place to live in town. Prices on the slopes are soaring more steeply than the Flatiron's mountain wall. In the past year the lowest prices on the foothills were in the $250,000s.

### Rental & Investment

The rental market is strong and investors can expect surprisingly good returns from well constructed apartments and four-bedroom homes.

## Why I live there

### Dale Gorney

Apache Junction gets younger every year, says Dale Gorney. The Realtor lives in a 1,700 square-foot ranch home near Idaho Road and Southern Avenue with her long-time boyfriend, Scott Taylor. "It's not just retirees," Dale says. "In fact, they're probably getting tired of us."

Scott moved there from Gilbert to escape sprawl in 1995. AJ's population has more than doubled since then. "It still has a small-town feel, but it probably won't stay that way forever," says Scott, who owns a marketing and art firm called DST Creative.

That might change the small-town character he loves a bit, but not enough to make him leave. "I fell in love with the Superstitions the first time I saw them," Dale agrees.

## Smart Buy ⊘

You can buy an executive home on the foothills of the Superstition Mountains for about half the price of the same home next to the McDowell Mountains in North Scottsdale. This place is spectacular and future prices will surely reflect that.

## At a Glance...

### House Prices

**Townhouse**

| Bedrooms | 🛏 🛏 |
| --- | --- |
| Price | $100,000 - $200,000 |

**Family home**

| Bedrooms | 🛏 🛏 |
| --- | --- |
| Price | $150,000 - $250,000 |

**Family home**

| Bedrooms | 🛏 🛏 🛏 |
| --- | --- |
| Price | $250,000 - $500,000 |

**Family home**

| Bedrooms | 🛏 🛏 🛏 🛏 |
| --- | --- |
| Price | $250,000 - $600,000 |

**Executive home**

| Area | Min. 4,000 sq. ft. |
| --- | --- |
| Price | $800,000 - $900,000 |

**Trailers**

| Sale Price | $100,000 - $200,000 |
| --- | --- |

### Rentals

**Apartment**

| Bedrooms | 🛏 🛏 |
| --- | --- |
| Price | $450 - $600 month |

**Townhouse**

| Bedrooms | 🛏 🛏 |
| --- | --- |
| Price | $600 - $800 month |

**House**

| Bedrooms | 🛏 🛏 🛏 |
| --- | --- |
| Price | $900 - $1,000 month |

### Travel Times

Distance to downtown Phoenix: 44 miles

To downtown Phoenix:
Peak: 45 – 60 minutes
Off-peak: 35 – 40 minutes

To the airport:
Peak: 35 – 40 minutes
Off-peak: 30 minutes

*East Valley*

Chandler has an easygoing feel. Palms waving in the air. Fresh-cut grass and the distant whicker of mowers. Burgers hissing on grills. Kids playing Marco Polo in pools. Everything's alright. You can relax here. This is great living with no problems.

Chandler was a rural area until the early 1990s. Then subdivisions spread like alien colonies in a science fiction movie. You'd drive by a cotton field and nine months later it was "Sparkling" Falls, with four models open for viewing. The country feel has lasted, however. Chandler still has lots of horse properties and that relaxed have-a-steak-and-another-beer all-American appeal.

Now Chandler is a regional technology powerhouse. Computer giant Intel announced plans in July 2005 to build a $3 billion chip plant in Chandler. The plant will employ 1,000 techies with salaries averaging $40,000. The company is already Chandler's largest employer, with 9,500 well-paid workers.

Intel, Microchip, and the rest of the local brainpower industries have drawn smart employees from all over the globe. Thousands of Asians have moved to Chandler, attracting some of the Valley's best Asian restaurants and supermarkets.

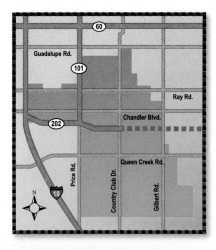

Total Population: 224,000 approx.
Median Age: 30 years
Median Household Income: $71,000 p.a.

## Who Lives There?

Chandler's residents tend to be young (median age 30). Thanks to the thousands of high-tech jobs in the city, they're also well-off. The average household income is $71,456, higher than wealthy Scottsdale's median income of $62,000.

The typical resident is employed, pretty well-paid, with a couple of kids, owns their own home and is community–involved, and likes to have a lot of fun. Chandler folks are active outdoors. There are a lot of horse properties down south, Harleys abound on weekends, and sports are popular. A Chandler executive is much more likely to take his big boat to Lake Powell or Havasu than to play golf.

Demographics follow the rest of the state – it's mostly Anglo, with the next largest group Hispanic – with one exception. Chandler has a comparatively large Asian population. A Chinese Cultural Center was built at Ray and Alma School Roads. Foreigners on multi-year work visas live and buy homes in Chandler.

## Homes

Chandler homes are stucco-and-tile of varying degrees. Most have swimming pools and attractive desert landscaping, but do not expect aesthetically significant architecture. These are big, comfortable homes perfect for raising families; but they're not *Phoenix Home and Garden* showplaces.

The city does not have an historic district. Horse properties abound in southern Chandler, however. The poshest parts of the city are the San Marcos Estates, west of the resort founded by Dr. A.J. Chandler, and a master-planned community called Ocotillo.

For people who live to fly, Stellar Airpark has 65 homes where you can get in your plane, open the garage door, taxi out to the private runway, and take off.

To date, Chandler's only housing option has been single-family detached homes. Now a 15-story tower with 11 floors of lofts, luxury condos and penthouses is in the works to rise beside Chandler Fashion Center. Prices will range from $300,000 to $4 million.

# Amenities

### Schools ★★★★

Three district boundaries run through Chandler. The main school district is the Chandler Unified District with a total of 30 schools, including three high schools. Kyrene Elementary District and Mesa Unified District also have primary schools in Chandler.

The Chandler Unified District is one of the fastest growing districts in the State. In the 1990s, the district opened seven schools, and since 2000, it has opened another five schools. About one-third of the schools are rated "excelling," the others are either "highly performing" or "performing plus."

Most schools are very well resourced. You can imagine what your kid's schools are equipped with when Intel and Microchip are in the district.

## Shopping & Dining ★★★★

In the past five years about five million square feet of retail has been built in Chandler. Scottsdale-caliber shopping hit Chandler a couple of years ago with the Chandler Fashion Center, a monstrous mall featuring a 20-screen multiplex, Nordstrom's, Dillards, Sears, six sit-down restaurants, and 180 stores including Banana Republic, Eddie Bauer, J. Crew, and Victoria's Secret. Chandler is blessed with eateries that define the term "destination dining."

C-Fu Gourmet, the Valley's best Chinese restaurant, is in Chandler. C-Fu's dim sum, or Chinese brunch, is amazing. Crabmeat dumplings, eggplant stuffed with shrimp, pan-fired pot stickers, and barbecued pork buns are a few of the small dishes. Extended families and hulking ex-soldiers with tiny Asian wives pack the place on Sunday mornings.

Chandler is also home to two of the Valley's best Mexican restaurants. Guedo's Taco Shop has a small menu of tacos, tortas, burros, and cheese crisps. What distinguishes Guedo's is that these are some of the best tacos and tortas you've ever had in your life. *The New York Times* and *Gourmet* magazine have both plugged Guedo's.

Espo's Mexican Food at 3887 W. Chandler Blvd. has been wildly popular since 1974.

Located beside a small market and run by the same family, Espo's makes a green chilli burrito you'd crawl over shattered glass with broken legs to eat.

## Leisure ★★★

Chandler celebrates its past with the annual Ostrich Festival held each March. Ostrich races (one cowboy said it's like riding a basketball), a carnival with rides, classic rock and country bands, and ostrich burgers make it a crowd-pleaser.

Chandler Center for the Arts, a 1,150-seat hall and 2,000 square foot exhibition gallery, features popular performances like the Glenn Miller Orchestra and Ballet Etudes.

To gamble, head to Vee Quiva Casino on the Gila River Reservation west of Interstate 10. San Tan Mountain Regional Park has more than 10,000 acres of pristine lower Sonoran Desert to hike and meander.

# Real Estate

## Trends

Initial sales on a 54-unit townhouse complex in downtown Chandler have been strong, and two other developers may soon build similar projects. 123 Washington features two- and three-story models, both with two-car garages, high ceilings and granite

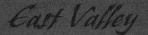

countertops. Opening prices ranged from $269,000 to $316,000. City officials are more interested in creating a vibrant, residential downtown than a night-spot nexus or business mecca.

## Rental & Investment

If you're buying for appreciation, pundits recommend buying homes close to Chandler Fashion Center; with freeway proximity; near elementary schools; or in newer communities. Three- or four-bedroom houses are the best bets for capital growth.

### Local Hero
### Lee Lee Oriental Supermarket

The Valley's best Asian supermarket is in Chandler. Lee Lee Oriental Supermarket at 2025 N. Dobson Road is the size of a big-box store. Inside you'll find Thai, Korean, Japanese, Vietnamese, Cambodian, Indian, Filipino, Indonesian, and all Chinese provincial foods and ingredients. If Asian food and cooking isn't your thing, Lee Lee is still worth shopping because of unbelievably low prices on meat and fresh seafood. It's a great place to go on Sunday afternoon to waddle down the aisles after gorging on dim sum across the street at C-Fu Gourmet.

## At a Glance...

## House Prices

### Townhouse
| Bedrooms | |
|---|---|
| Price | $150,000 - $350,000 |

### Family home
| Bedrooms | |
|---|---|
| Price | $200,000 - $400,000 |

### Family home
| Bedrooms | |
|---|---|
| Price | $250,000 - $400,000+ |

### Family home
| Bedrooms | |
|---|---|
| Price | $350,000 - $550,000 |

### Executive home
| Area | Min. 4,000 sq. ft. |
|---|---|
| Price | $700,000 - $1,100,000 |

## Rentals

### Apartment
| Bedrooms | |
|---|---|
| Price | $600 - $900 month |

### Townhouse
| Bedrooms | |
|---|---|
| Price | $900 - $1,200 month |

### House
| Bedrooms | |
|---|---|
| Price | $1,000 - $1,500 month |

## Travel Times

Distance to downtown Phoenix: 14 miles

To downtown Phoenix:
Peak: 60 minutes
Off-peak: 35 – 45 minutes

To the airport:
Peak: 35 – 45 minutes
Off-peak: 30 – 35 minutes

# Gilbert ★★★★★

Gilbert, once dubbed the "Hay Capital of the World," is the nation's fastest-growing city. Once a sleepy farm hamlet of 1,971 residents dozing in a half-forgotten corner of the Valley, now more than 165,000 people live in Gilbert. Local news stories endlessly decry, "Gilbert Losing Its Rural Soul." The fact is the rural soul is gone. Ten years ago, being stuck in traffic on Warner Road meant inching behind a tractor trundling towards a cotton field or waiting at the single traffic light. Not any more. Planners for the 76-square-mile town estimate build-out in 2030, with a population of 290,500. That's a long line to get into Olive Garden on a Friday night.

They're flocking to Gilbert for low-priced brand-new homes, good schools, easy freeway access, and proximity to major employers like Intel and Motorola. Freshness is a big seller for Gilbert families. There isn't any urban blight because there wasn't any "urban" to become blighted in the first place. Almost the entire town emerged from the ground fully formed like a Hopi mud spirit.

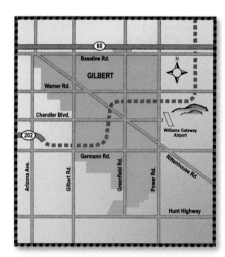

Total Population: 165,000 approx.
Median Age: 30 years
Median Household Income: $68,000 p.a.

## Who Lives There?

Gilbert residents tend to be in management, the professions, sales, or office work of one sort or another. They're young families starting out; the median age is 30. They earn good salaries, between $50,000 and $100,000.

If funky architecture, tattooed baristas, conceptual art galleries, and sternum-thumping nightclubs are your thing, head west. The same goes for boulevardiers who want to drop $600 on dinner and wine a few times a week after wearying of collecting paintings. This is not your place.

Gilbert is a conservative town. People get up and go to church on Sunday at about the same time half of Tempe is going to bed. Gilbert is soccer-mom and football-dad country: quiet, clean, and risk-free.

Gilbert has a sizeable Mormon population.

## Homes

Homes in Gilbert sell for two reasons: they're low-priced and brand-new. No headaches, everything's going to work, and you won't have to replace the roof in 24 months.

There is a wide variety of stucco-and-tile with big living rooms and garages, but stucco-and-tile is your only choice. For buyers a few rungs up from starting out, acre horse properties and lakefront homes (the lakes are man-made) are available.

# Amenities

### Schools ★★★

Two school districts cover the Gilbert area—Gilbert Unified and Higley Unified. Most students attend one of the 25 elementary, six junior high, or four traditional high schools that comprise the Gilbert Unified District. Higley is a much smaller district, and currently has only four elementary/middle schools and two high schools. It is also one of the fastest growing school districts in the state.

Highland High School is a 2004 National Blue Ribbon School, and the school's band was selected to march in the 2004 Macy's Day Parade.

Gilbert is also home to a non-traditional high school, the Gilbert Public Schools Technology and Leadership Academy. Founded in 2003, this school is a partnership between the district and the United States Air Force and emphasizes leadership training and technology.

### Shopping ★★★

The town is getting its first Home Depot and Target, as well as a mall with a power center. Crossroads Towne Center, a 140-acre regional entertainment and power center at the Santan Freeway and Gilbert Road, is slated to have a Super Target, Barnes & Noble, Petsmart, Pier One Imports, and other national retailers. The first phase opened in March 2005.

Upscale mall developer Westcor is building a 1.3-million-square-foot mall. SanTan Village Mall at the SanTan Freeway and Williams Field Road will have office and residential space. It's intended to be similar to the swanky Kierland Commons in Central Scottsdale. About 125 stores will join Dillard's and Robinson's-May. Harkins is opening a multiplex, too.

Besides posh shopping, Gilbert's first hospitals are coming too. Gilbert Emergency Hospital opened at Power Road south of Ray Road in 2004. The $10 million facility exclusively treats emergency cases. Mercy Gilbert Medical Center, a 20-bed, 300,000-square-foot acute-care hospital, is under construction at Val Vista Drive and Pecos Road.

# Gilbert

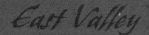

*East Valley*

## Leisure ★ ★ ★

Hiking in Tonto National Forest or the Superstition Mountains, and boating and water-skiing on Canyon and Apache Lakes, is a short drive away. Gilbert has nearly 600 acres of public parks with ball fields, picnic areas and pools. Gilbert doesn't have resorts, night-clubs, or art galleries, but the bright lights of downtown Phoenix and Scottsdale are only 22 miles away.

# Real Estate

## Trends

Most of the big master-plan community builders have opened shop in Gilbert. They've built thousands of homes and thousands more are coming down the pipeline.

For example, the company behind Scottsdale's DC Ranch and the new mega-master-plan Verrado west of Phoenix, Sunbelt Holdings, is well on the way to completing its 1,414-acre Power Ranch community at Power and Queen Creek Roads. Power Ranch is expected to be home to between 10,000 to 15,000 residents at build-out. About 5,400 homes will sit along tree-lined streets with nine parks, lake, clubhouse, soccer complex, trails, and 140 acres of retail and commercial space.

That's the biggest subdivision in the works. There are about a dozen smaller, but still significant, other developments rising from the ground. Almost none of them sell to investors, but there's enough churn to gain a beachhead. School quality and almost-new homes keep Gilbert hot for families.

## Rental & Investment

Gilbert's position in the path of progress, coupled with good schools, easy freeway access, and proximity to major employers, will always maintain home values. Expect to pay about $1,200 a month to rent a three-bedroom home.

## At a Glance...

### House Prices

**Townhouse**

| | |
|---|---|
| Bedrooms | 🛏 🛏 |
| Price | $250,000 - $400,000 |

**Family home**

| | |
|---|---|
| Bedrooms | 🛏 🛏 |
| Price | $250,000 - $300,000 |

**Family home**

| | |
|---|---|
| Bedrooms | 🛏 🛏 🛏 |
| Price | $250,000 - $400,000 |

**Family home**

| | |
|---|---|
| Bedrooms | 🛏 🛏 🛏 🛏 |
| Price | $300,000 - $450,000+ |

**Executive home**

| | |
|---|---|
| Area | Min. 4,000 sq. ft. |
| Price | $700,000 - $900,000 |

**Family home in Power Ranch**

| | |
|---|---|
| Bedrooms | 🛏 🛏 🛏 🛏 🛏 |
| Price | $400,000 - $800,000 |

### Rentals

**Apartment**

| | |
|---|---|
| Bedrooms | 🛏 🛏 |
| Price | $900 - $1,000 month |

**Townhouse**

| | |
|---|---|
| Bedrooms | 🛏 🛏 |
| Price | $900 - $1,200 month |

**House**

| | |
|---|---|
| Bedrooms | 🛏 🛏 🛏 |
| Price | $1,000 - $1,500 month |

### Travel Times

Distance to downtown Phoenix: 22 miles

To downtown Phoenix:
Peak: 40 – 45 minutes
Off-peak: 28 minutes

To the airport:
Peak: 35 – 40 minutes
Off-peak: 25 – 30 minutes

including Johnson Ranch

Downtown Queen Creek got its first stoplight in 2004, and cable Internet has yet to make its debut. Queen Creek is the last of the rural East Valley communities to be developed. A fair number of potato and cotton farms remain. Cotton can't grow on $70 million pieces of property for long, however; most of the farms will inevitably be developed. For now, giant farm machinery timidly ventures into manic traffic streams of Starbucks-fuelled go-getters.

Horse properties are a big part of Queen Creek's culture. This is a modern Arizona cowboy town. You can join breakfast horse rides with the mayor. There's a roping school. For now the population is about 20,000, but it's expected to hit 100,000 by 2010. Officials are planning redevelopment of the tiny town center. It's a thoughtfully-run place and affordable, even if far on the fringes.

Young families in their twenties are flocking out for affordable new houses. Johnson Ranch is attracting middle-class Republican California families and Midwestern retirees.

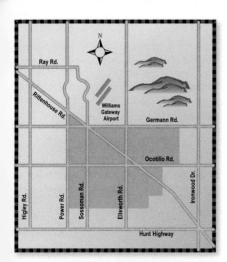

*Total Population: 20,000 approx.*
*Median Age: 31 years*
*Median Household Income: $64,000 p.a.*

## Who Lives There?

There are still some farmers who refuse to change. It's also one of the last refuges of the modern Southwestern urban cowboy. No ranch and he commutes to a job in construction management, but there's a truck, a trailer, and two mares in the backyard that he and the old lady take out in the Santans on the weekend. You want another beer or are you good?

## Homes

Affordability is driving new housing in Queen Creek. The majority of buyers are heading for Johnson Ranch, where you can buy a brand-new 1,600 square-foot four-bedroom home for about $300,000.

About 6,000 homes from the $200,000s to the $500,000s will surround a golf course, a lake, and an elementary school on 2,000 acres with a view of the Santan Mountains. Johnson Ranch also has parks, pools, playgrounds, basketball and tennis courts, and recreation centers.

Horse properties are hard to come by, according to agents. The equestrian crowd is well-entrenched and shows no signs of moving. The Orchard Ranchettes has more than 800 one-acre lots for the bit and bridle set, and Will Rogers Equestrian Ranch has homes with smaller lots around shared stables and an arena.

# Amenities

### Schools ★★★

A mix of old and new, rural and suburban, Queen Creek schools overall are good schools. Queen Creek Unified District is at the forefront with four elementary schools, a middle school and a high school. Jack Barnes Elementary is the first Queen Creek District school to get the state's highest rating, "excelling." Of the more established schools, Queen Creek Middle School shines as a "highly performing" school that uses computers not only for research but also for PowerPoint presentations by students.

Other districts with schools in Queen Creek are Florence Unified School District with three elementary schools, J. O. Combs School District with an elementary school and a middle school, and Coolidge Unified District with the newly built San Tan Heights Elementary School.

### Shopping & Dining ★

The nearest place to buy clothes, books, and sheets is Superstition Springs Center

in south Mesa, about 12 to 15 minutes north. (It also has a movie multiplex.)

Down at Johnson Ranch a huge Fry's grocery store with a drive-through pharmacy anchors a neighborhood center with a Bank of America branch. There is a wide variety of restaurants and services, and there's a Walgreen's Pharmacy at the west end of Johnson Ranch. Beyond that, get in the car or get on the Internet.

Every barrio, country club, and enclave in the Valley has its quasi-official Mexican joint, the place where locals go for red enchiladas, beer, and a minimum of tomfoolery involving sombreros. In Queen Creek, that's Rudy's Mexican-American Food on South Ellsworth.

There are a few cafes (in Queen Creek that still means breakfast, burgers, and drip coffee, not triple-foam soy mocha lattes and cranberry scones), but that's it for now.

### Leisure ★★★★

Queen Creek doesn't have an arena or an orchestra, but it has other pleasures. San Tan Mountain Regional Park is open during the day. There are no designated trails. Visitors hike and ride horseback on existing paths that have been worn over the years.

Schnepf Farms is a 225-acre farm-turned-attraction run by a fourth generation farmer and former Queen Creek mayor. There's a bakery, u-pick crops like pumpkins, chiles, and apples, a festival site, and a train to tour the farm. The Biltmore hotel buys their peaches here.

The annual Tour de Farm bike ride ranges from Florence to Queen Creek and ends at Schnepf Farms. Queen Creek also has

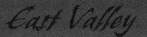 
four private golf courses where the public is welcome.

# Real Estate

## Trends

Queen Creek isn't exactly nowhere, but if you stand on a rock you can see nowhere. Unstable gas prices, a 36-mile drive to Phoenix, and a lot of new house for a little money are three factors to discuss when buying here.

There are plenty of homes for sale. Circle G Ranch and Pegasus are two of the custom-home communities. Acre lots run to about $250,000; tack on another $550,000 for a home.

Resales are a bit overpriced, agents say, but expect a market correction by the second half of 2006. There are no condos, townhouses, or any kind of multifamily housing in Queen Creek.

## Rental & Investment

Rental homes are plentiful; you'll pay about $1,000 a month to live in a brand-new 2,200 square foot home.

# Look Out! ⊙

Queen Creek's housing boom has put homes in areas where fissures as deep as 20 feet and hundreds of feet long appear after heavy rains. Sellers are required to disclose any geological hazards to buyers, according to the state. However, the state's maps are woefully outdated and there are no plans to draw new sets. Watch out for property along Hunt Highway and in the Santan Mountain foothills, according to geologists. Our advice: if in doubt, hire a consulting hydrologist or geologist before the words "money pit" acquire a new meaning.

## At a Glance...

### House Prices

**Townhouse**
Very few townhouses available

**Family home**
Bedrooms
Price                $200,000 - $300,000

**Family home**
Bedrooms
Price                $250,000 - $350,000

**Family home**
Bedrooms
Price                $300,000 - $450,000

**Executive home**
Area                Min. 4,000 sq. ft.
Price                $600,000 - $800,000

### Rentals

**Apartment**
Very few apartments available

**Townhouse**
Very few townhouses available

**House**
Bedrooms
Price                $900 - $1,200 month

## Travel Times

Distance to downtown Phoenix: 36 miles

To downtown Phoenix:
                Peak: 1 hour 30 minutes
                Off-peak: 1 hour

To the airport:
                Peak: 1 hour 20 minutes
                Off-peak: 1 hour

# Tempe ★★★★★

Tempe is the Valley's oldest city. It was founded ten years before Phoenix and named by the same alcoholic English aristocrat, Lord Darrell Duppa. Today's Tempe is a national party landmark, original home to the Fiesta Bowl, an enormous New Year's Eve street party, an Ironman triathlon, at least one Super Bowl to date, arts festivals, Arizona State University (ASU) games, an ersatz Mardi Gras, and spring baseball training.

But there's more to Tempe than just ASU. Great schools and parks, eye blink access to Sky Harbor, freeway convenience, more than 200 high-tech companies and 750 manufacturing firms, the nation's fifth-largest university: it all adds up to one of the Valley's most popular cities to live in. And it's getting even more popular, thanks to Tempe Town Lake. Inflatable dams hold 220 acres of water in a two-mile stretch of the Salt River bed. Kayaking, sailing, and fishing are popular activities.

The 3,000-seat Gammage Auditorium, designed by Frank Lloyd Wright, is the Valley venue for road-company productions of Broadway hits.

*Total Population: 161,000 approx.*
*Median Age: 29 years*
*Median Household Income: $42,000 p.a.*

## Who Lives There?

Tempe people tend to be liberal, due to the university's influence. It was the first Valley city to have a gay mayor. Democratic presidential candidates often hold rallies in Tempe. Organic grocery stores are popular.

In north Tempe near the university, students and academics rule the roost.

Farther south you'll find America West/ US Airways executives, airline pilots, consultants, Intel managers and other tech professionals.

## Homes

Professors and old Tempe families live in renovated houses in a charming old neighborhood west of ASU. East of campus is called Sin City, where thousands of students live in crumbling rat-maze apartment complexes. South of the university, are frame, stucco, and block homes built in the 1960s and 1970s. Most of these neighborhoods are a mixed bag, at best.

Heading south, homes and neighborhoods become more expensive. Warner Ranch sports million-dollar homes. Horse properties are plentiful in south Tempe, but rarely come on the market. South of Broadway, Mill Avenue's madding crowds and kamikaze student drivers dissipate into quiet, neat family-oriented neighborhoods.

# Amenities

### Schools ★★★★

The Tempe School District has elementary and middle schools. About one-third are rated "performing," the rest are "performing plus" or "highly performing." There is a school for students with significant developmental challenges, a back-to-basics school, and even a school for students having difficulty succeeding in their neighborhood school.

There are also six Kyrene Elementary District schools in Tempe. Kyrene schools are recognized as some of the State's top schools, consistently scoring high on standardized tests.

High school students attend schools in the Tempe Union High School District—Corona Del Sol, Desert Vista, Marcos De Niza, McClintock, Mountain Pointe or Tempe high schools. McClintock High School is home to The Payne Academy, a public school program designed for gifted students with a rigorous curriculum and many enrichment programs.

### Shopping & Dining ★★★★★

Mill Avenue is the place to stroll, stop for a latte or lunch, or see a movie at the 11-screen cineplex. There are more than 60 retailers along Mill, most with merchandise geared for the college crowd. Arizona Mills Mall (at the juncture of highways 60 and 10) has more than 170 outlet stores, restaurants and a 24-screen cineplex. Tempe is home to Arizona's only Ikea home furnishings store.

Eastside Records ROCKS! Go in here, tell 'em you're interested in whatever group, and they'll tell you the seminal recordings to listen to. They have a huge blues collection, too. "We don't carry any bluesman not named after a state or an affliction," the owner says. Fans of Blind Lemon Jefferson and Mississippi John Hurt, welcome home.

Monti's La Casa Vieja on the riverbank is the oldest restaurant in town. It's also the oldest continuously occupied building in the Valley, built in 1871. Try to get a table in one of the original rooms to soak up some serious old Arizona vibes.

Casey Moore's Oyster House on Ash and Ninth Streets is another Tempe favorite. It's reputedly haunted.

# Tempe

## Local Hero: Arizona State University

ASU is the 900-pound gorilla in town. More than 44,000 students attend and spend in Tempe, plus tens of thousands more professors, staff, and researchers. Once famous for its status as one of Playboy's Top Five Party Schools, ASU has worked hard to break away from that image in recent years, under an aggressive ex-Ivy League president. Admission now requires more than a pulse. Research has been ramped up. One of the faculty members won a Nobel Prize for economics. The creative writing program is one of the best in the country. Porn movies are forbidden to be filmed on frat row anymore. Alumni barely recognize the place.

## Leisure ★★★★

Event entertainment in Tempe is so relentless that one marvels to find a child without a painted face. Almost all of this frenzy is clustered around Mill Avenue, a nexus of nightclubs, bars and restaurants. If you like Rush Street in Chicago or the French Quarter during Mardi Gras, you'll love Mill. (The Tempe police made a special announcement declaring Mardi Gras breast-flashing would not be tolerated.)

The Anaheim Angels play Cactus League spring training games through March at Tempe Diablo Stadium. Baseball, sunshine, and hot dogs are a great way to spend a day skipping work.

# Real Estate

## Trends

One solid reason behind Tempe's popularity is its location. People in the East Valley are tired of long commutes and want to live closer to Phoenix. Some parents of ASU students buy their kids homes near campus. Tempe is a well run city with great public sports and education, and lots of parks.

The hottest new developments in Tempe are the luxury high-rises on Mill Avenue and beside Tempe Town Lake. Edgewater's first phase may be sold out, but there are three more towers planned. ASU professors, America West/US Airways executives, empty nesters, and out-of-staters buying second homes are snapping up lakefront units. On the other side of the lake, North Shore Condominiums, a five-story tower, will have 134 units when completed.

The Centerpoint Condominiums are being built on five acres at Mill Avenue and Sixth Street. The four-phase, mixed-use development will start with one 22-story, followed by three 30-story residential buildings. These first two buildings will be Tempe's tallest. The project is also bringing the first grocery store to downtown Tempe in more than a decade, a 16,000-square-foot gourmet grocery, deli and café. Units are expected to start from about $250,000.

Apache Boulevard has been a strip of seedy bars and tire shops for decades. The city has now designated it a redevelopment zone, and projects coming down the pipe include new market-rate multi-housing. Light rail will run down the street.

## Rental & Investment

Tempe is not a good place to rent. The presence of the university skews rental costs towards proximity to ASU. North Tempe is rife with slumlords who charge criminal prices to live in places worse than Somalian slums. Leasing in the better quality apartment complexes involves an array of exotic surcharges and deposits which, needless to say, you will never see again. Whether you're a student or not, rent in another city.

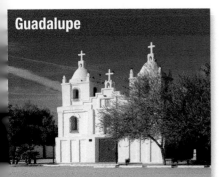

### Guadalupe

Guadalupe is a square-mile Pascua Yaqui and Hispanic community in the southwest corner of Tempe at the foot of South Mountain. When Mexican dictator Porfirio Diaz attacked and enslaved Yaqui Indians during the 1880s, they fled to the United States. The first place the tribe settled was Guadalupe.

In the center of town there is a large traditional plaza bordered by Our Lady of Guadalupe Catholic Church and the Yaqui Temple. The Yaquis are Catholic Indians, blending both religions and holding ceremonial rites each Easter in the plaza. They perform the famous Deer Dance, originally done for good hunting. A man wearing a deer head like a crown takes on the persona of a hunted deer and is sometimes killed by clowns portraying coyotes or wolves. Everyone is welcome at the dances, but pictures and video are not permitted.

## At a Glance...

### House Prices

#### Townhouse
| Bedrooms | |
|---|---|
| Price | $200,000 - $350,000 |

#### Family home
| Bedrooms | |
|---|---|
| Price | $200,000 - $300,000 |

#### Family home
| Bedrooms | |
|---|---|
| Price | $250,000 - $350,000 |

#### Family home
| Bedrooms | |
|---|---|
| Price | $350,000 - $600,000 |

#### Executive home
| Area | Min. 4,000 sq. ft. |
|---|---|
| Price | $700,000 - $900,000 |

#### High-rise Condominium
| Size | 500 to 3,000 sq. ft. |
|---|---|
| Price | $275 to $400 per sq. ft. |

### Rentals

#### Apartment
| Bedrooms | |
|---|---|
| Price | $700 - $900 month |

#### Townhouse
| Bedrooms | |
|---|---|
| Price | $800 - $900 month |

#### House
| Bedrooms | |
|---|---|
| Price | $1,000 - $1,500 month |

### Travel Times

Distance to downtown Phoenix: 9 miles

To downtown Phoenix:
Peak: 15 – 20 minutes
Off-peak: 10 – 15 minutes

To the airport:
Peak: 10 – 15 minutes
Off-peak: 5 – 10 minutes

# Northeast Valley

Gorgeous Sonoran highlands, saguaro forests, verdant golf courses, and high-priced cars: the Northeast Valley is a Southwestern kingdom of desert chic. At neighborhood dinner parties you're likely to spot a blonde trophy wife in $30,000 worth of fringed suede buckskin. You live in a $1 million home? Ho-hum. If you want to turn heads here, you'll need triple-figure acreage, an eight-figure portfolio, or a daily helicopter commute.

Turn away from the mega-wealthy in custom homes designed by celebrity architects to families in master-planned communities like Grayhawk, Terravita and McDowell Mountain Ranch and you're still looking at privileged lives. Schools are top-notch. Everything from a butterflied leg of lamb to couture is

ten minutes away. Swedish masseuses, private sommeliers, home botanist visits (would you trust the maid to water the $900 palm in the dining room?). An unctuous legion of luxury is marshaled at the ready.

The Tonto National Forest and the Fort McDowell Yavapai reservation lock in the area's northern boundaries. All the major development battles were fought long ago. Any shock over North Scottsdale Road's commercialization is a bit disingenuous; the shopping centers and office complexes were in the city's General Plan more than a decade ago. The acreage around the Loop 101 and Scottsdale Road interchange is destined

## If you want to turn heads here, you'll need triple-figure acreage, an eight-figure portfolio, or a daily helicopter commute

to become the Southwest's premiere retail location. Rawhide Western Town sold its 160-acre site to a developer who plans to build 700 townhouses, patio homes and courtyard homes; six units per acre.

Scottsdale (and its stricter zoning regulations) occupies the eastern side of Scottsdale Road; the western side belongs to Phoenix. Discussions between Scottsdale and Phoenix about zoning and sharing sales tax revenues have not fared much better than Middle Eastern peace talks.

The old characters of North Scottsdale – the down-home Arabian breeder and the broken-down cowboy painter – will be gone forever, replaced by the retired business mogul and the golf pro.

The two main arteries off the Loop 101 Freeway to Cave Creek, Carefree, Rio Verde, and North Scottsdale – Scottsdale and Pima Roads – have been widened. At this point both roads move reasonably quickly. (Pima Road can be a parking lot during peak hours. One evening cars idled so long on Pima a huge coyote loped between them on his way down from the McDowell Mountains to Grayhawk for a housecat supper.) Build-out is hitting from Cave Creek to Fountain Hills, so traffic patterns won't look very different in the future, i.e. not that bad. Any Californian would wonder what all the complaining is about.

# Carefree ★★★★    *Northeast Valley*

Carefree is a small resort town north of Scottsdale and was one of Arizona's first planned communities. Two partners bought a goat ranch and 2,000 acres in the mid-1950s, then chose a saccharine array of street names like Easy Street and Tranquil Lane. (Ho Road clearly has not withstood the test of time.)

Names notwithstanding, it's a gorgeous town surrounded by dramatic mountains and dotted with prehistoric boulder stacks and lush desert vegetation. Natural beauty and exclusive custom homes help make Carefree the second most expensive area in metro Phoenix, surpassed only by Paradise Valley. Wildlife like coyotes, javelina, and jackrabbits roam the quiet roads. (Actually, wildlife roams everywhere. The town lists no less than nine numbers to call to have snakes, coyotes, and other wild innocents hauled away.)

Carefree is about quiet and wealthy desert living, without Scottsdale's frenzy and traffic. Carefree's culture is as much golf-and-gallery as Cave Creek's is saloon-and-cowboy.

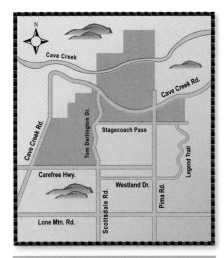

*Total Population: 3,500 approx.*
*Median Age: 55 years*
*Median Household Income: $89,000 p.a.*

## Who Lives There?

About 3,300 people live here. Most residents are retired, and some are well-to-do snow-birds who show up for the winter months. Californians and Easterners outnumber the Midwesterners who used to make up most of the population. Lucille Ball used to vacation at the Carefree Resort. Television star Dick Van Dyke lived in Carefree for awhile. Think slow-moving late-model Cadillac sedans with the wives in the back seat.

## Homes

Three, four, five, even $6 million dollar homes are common in Carefree. Santa Fe contemporary is a popular style. Traditional homes can feature Southwestern-style exposed wooden beams, courtyard fountains, outdoor fireplaces, and wall niches for santos. Condos and townhouses built in the 1970s can run into the high $200,000s and above. There's hardly anything available in mid-range single-family homes in Carefree.

# Amenities

### Schools ★★★★★

Students in Carefree attend schools in the Cave Creek Unified School District. Black Mountain Elementary School is the Carefree primary school for children through fifth grade. This school emphasizes technology with network capabilities, Internet access, laptops and smartboards.

Students sixth through eighth grade attend Desert Arroyo Middle School, which has a 20-acre desert education preserve. Two Desert Arroyo teachers were recently nominated for Disney Teacher of the Year.

Cactus Shadows High School ranked as one of the top five schools in the State with its 2003 AIMS testing results. Athletically, Cactus Shadows Falcons are 4A State Champions in Girls Golf, Girls Volleyball, and Competitive Cheer.

### Shopping & Dining ★★★

There aren't any big malls, and never will be, in Carefree. Shopping consists of a boutique-and-gallery-heavy complex at the town center at Cave Creek and Scottsdale Roads. You'll find expensive paintings of wistful Indian maidens, life-size rusted metal horses, crystals, and wind chimes. It's very popular with tourists and ladies who lunch. AZ Wine is an excellent wine shop.

A brand-new shopping center about a mile and a half down Scottsdale Road has everything to keep a home stocked with steaks and dry-cleaned shirts.

The town center at Cave Creek and Scottsdale Roads has several intimate restaurants, including an excellent tapas bar. There's also a bar and grill, if you're not feeling intimate and just want to yell at the Arizona Cardinals while they lose another game. Fine dining at the Carefree Resort and The Boulders Resort & Spa is around the corner for special nights.

## Leisure ★★★

A hike to the Sears-Kay Ruin, a 40-room Hohokam village about seven miles northeast of town, offers a look at how people lived before the advent of granite countertops and central vacuum systems. Bartlett Lake is close by for boating and fishing. Naturally this is golf country; about five courses are nearby. The

## At a Glance...

### House Prices

**Townhouse**

| | |
|---|---|
| Bedrooms | |
| Price | $300,000 - $400,000 |

**Family home**

| | |
|---|---|
| Bedrooms | |
| Price | $200,000 - $300,000 |

**Family home**

| | |
|---|---|
| Bedrooms | |
| Price | $250,000 - $400,000 |

**Family home**

| | |
|---|---|
| Bedrooms | |
| Price | $400,000 - $700,000+ |

**Executive home**

| | |
|---|---|
| Area | Min. 4,000 sq. ft. |
| Price | $1,000,000 - $2,000,000 |

### Rentals

**Apartment**

| | |
|---|---|
| Bedrooms | |
| Price | $900 - $1,500 month |

**Townhouse**

| | |
|---|---|
| Bedrooms | |
| Price | $1,200 - $2,500 month |

**House**

| | |
|---|---|
| Bedrooms | |
| Price | $2,500 - $4,000 month |

### Travel Times

Distance to downtown Phoenix: 35 miles

To downtown Phoenix (via the Loop 101 Freeway and State Route 51):

Peak: 1 hour 15 minutes
Off peak: 45 minutes

To the airport (via the Loop 101 and 202 Freeways):

Peak: 1 hour 20 minutes
Off-peak: 45 minutes

town also borders the immense Tonto National Forest.

# Real Estate

## Trends

A few luxury projects are being built in Carefree. Gated Carefree Ranch will feature 42 custom home sites on 900 acres; some areas are already sold out. An upscale 22-unit condo complex called Happy Hollow Villas is under construction. With North Scottsdale approaching buildout, expect prices in Carefree to rise along with the rest of the northeast Valley.

## Rental & Investment

There are two apartment complexes in Carefree, both renting two-bedrooms for about $900 per month. Vacation villas are prohibitively expensive if you're not on vacation – usually around $550 per day.

Investing in Carefree will always be solid because of the area's status. Nothing here is likely to depreciate.

ave Creek didn't get electricity or phones until 1946. The small town north of Scottsdale still has plenty of Old West feel. Many roads are dirt. Honky-tonks with names like the Buffalo Chip Saloon and the Horny Toad line the main drag. It's not uncommon to see people on horseback clopping through town.

That rustic Western ambience has not happened by accident. Wags like to say "Cave" stands for "Citizens Against Virtually Everything." Creekers like their roads dirt, their businesses small, and Scottsdale at arm's length.

It's the home of the rugged individualist. The first Creekers were miners crazy enough to dig in Apache country. Cowboys held sway until the 1970s, when artists discovered it. Those two factions were joined by people craving the peace and solitude of desert living. All three became as vicious as a cornered javelina about building so much as a tool shed.

And that is why Cave Creek is such a beautiful place to live today; preserved with foresight and passion, it may well represent the best in true Arizona living.

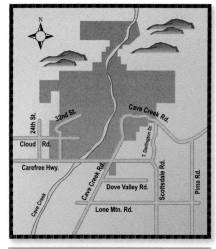

Total Population: 4,500 approx.
Median Age: 44 years
Median Household Income: $60,000 p.a.

## Who Lives There?

The mayor of Cave Creek once told a local newspaper he was reading a Buddhist guide to sex. Hells Angels founder Sonny Barger lives here. Welcome to Cactus & Cowboy Country, with a twist.

There are the old Creekers, mostly horse people, who have been up there forever and love the land. Wealthy people from the nearby ultra-luxury master-plan, Desert Mountain, are keeping their membership privileges and moving to Cave Creek. They want both elbowroom and golf. Young families are moving in for the excellent Cave Creek School District and nearby charter school, Foothills Academy. The artists have found no reason to leave.

In Cave Creek you'll find people who have run multi-million dollar corporations out on the golf course next to someone on a retirement salary thrilled they bought here ten years ago.

## Homes

Like the residents, Cave Creek homes are an interesting mix. Properties range from trailers in the desert to multi-million dollar luxury homes. What they all have in common is expensive land beneath them. Homes not in demand today are being replaced by custom housing.

Trailers used to sit next to $2 million homes, but that's disappearing because the value of the land has brought up the value of the construction. You're not going to find $200,000 homes in Cave Creek. It's more of a resort community now. Land prices are comparably expensive. An acre costs around $400,000.

The lucky few will chance upon a $400,000 two-bedroom two-bath home, which is four or five decades old. A sizeable chunk of land may come with it, but at that price not with a mountainside view. In the older areas of Cave Creek like Black Mountain you may squeak in some homes for $350,000.

## Amenities

### Schools ★★★★

Lone Mountain Elementary School strives for technological efficiency. The school

has a 30-station computer lab and four to six computers in each classroom. Desert Willow Elementary School offers a variety of enrichment programs including Scouts and after-school kickball and basketball.

Sonoran Trails Middle school, rated "highly performing," has two, 30-station computer labs. "Excelling" Desert Arroyo Middle School has a 20-acre desert education preserve.

Cactus Shadows High School ranked as one of the top five schools in the state in test results. The high school excels athletically as well.

### Shopping & Dining ★★★★

Cave Creek's saloons are some of the best in the Valley. Harold's Cave Creek Corral, the Buffalo Chip Saloon, the Horny Toad, and Crazy Ed's Satisfied Frog are all worth a visit. Unlike Tombstone saloons, the food's really good, too. In the 1960s

Harold's had a pet tiger and an owner who fired a pistol into the ceiling when the bar got too loud.

Hot newcomers are the Tonto Bar & Grill at the Rancho Manana Golf Course and Binkley's Restaurant. Locals are raving about the grill. Binkley's is turning into destination dining.

Art galleries and studios are scattered along Cave Creek Road; the town has an art night similar to Artwalk in Scottsdale or First Fridays in Phoenix. Cave Creek has some great pottery places. The Town Dump is junker's heaven. New boutiques with pricey goodies are opening to serve the new residents who pay cash for their million-dollar second homes.

For mega mall shopping, Desert Ridge is 20 minutes away. Where else could you see a bobcat in your driveway and 20 minutes later be in Barnes & Noble?

For Cave Creek Fiesta Days, a three-day rodeo and parade in early April, bring the kids, cooler, and lawn chairs. Americana at its best.

## Real Estate

### Trends

Buyers are keeping that 1940s or 1950s ranch house, and rehabbing it as a guesthouse. It also works as caretaker's

quarters, with a beautiful custom home as the main quarters.

If you're not in the caretaker-hiring tax bracket and still want to live in Cave Creek, there are small apartment-style condos in the $250,000 to $350,000 range. Condo conversions are popular in Cave Creek right now. If you buy a condo in a high-traffic area and later move into a single-family home, you can easily rent to snowbirds or vacationers.

Buyer demand has pushed appreciation up to rates ranging from 20 to 50 percent per year, depending on the property. No major master-planned developments are in the works, so appreciation will likely remain high.

Cave Creek has turned into a resort community for the wealthy. If you can find an older down-at-heel three-bedroom house in the $300,000s, buy it. The house may be a dump, but the dirt underneath it is only to going to appreciate.

Older teardowns and ranch land, way off the beaten path, split into smaller building lots, are good buys. If prices sound high, imagine what Scottsdale prices sounded like ten years ago and where they are now.

### Rental and Investment

There are a couple of luxury apartment complexes in Cave Creek – Azure Creek and Terra Vista – with gourmet kitchens, soaking tubs, high-speed Internet access, built-in bookshelves, and other features. Rents range from the $900s to $1,100 a month, depending on size. Vacation rentals are in high demand, but prices are prohibitive for long-term residents.

## Look Out! ①

Black Mountain has the highest concentration of venomous snakes in the world, according to a local expert.

## Local Hero: Spur Cross Ranch

A golf course, resort, and hundreds of homes were planned for the Spur Cross Ranch Conservation Area. Thanks to a grassroots movement, though, 2,100 acres of upper Sonoran desert became the newest addition to Maricopa County's park system.

Just outside Cave Creek, Spur Cross Ranch offers hiking, mountain biking, and equestrian trails. (For those who don't own their own horse, a privately run stable rents horses for use within the park.) The trails range in length from 1.2 miles to 4.6 miles.

During winter months, Cave Creek flows through the park, where there is evidence of prehistoric inhabitants and remnants of early Arizona mining and ranching. Visitors will see petroglyphs and find pottery sherds (do not remove anything from the park, though—it's considered theft). Ranger-led hikes permit access to the Hohokam ruins.

Wildlife in the area varies. Near the creek, it is possible to regularly see deer, rabbits, and coyotes. Mountain lions are occasionally seen, as well as snakes and tarantulas.

## At a Glance...

### House Prices

**Townhouse**
Bedrooms
Price $150,000 - $300,000

**Family home**
Bedrooms
Price $300,000 - $600,000

**Family home**
Bedrooms
Price $400,000 - $700,000

**Family home**
Bedrooms
Price $500,000 - $800,000

**Executive home**
Area Min. 4,000 sq. ft.
Price $900,000 - $2,000,000

### Rentals

**Apartment**
Bedrooms
Price $800 - $1,100 month

**Townhouse**
Bedrooms
Price $1,000 - $2,000 month

**House**
Bedrooms
Price $1,400 - $2,500 month

### Travel Times

Distance to downtown Phoenix: 32 miles

To downtown Phoenix:
Peak: 1 hour 15 minutes
Off peak: 42 minutes

To the airport: Peak: 1 hour 20 minutes
Off-peak: 45 minutes

# Fountain Hills ★★★★★ *Northeast Valley*

ountain Hills sits off by itself in the northwestern corner of the Valley. Surrounded by a mountain range and two Indian reservations, it has a distinctly small-town sense of place. It's kind of sleepy; there's not much entertainment (or crime); and its central feature – the World's Tallest Fountain – harkens to the roadside-attraction park-and-gawk genre of Americana. What residents want more than anything is for a movie theatre to come to town. "You definitely have a slower pace of life here," one agent says.

Residents love the fact Scottsdale's bright lights are only 20 minutes away, but Scottsdale's construction, traffic, and manic pace don't follow them back over the mountain. While there's no multiplex in Fountain Hills, there is plenty of golf and wilderness. Superstition Mountain views are extraordinary; agents talk about how easy it is to sell Fountain Hills in winter when Four Peaks is covered in snow.

Vacant lots are available. Because there is no requirement to build, quite a few people invest in lots and hold them. Teardowns - a universal sign you've bought wisely - just started in Fountain Hills.

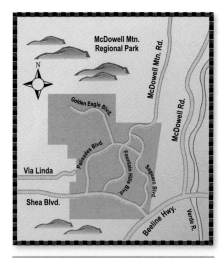

Total Population: 24,000 approx.
Median Age: 46 years
Median Household Income: $61,000 p.a.

## Who Lives There?

Fountain Hills is popular with wealthy Midwesterners because the safety and small size reminds them of their hometowns. The million dollar-plus custom homes draw empty-nesters who want upscale living but not trophy wives backing Hummers into their landscaping.

About 60 percent of the 24,000 residents commute to work all over the Valley. Starter families are almost priced out of Fountain Hills, except in the condo market. (Even those cost about $250,000 for a two-bedroom condo with about 1,300 square feet.) Established families with teenagers continue to move to the town.

## Homes

This is not cookie-cutter country. Seventy-five percent of the homes are custom-built.

Besides Phoenix, Fountain Hills has the most diverse housing stock in the Valley. There's little danger of coming home after a night out and trying to unlock your neighbor's door.

Lots are big and streets are wide. Developer MCO Properties also plugged in a lot of open space and maintained the view corridors. The town is built on a series of small hills and ridges, so neighborhoods aren't grids of monotony. It's not a Gucci ghetto, either; town homes and patio homes put some diversity into the area.

# Amenities

### Schools ★★★★
The Fountain Hills Unified School District has earned a reputation for excellent academic programs. It is a small district with high levels of parent and community involvement.

Students in Fountain Hills begin their academic career at McDowell Mountain Elementary in kindergarten, first, and second grades. The school also has a preschool program.

For third, fourth, and fifth grade, students attend Four Peaks Elementary. Four Peaks offers students many extracurricular activities including computer, newspaper, Spanish, and drama clubs.

Fountain Hills Middle School educates sixth through eighth graders and is recognized as "excelling." It has an inter-scholastic athletics program, wireless mobile computer labs, and a technology-based media center.

Fountain Hills High School shines both academically and athletically. Instruction focuses on college preparation with 93 percent of its graduates going on to college. In athletics, the 2005 Boys Basketball team won the 3A State Championship, and the baseball team finished its season as state finalists.

### Shopping & Dining ★★
Grocery stores, dry cleaners, and other daily necessities are plentiful in Fountain Hills. There aren't any malls, but downtown has a few art galleries.

A British expat couple runs The Codfather, a traditional fish-and-chips shop. They're the only place in the Valley with the guts to put kidneys in their steak and kidney pies. Italian food reigns supreme in Fountain Hills; it seems every other restaurant is a ristorante. For fine dining, Alchemy at the Copperwynd Resort gets good notices.

### Leisure ★★★★
Gambling is five minutes away at Fort McDowell Casino, as is an award-winning golf course. Saguaro Lake, with its soaring cliffs, swimming areas, and picnic grounds, is a better place to take the kids.

The town also has two huge fairs each year: the Great Fair in February and the Fountain Festival of Arts and Crafts in November.

If the call of the wild beckons, the Superstition Mountains and the rest of the Tonto National Forest are at your back door. Bring ropes, boots, water, and pain tolerance.

# Real Estate

## Trends

The first Fountain Hills home to crack the $3 million mark sold last year. One of the reasons home prices are jumping is because Scottsdale people are moving to Fountain Hills for the quiet. A 2,700 square foot single family home averages about $600,000. In the Eagle's Nest subdivision vacant lots start at about $500,000. Completion of the Loop 101 also kick-started Fountain Hills home prices.

Fountain Hills will be sold out in seven or eight years. Whether the town expands depends on the possible sale of state land to the north. Existing planned development will be complete in about 2010. Expect prices to rise even higher if the state doesn't sell the land.

## At a Glance...
## House Prices

**Townhouse**
Bedrooms
Price                    $200,000 - $400,000

**Family home**
Bedrooms
Price                    $350,000 - $500,000+

**Family home**
Bedrooms
Price                    $450,000 - $700,000

**Family home**
Bedrooms
Price                    $700,000 - $1,000,000

**Executive home**
Area                     Min. 4,000 sq. ft.
Price          $1,400,000 - $2,400,000

## Rentals

**Apartment**
Bedrooms
Price              $1,000 - $2,500 month

**Townhouse**
Bedrooms
Price              $1,000 - $2,500 month

**House**
Bedrooms
Price              $1,500 - $3,000 month

## Travel Times

Distance to downtown Phoenix: 31 miles

To downtown Phoenix (via the Beeline Highway & Loop 202 Freeway):
Peak: 50 minutes – 1 hour
Off-peak: 37 minutes

To the airport (via the Beeline Highway & the Loop 202 Freeway):
Peak: 45 minutes – 1 hour
Off-peak: 30 minutes

To the Loop 101 Freeway:
Peak: 25 minutes
Off-peak: 18 minutes

Paradise Valley is one of the country's 50 wealthiest communities, and one of only three ritzy ZIP codes not on either coast. Stars of stadium, screen, and boardroom all live here. Paradise Valley evokes Shangri-La. Sitting atop mountains in the middle of the city; it seems to float above the rest of the Valley. The desert setting is idyllic and the views are forever.

Wealthy people have always been attracted to the area because of its natural beauty, large lots and proximity to town. Here they can have it all: privacy, expansive living, views, and easy commutes.

Paradise Valley started out as a rural spot with a few genteel dude ranches, where residents rode their horses to visit neighbors. Most of the horses are gone now, and many of the five-acre parcels have been subdivided, but commerce remains limited to churches, schools, resorts and medical offices. Anything not residential requires a special-use permit, including the $12,000 pigeon coop boxer Mike Tyson built behind his home last year.

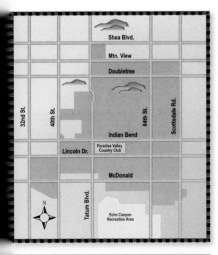

*Total Population: 14,000 approx.*
*Median Age: 46 years*
*Median Household Income: $150,000 p.a.*

## Who Lives There?

Paradise Valley has a lengthy roster of celebrity residents. Statesman and river rat Barry Goldwater, columnist Erma Bombeck, and sprinter Jesse Owens were some of the town's original stars.

Former Vice President Dan Quayle, broadcaster Hugh Downs, rockers Alice Cooper and Stevie Nicks, Family Circle cartoonist Bil Keane, baseball and basketball stars, and heirs to the Campbell Soup and Spam fortunes all live in Paradise Valley. Muhammad Ali recently bought here. Porn star Jenna Jameson and her husband live here in a 10,000 square foot home.

Celebrities like the quiet and seclusion. They feel safe. About 60 percent of Paradise Valley transplants come from out of state. Some are CEOs from the Midwest.

They spend the winter here and plan to move here full time when they retire.

## Homes

Architecture is an interesting jumble of styles. Brick ranches built in the 1950s, front yards thick with cactus and bramble, sit next to pillared white McMansions with manicured lawns and topiaries. Modern masterpieces of glass and steel cling to hillsides. Many properties are well-hidden behind private gates, long driveways and thick oleander hedges. Desert landscaping is a hallmark. Rabbits and quail are common sights skittering behind creosote bushes.

The gap between Paradise Valley and the also-rans is substantial. Paradise Valley homes cost twice as much as those in Carefree and almost three times more than Scottsdale homes.

## Amenities

### Schools ★ ★ ★ ★ ★
Excellent schools are another advantage of living in Paradise Valley. Most students attend elementary, middle and high school in the Scottsdale Unified School District. These schools rank among the state's best, consistently rated as "high performing" and "excelling."

Elementary students attend Kiva or Cherokee (both "excelling"). Middle schoolers go to Mohave ("highly performing") or Cocopah ("excelling"). Chaparral and Saguaro High Schools (both "excelling" schools) educate the community's high schoolers. Chaparral had 24 National Merit Semi-finalists in 2000, and Saguaro recently reported the highest average ACT scores in the state.

Paradise Valley is also home to four private schools. Tesseract and Camelback Desert Schools offer instruction for preschool through eighth grade while Phoenix Country Day School and Kachina Country Day School continue through 12th grade.

### Shopping & Dining ★ ★ ★ ★
For high quality deli and grocery shopping, there is an AJ's Fine Foods at both ends of PV: one at 44th Street and Camelback Road and one at Lincoln Drive and Scottsdale Road. For stocking up on staples, you'll find a major grocery store north on Shea Boulevard and east on Camelback. Paradise Valley Mall and

its satellites offer department and big-box retailers. Biltmore Fashion Park and Scottsdale Fashion Mall are only three miles from the center of town if you crave an A-list shopping experience.

El Chorro Lodge has sandstone and copper flowing through its veins, a true Arizona classic with lauded outdoor dining and old Valley charm. Sanctuary on Camelback Mountain Resort and Spa is New York- or LA-caliber chic, and elements, the resort's signature restaurant, plates fine Asian-American fusion at a very reasonable price for fine dining.

## Leisure ★★★★★

The 200-acre Paradise Valley Country Club was established in 1953 and has just completed a $28 million renovation. It's a club in the old tradition. If you want to join, two current members, who have known you for at least two years, must submit your name. The membership fee is unpublished.

Some of the Valley's earliest resorts opened in Paradise Valley. The Camelback Inn opened in 1936. The Hermosa Inn was built in 1930 as a home and guest ranch. The Sanctuary on Camelback Mountain started life as a tennis club in the 1950s, and is now an intimate resort and spa. El Chorro Lodge opened in the 1930s as the Judson School for Girls.

Try rappelling the 400'+ north face of Camelback Mountain's west end. It'll put hair on your chest. Peregrine falcons soar mere feet over your head and look you right in the eye while you're anchoring to the palo verdes. Over the edge SUVs look like M&Ms.

## Real Estate

### Trends

Paradise Valley is ripe for tear-downs. The location is desirable and unique, many of the homes are older. An empty acre (if you can find one) costs about the same as an acre with an older home. Razing permits

### Local Hero: Camelback Mountain

Camelback Mountain is the heart of the Valley. It looks like a camel stretched out with its chin on the desert floor. It's a beautiful 2,704-foot high pile of red Tertiary sedimentary beauty perched on top of a big hard hump of Precambrian granite. Climb to the top via the Echo Canyon trail off McDonald Drive. It's a real mankiller, one of the most difficult trails in Arizona. The view is sublime. Climbers: check out the Praying Monk on the north slope if you're in the mood for something really testing.

Local businessman Gary Driggs is Camelback's Obi-Wan. He was one of the first to climb the Monk, in 1951. Driggs' vision and perseverance played the key role in preserving the mountain from development. His successful efforts in this arena culminated in a dinner held in the late 1960s where he convinced then-First Lady, Lady Bird Johnson, to hike the Cholla Trail wearing high heels. Driggs also arbitrated between homeowners and hikers to preserve the Echo Canyon trail. Without his efforts, Phoenicians would only look up at Camelback, not down from it.

Recreation aside, Camelback Mountain casts a powerful spell. Try walking out of a noisy party some night, standing in the back yard, and pondering this symbol of permanence. You'll understand why homes with views of this magnificent mountain are valued so highly.

almost tripled in the past three years. Now many vacant lots cost the same, whether or not they have a 1950s brick ranch on them.

Luxury condos made their Paradise Valley debut in fall 2005 with Bella Terra. The 240-unit project at Shea Boulevard and 54th Street features one-, two-, and three-bedroom condos starting in the low $200,000s. Granite countertops and state of the art kitchens are standard. Select units have fireplaces, crown molding, and nine foot ceilings.

## Rental & Investment

There are homes for lease in this celebrity-studded town, at appropriately stellar rents: think 5,000 square feet with a heated pool and spa and mountain views for $10,000 per month. That's not a misprint. Condos – a rarity in Paradise Valley - are slightly more reasonable (in the town's context): two bedroom, two bath, furnished for $2,600 per month.

## Look Out! ⓘ

When the town incorporated in 1961 it set its mission: "to maintain a residential community in a quiet and country-like setting with little government intervention." Pay close attention to those last three words.

Residents are responsible for signing up and paying for their own water, garbage pickup, and fire service. One recent newcomer wondered why her garbage hadn't been picked up in three weeks.

A few other risks of PV living:
Town water pipes are woefully outdated; this has led to pressure problems during house fires. Updating is ongoing, so traffic disruptions are common. Town officials have a tendency towards a fuddy-duddy mentality; getting building plans approved can be unbelievably arduous.

## At a Glance...

## House Prices

### Townhouse
| | |
|---|---|
| Bedrooms | 🛏 🛏 |
| Price | $400,000 - $600,000 |

### Family home
| | |
|---|---|
| Bedrooms | 🛏 🛏 |
| Price | $700,000 - $1,000,000 |

### Family home
| | |
|---|---|
| Bedrooms | 🛏 🛏 🛏 |
| Price | $1,500,000 - $2,500,000 |

### Family home
| | |
|---|---|
| Bedrooms | 🛏 🛏 🛏 🛏 |
| Price | $2,000,000 - $3,000,000 |

### Executive home
| | |
|---|---|
| Area | Min. 4,000 sq. ft. |
| Price | $4,000,000 - $6,000,000 |

## Rentals

### Apartment
Very few apartments in Paradise Valley. If you can find one, you'll pay up to $3,000 a month.

### Townhouse
Very few townhouses in Paradise Valley. If you can find one you'll pay up to $1,200 a month.

### House
| | |
|---|---|
| Bedrooms | 🛏 🛏 🛏 |
| Price | $6,000 - $8,000 month |

## Travel Times

Distance to downtown Phoenix: 14 miles

To downtown Phoenix:
Peak: 20 – 30 minutes
Off-peak: 20 minutes

To the airport:
Peak: 15 – 30 minutes
Off-peak: 10 – 15 minutes

Rio Verde, northeast of Scottsdale at the northern tip of the McDowell Mountains, is as rural and beautiful as anything you'll find in the Southwestern outback. Say "Arizona" to a German, an Eskimo, and a New Yorker, and all three will picture Rio Verde.

It's a saguaro forest at the top of the eastern slope of the Verde River. Views of the Superstition Mountains in the east are amazing. Sunsets here are the stuff of postcards. Javelina, coyotes, mule deer, and mountain lions ghost behind the sage.

Most Rio Verde folks are serious horse people. If roping, polo, or trail riding are your passions, move here. You'll have a lot of instant friends. In the past decade Rio Verde has become a haven for riders chased out of Scottsdale by development.

The 20-square-mile area is a county island. Because Rio Verde has not (and probably never will) incorporate into a city, you're on your own. There are no water lines, sewers, paved roads, streetlights, garbage pickups, schools (except a cowboy college), or aesthetic rules. All that's your problem.

While there is no government, a very smart local horseman's association has in recent years represented the community.

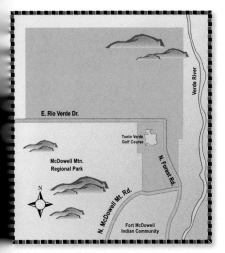

Total Population: 1,800 approx.
Median Age: 69 years
Median Household Income: $86,000 p.a.

## Who Lives There?

Almost no one lived in Rio Verde until recently. The 1990 census counted 33 residents. About 1,800 live here now. Officials estimate a population of 3,800 by 2020.

Philanthropists, retirees, cowboys, and business-people, live in Rio Verde. What almost all of them have in common is horses. There's a lot of expensive horseflesh nibbling Rio Verde sage.

If you want to live in the desert but feel you can do so without owning a horse, you'll be in the minority but not alone. There are plenty of people who aren't bowlegged and just want natural beauty.

There are a few families living in the area (see Schools below). A number of residents commute to work at the office complexes flanking the 101 Freeway or in central Scottsdale.

## Homes

Free rein has made Rio Verde a bizarre rural enclave. One of the Valley's richest men owns a mansion there in the middle of 200 acres. His nearest neighbor lives in a trailer surrounded by junk and crowned with a blue tarp held down by tires.

That's an extreme example. Most residents live in quality homes, ranging from stucco and tile to custom showplaces. Because the area is so newly settled, the majority of homes are five years old or less. Lots are huge; most people can't see their neighbors, and that's the way they like it. It's a place to enjoy quail and rabbits. Naturally the horse crowd has barns and corrals.

A few cowboys still live in swamp-cooled trailers out in the palo verdes, with a generator and a tank for hauled water. You've either got to be tough or well-off to live in Rio Verde.

# Amenities

## Schools ★★

There are no schools as such in Rio Verde. Most students attend schools in the Cave Creek Unified School District, located west and northwest of the planning area. Fewer than 25 kids go to school in the Fountain Hills district. (When there are 25 or more, that district plans to start a bus service.) Fountain Hills operates two elementary schools, a middle school, and a high school.

The Scottsdale school district offers open enrollment for Rio Verde students at an elementary and a middle school. There are two buses each morning and afternoon. Kids can also attend a Paradise Valley district school in the Grayhawk subdivision north of the Loop 101 Freeway.

## Shopping & Dining ★

Rio Verde isn't about the conveniences. There are no stores or restaurants or gas stations. For dinner, you can drive about 20 miles to Cave Creek to hit one of the saloons or enjoy an elegant meal at The Boulders Resort & Spa. Posh restaurants on Pinnacle Peak and Pima Roads in North Scottsdale are 16.5 miles away.

Fountain Hills is 10.5 miles away, and has large grocery stores, Starbuck's and all the other trappings of civilization. For clothing or a movie, it's about 22 miles to the Loop 101 North Freeway and four more miles west to the vast Desert Ridge Marketplace.

## Leisure ★★★★

Folks who live in the Rio Verde desert have a vast playground right outside their front doors, that's why they live there. Riding horses through the land is their true joy. Rio Verde has big sky and mountain views in every direction. McDowell Mountain Park is nearby, but residents pretty much stick to their own property. You won't see Rio Verde residents roaring through the wilderness on ATVs. These residents prefer transportation that's quiet and has four legs.

Folks with a passion for beautiful vistas and golf can have both in Rio Verde and Tonto Verde golf communities. Both golf courses have homes ringing the fairways, at prices below what you'd pay for a similar property and site 10 miles east in Troon North.

## Rural Issues

Living in the country requires more than a fair bit of rugged individualism. Here's a Rio Verde primer:

**Water:** This is the first thing you ask your agent about. In Rio Verde water comes from private wells, a small private water company, or it's hauled in by truck. If you're at all in doubt about how to interpret water information, hire a water lawyer or hydrologist.

**Fire protection:** Rio Verde residents are establishing a fire district. Emergency medical service and sheriff's patrols are provided by the county.

**Phone and electric:** Both are available. Cell service is spotty due to the mountains.

**Trash:** You need to call the private Waste Management Corporation and set up an account.

**Floods and mud:** You'll need a vehicle with high clearance and / or four wheel drive. Don't even think about driving a sedan on these roads when the washes run.

**Sewer:** You'll need a septic tank.

**Streetlights:** No way. Residents like seeing the stars at night.

**Cows:** Until a new law kicks in in 2006, Rio Verde is open range. Cows, horses, and other critters roam the roads. There have been a few BMW-livestock collisions, so don't speed at night.

## Look Out! ⊙

State water officials have no idea how much water is available in Rio Verde. If you build in Rio Verde, you're going to have to have a test well drilled to find out how much water is available, and what the quality is. "In general, wells have been more successful producing water in the western half of the planning area than in the eastern half," says one report.

## At a Glance...

## House Prices

### Townhouse
| | |
|---|---|
| Bedrooms | 🛏 🛏 |
| Price | $400,000 - $500,000 |

### Family home
| | |
|---|---|
| Bedrooms | 🛏 🛏 |
| Price | $500,000 - $700,000 |

### Family home
| | |
|---|---|
| Bedrooms | 🛏 🛏 🛏 |
| Price | $550,000 - $800,000 |

### Family home
| | |
|---|---|
| Bedrooms | 🛏 🛏 🛏 🛏 |
| Price | $700,000 - $900,000 |

### Executive home
| | |
|---|---|
| Area | Min. 4,000 sq. ft. |
| Price | $800,000 - $900,000 |

## Rentals

### Apartment
This small, rural community has very few apartments.

### Townhouse
They are scarce, but you may find a town-house for rent at about $1,000 a month.

### House
This small, rural community has very few homes for rent.

## Travel Times

Distance to downtown Phoenix: 42 miles

To downtown Phoenix:
Peak: 1 hour 15 minutes
Off-peak: 50 minutes

To the airport:
Peak: One hour
Off-peak: 45 – 50 minutes

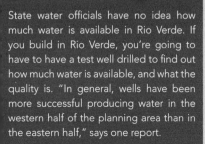

West Valley

The West Valley is where the East Valley was 20 years ago. It's a somewhat motley and remote collection of cotton and alfalfa fields interspersed with dairies and horse ranches. Growers' lavish horse properties lay like islands in the fields, powerboats parked beside barns. Farm workers have Saturday swap marts on dirt lots with meat smoke and norteno music swirling. Downtowns are dusty and utilitarian; think of good old boys in overalls and John Deere gimme-caps.

Amidst all this, amidst the white flies and dust blowing in from the western deserts, thousands and thousands of affordable new homes are being built. Goodyear's Palm Valley development will feature more than 13,500 homes when it's complete in two years.

The state Department of Economic Security predicts that the two largest cities in the West Valley (Avondale and Goodyear) will grow 34 percent in the next seven years.

Freeways are crucial to accommodating all this growth. Loop 303 is a quick slingshot to downtown. Interstate 10 will be widened out in Goodyear. With the massive development planned for the northeastern White Tanks, the Sun Valley Parkway is almost guaranteed to eventually go from two lanes with stoplights to a mega-artery like the rest of the loop system.

Land is more affordable in the West Valley, which is key to rapid development. Shopping is hot on the heels of

## amidst the white flies and dust blowing in from the western deserts, thousands and thousands of affordable new homes are being built

houses. Upscale mall creator Westcor is developing a state of the art mixed-use regional shopping center in Goodyear. Estrella Falls will also include multi-family residential developments like townhouses or apartments, offices, and Westcor's signature elaborate landscaping and design. The old boy in the overalls and the John Deere gimme-cap will soon be able to get an appletini and some sashimi.

What looks like the boonies now will look completely different in 20 years. As the west side of the Valley grows, these areas won't seem so far from the center of the metropolis. Once upon a time Mesa and Gilbert were the far fringes of civilization. Now look at them. No more dust or white flies there. That's what's in store for the West Valley.

Market forces will have redeveloped town centers and attracted new businesses. Landscaping will have filled out. The West Valley will be home to an enormous football stadium hosting a Super Bowl. Fifth-generation chi-chi foo-foo like dog psychics and artisan cheesemakers will have opened their doors. It's an area which is a good buy right now. Home values will only appreciate as the finer things in life roll this way.

Avondale is one of the Valley's most intriguing cities because of what might be there, rather than what is. It has affordable new homes, a quaint historic downtown, and residents and leaders who don't want the vacant spaces filled in with junk.

Residents and leaders bit the head off a second Wal-Mart attempting to sneak in. Residents stood up at city council meetings and said they didn't build golf course homes to live across the street from a Wal-Mart. They wanted an AJ's Fine Foods or a Crate & Barrel. "Avondale Boulevard is going to be special," the mayor said. "We're telling interested retailers that you just can't put in a big box." "How about it going south of Buckeye?" one citizen suggested.

Avondale has a nice little old downtown with an antique store, an excellent Western bookstore, a park, a Mexican bakery, and other walkable features. The city has put effort into retaining downtown's genuine Arizona charm, and it will only improve. Look for this to be the coolest spot in the entire West Valley 20 years from now. In 30 years it'll have boutiques and Starbuck's.

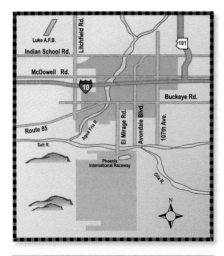

*Total Population: 60,000 approx.*
*Median Age: 27 years*
*Median Household Income: $49,000 p.a.*

## Who Lives There?

About 60,000 people live in Avondale, with half over and half under 27. Young families and career-starters who commute across the Valley, buy in Avondale. Farm workers live here in the older neighborhoods. Farmers still milk cows, raise thoroughbreds, and grow cotton. Medical workers from the area's two new hospitals have a short drive to work.

## Homes

This is the land of spacious affordable homes. They're stucco-and-tile, with different sizes and shapes and prices. SUVs, kids on bikes, a garage, and an afterthought front door. The average home costs about $160,000.

Older Avondale neighborhoods tend to be 1970s architecture showing its age and homes with second- and third-generation additions, some built with slightly suspect skill and materials. There are horse properties, of course, and a few large older luxury homes, which belong to growers and ranchers.

# Amenities

### Schools ★★★

The school system in Avondale can be a bit confusing. There are four elementary school districts with schools within the city limits—Avondale, Littleton, Litchfield, and Pendergast—and two high school districts, Agua Fria and Tolleson.

Anyone moving to Avondale with school age children will need to spend some time investigating the school system. Don't assume that your children will attend the neighborhood elementary school because the grades taught at each school vary. For example, Rio Vista Elementary School teaches students from pre-kindergarten through eighth grade while Michael Anderson Elementary School goes only through the second grade.

Avondale has two high schools. Westview High School (rated "highly performing") in the Tolleson Union High School District has a strong extracurricular activities program. Westview offers a model United Nations club as well as culinary arts, drama and fashion clubs.

The Agua Fria Union High School District expects to double from three to six high schools by 2010. Desert Edge and Millennium high schools are rated "performing plus," Agua Fria is rated "performing." The girl's basketball team has been to the State playoffs for the past three years, and the football team has six State championship titles as well as five additional playoff appearances. Agua Fria also has an Air Force Junior ROTC program.

A Montessori pre-school opened in the Avondale district last year.

### Shopping & Dining ★

The new shopping centers, near Interstate 10, are the only options at this point. You have to drive to the Palm Valley centers in Goodyear, which is right next door, for quality shopping. As far as dining goes, it's Mexican at Raul and Teresa's on Main Street or mall chains like El Paso Barbeque Company or TGI Friday's.

### Leisure ★

Burning fossil fuels down at Phoenix International Raceway is enormously

popular. Two NASCAR races bring in more than 150,000 people, and Formula One races are also held.

Friendship Park is a huge regional park with 10 soccer fields and other features.

The Estrella Mountains form the city's southern boundary. They're one of the Valley's wildest and least-trodden mountain ranges. No one ever goes there. The terrain is very challenging – a great place to explore in solitude and silence.

# Real Estate

## Trends

While Avondale is known for its affordable homes, two high-end developments are coming. Upscale development is being encouraged by the city, so residents won't have to move out to move up. Avalon Estates will have some of the city's most expensive housing, averaging $450,000. Roosevelt Park homes will face each other over shared courtyards maintained by the homeowners association. Drivers will reach garages through alleys and park in back of homes.

## Rental & Investment

Park Shadows may be one of the prettiest apartment complexes in the Valley. It's an idyllic park with tall trees, 267 ivy-covered cottages, and swimming pools. It's decades old and quite affordable (a three-bedroom cottage rents for $810 a month), but very pleasant.

## At a Glance...

## House Prices

### Townhouse
Currently very few townhouse omplexes in Avondale. Those available range in price from $70,000 to $90,000.

### Family home
| Bedrooms | 🛏 🛏 |
|---|---|
| Price | $200,000 - $300,000 |

### Family home
| Bedrooms | 🛏 🛏 🛏 |
|---|---|
| Price | $250,000 - $350,000 |

### Family home
| Bedrooms | 🛏 🛏 🛏 🛏 |
|---|---|
| Price | $300,000 - $400,000 |

### Executive home
| Area | Min. 4,000 sq. ft. |
|---|---|
| Price | $350,000 - $450,000 |

## Rentals

### Apartment
Currently very few apartment complexes in Avondale.

### Townhouse
Currently very few townhouse complexes in Avondale.

### House
| Bedrooms | 🛏 🛏 🛏 |
|---|---|
| Price | $800 - $1,200 month |

## Travel Times

Distance to downtown Phoenix: 18 miles

To downtown Phoenix:
Peak: 35 – 40 minutes
Off peak: 23 minutes

To the airport:
Peak: 35 – 45 minutes
Off-peak: 26 minutes

**B**uckeye has always been the Green Acres of the Valley, a place where the mayor wears a big brass belt buckle with his name — "RAY" — on it. This is farm country: white flies in spring, cotton in the fall, and dust all the time. Bola ties, skin cancer, and Western-cut shirts are always in fashion in Buckeye.

Buckeye is a very tight-knit place. When a local kid wins a 4-H grand champion ribbon, the community pitches in to help support competition. Even if residents don't have alfalfa or cotton farms, they have horse properties so their kids can learn to ride or raise animals for 4-H. It's always been more a part of rural Arizona than metro Phoenix. "I think what's made Buckeye unique is that we're so far from Phoenix we've maintained our identity," says a lifelong resident. "I can see that changing." Buckeye has grown from 8,000 to 35,000 people in the past years, and in eight years is expected to have a population of about 150,000.

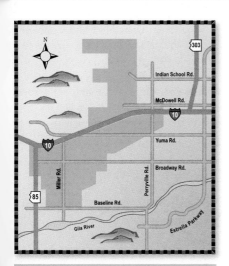

*Total Population: 35,000 approx.*
*Median Age: 30 years*
*Median Household Income: $35,000 p.a.*

## Who Lives There?

There are more than 240,000 homes planned in Buckeye in 12 master-plans, some as big as 36,000 acres. Finding a new home isn't a problem. A four bedroom, two bath 1,300 square foot home costs right around the high $180,000s. That's in a master-plan with an 18-hole public golf course, a lake, trails, shopping, parks, and outdoor recreation areas. High end is in the $300,000s.

## Homes

Acre-lot irrigated neighborhoods are wildly popular in Buckeye for keeping livestock. Not only are the old horse properties thriving, new semi-custom to custom homes in the $400,000 range are being built on large lots specifically for

equestrians. The last horse development sold out immediately.

# Amenities

### Schools ★★★

Buckeye's schools run the gamut from brand new schools like Sundance Elementary School to Buckeye Union High School, which graduated its first class of two students in 1921. Standardized test scores vary as well, ranging from below average in Buckeye Elementary and Union High School Districts to above average in the Liberty Elementary District.

As soccer moms and minivans move into what has traditionally been an agricultural community, these schools are working to meet suburban expectations. One example of this is Rainbow Valley Elementary School, which has developed an award winning cultural exchange program with Banamichi, Mexico, called Banamichi Club.

### Shopping & Dining ★

The Butcher & The Farmer market has been downtown for decades. (Most of the locals visited the new Fry's center once or twice, then went back to the B & F.) Downtown also has a Western wear store selling boots, hats, and Wranglers; a pharmacy, a florist, and other thriving small businesses. The Fry's shopping center has a video store, a bank, and restaurants with sandwiches, Chinese, and pizza.

"And of course we have hamburgers and Mexican," an old timer says. "We could use a good steak restaurant."

### Leisure ★★

All the master plans have their own recreation centers, parks, pools, and golf courses. The town has a youth center, a skate park, and a new aquatic center. The town library just got an addition, too. In a small town everything either revolves around the park or the school, and the two are close together here.

The Estrella Mountains are due south for horseback riding and hiking. The town celebrates Countryfest in the fall, Pioneer

Days in the spring, and a traditional Fourth of July.

# Real Estate

## Trends

Vast master-plans are coming this way. Verrado is the first. Designed to be a traditional American small town, about 14,000 homes will be built over the next 20 years. Alleyway garages, tree-lined streets, small shops with apartments above, and no house more than two blocks from a park are a few Verrado features. Prices range from about $175,000 to $400,000, with about 100 home designs for variety.

The biggest master-plan in Arizona is coming to Buckeye. Douglas Ranch will cover 36 square miles about 25 miles northeast of downtown Buckeye. It's in the infrastructure planning stage. When finished, it could include 83,000 homes and 250,000 residents.

## Rental & Investment

There aren't any apartment complexes in Buckeye - yet. It's still too rural. However, house rentals are plentiful. Homes in Verrado rent for about $1,200 to $1,700 a month for a three to four bedroom. Rentals in Sundance cost a little less; about $900 for a three-bedroom and $1,150 for a four-bedroom.

Horse properties will always hold their value in Buckeye, making them the town's wisest real estate investment.

## At a Glance...

### House Prices

**Townhouse**
Currently there are no townhouse complexes in Buckeye.

**Family home**
Bedrooms
Price   $100,000 - $200,000

**Family home**
Bedrooms
Price   $200,000 - $300,000

**Family home**
Bedrooms
Price   $250,000 - $400,000

**Executive home**
Area   Min. 4,000 sq. ft.
Price   $800,000 - $900,000

### Rentals

**Apartment**
Currently there are no apartment complexes in Buckeye.

**Townhouse**
Currently there are not townhouse complexes in Buckeye.

**House**
Bedrooms
Price   $900 - $1,500 month

**House**
Bedrooms
Price   $1,000 - $2,000 month

### Travel Times

Distance to downtown Phoenix: 35.5 miles

To downtown:
Peak: 50 minutes – 1 hour
Off-peak: 40 minutes

To the airport:
Peak: 55 minutes – 1 hour 10 minutes
Off-peak: 45 minutes

Goodyear has a great sense of community. "Mayberry out West," a longtime resident says. Like its neighbor Avondale, it's a farm town with suburbanites in affordable new homes. (There's still plenty of farm left in both towns, however.) Community leaders led a successful grassroots effort to build a $10 million YMCA. It's the twin of its sister Avondale: a farm town becoming suburbia, populated by civic-minded people.

Goodyear is like Gilbert or Chandler 15 years ago. There's not much beyond homes, farms, a few shopping centers, and some golf courses, but any goody the American heart desires will come eventually. Expect master-plans like Garden Lakes and Palm Valley to become as prized as Mesa's Dobson Ranch in two decades.

Between Aviation Management Systems, Lockheed Martin, Lufthansa's training facility, and Luke Air Force Base, you won't be alone if you're in aviation. This has been a flying town since World War II.

No one seems to care about the guests of the state at Perryville State Prison. "They worry more about Palo Verde," an agent says, referring to the nuclear power plant 23 miles away.

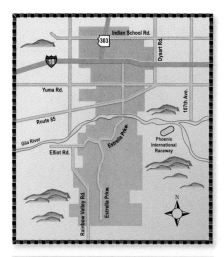

*Total Population: 37,500 approx.*
*Median Age: 36 years*
*Median Household Income: $57,000 p.a.*

## Who Lives There?

It's mainly families. There are a few retirees. Some East Valley residents have moved out to Goodyear to buy more house and be a little closer to downtown Phoenix. Nevadans and Californians have been joined by Floridians. Farm workers live in the older areas of town. There's a sizeable military population from Luke Air Force Base.

## Homes

The vast majority of Goodyear is brand-new. Originally it was a vast corporate cottonfield for Goodyear Tire & Rubber. The modern homes out here are typical suburban Valley starter homes: stucco-and-tile. Homes toward the south and west are the best value for money – think granite countertops, tile, and a pool for under $300,000.

Tycoon-caliber homes have appeared. "In my wildest dreams I never thought I'd see $1 million out here," an agent says.

Estrella Mountain Ranch is the original southwest Valley master-plan. Built by convicted white-collar scoundrel Charlie Keating about 20 years ago, it's at the foothills of the Estrella Mountains. About 7,000 people live there. It has two lakes, an 18-hole golf course, an amazing swimming and recreation center, a pizzeria, a gas station, and a high school. People who live there love it, despite a half-hour drive to an Italian restaurant.

Farther north, 9,000-acre Palm Valley will have 13,500 homes at buildout in two years. This master-plan has some of the Valley's most attractive production homes, with a Spanish Colonial Revival influence, garages minimized, and designs which will age well. The golf course has had a stellar reputation since it opened, too.

## Amenities

### Schools ★★★

Goodyear is served by a mix of school districts. Nonetheless, Goodyear has some

outstanding schools. The most celebrated of these is Western Sky Middle School, part of the Litchfield Elementary District. This school is both "highly performing" and a National Blue Ribbon School.

Liberty Elementary District has two schools in Goodyear. Estrella Mountain Elementary School is rated "performing plus." Avondale Elementary District has three schools in Goodyear: Desert Star ("performing plus"), and Pioneer and Wildflower (both "performing").

There are three high schools in Goodyear. Desert Edge High School and Millennium High School are both part of the Agua Fria Union High School District. Estrella

Mountain Foothills High School is part of the Buckeye Union High School District. This school has a unique culinary arts program where students operate an on-campus restaurant, El Lobo Café.

## Shopping & Dining ★★

More than four million square feet of major retail and mixed-use developments is coming to Goodyear in the next three years.

Westcor, the developer behind Scottsdale Fashion Square and the Valley's other swish malls, will bring the 300-acre Estrella Falls in 2008. Stores like Banana Republic and Victoria's Secret will appear in Goodyear.

The nearby Goodyear Centerpointe will feature stores like Petsmart, Borders, and Bed, Bath & Beyond when complete.

Palm Valley has already brought a pleasant series of shopping plazas to the area. Barnes & Noble, Kohl's, Target, and Lowes all anchor centers with smaller businesses.

Bella Luna is a highly-praised local Italian restaurant. For fine dining, the Wigwam Resort in Litchfield Park is nearby. Middlebrow chain restaurants like Chili's and Applebee's have opened in the new shopping centers.

## Leisure ★★★

Estrella Mountain Ranch offers a Phoenix Symphony Pops concert and a jazz festival in the spring. The White Tanks offer spectacular hiking and horseback riding. Trail riding is also popular in the Estrella Mountains.

# Real Estate

## Trends

Most new residents move into homes built in one of Goodyear's four master-planned communities. By 2010, officials estimate

the four major master-plans will add 18,000 new homes and 54,000 residents.

## Rental & Investment

Appreciation and rentals at Estrella Mountain Ranch have done very well in the past five years. Residents compare t to North Scottsdale at a quarter of the price.

Palm Valley has some resort-style luxury apartment complexes, with two-bedrooms renting at around $900 a month.

## Look Out!

We recommend having new homes thoroughly inspected, during construction, if possible, and documented with photographs. Like the south East Valley, new homes here are built on farmland. Expansive soil problems can crop up. Be cautious buying near Dysart and Glendale Roads; salt deposits in that area can wreak havoc with earth stability. Some subdivisions south of the interstate are showing repaired cracks in walls reaching up to second-story rooflines.

## At a Glance...

### House Prices

**Townhouse**

| Bedrooms | |
|---|---|
| Price | $100,000 - $150,000 |

**Family home**

| Bedrooms | |
|---|---|
| Price | $250,000 - $350,000 |

**Family home**

| Bedrooms | |
|---|---|
| Price | $300,000 - $400,000 |

**Family home**

| Bedrooms | |
|---|---|
| Price | $350,000 - $450,000 |

**Executive home**

| Area | Min. 4,000 sq. ft. |
|---|---|
| Price | $600,000 - $850,000 |

### Rentals

**Apartment**

| Bedrooms | |
|---|---|
| Price | $900 - $1,000 month |

**Townhouse**

| Bedrooms | |
|---|---|
| Price | $900 - $1,100 month |

**House**

| Bedrooms | |
|---|---|
| Price | $900 - $1,200 month |

### Travel Times

Distance to downtown Phoenix: 19.5 miles

To downtown Phoenix:
Peak: 35 – 45 minutes
Off-peak: 25 minutes

To the airport:
Peak: 38 – 48 minutes
Off-peak: 28 minutes

"Town." That's how Laveen residents refer to Phoenix. Laveen's actually within the city of Phoenix, but to local folks, casting glances across the Salt River, the place over on the north bank is "town."

Laveen is a 28 square-mile rural pocket in the southwest Valley butting up against South Mountain and the Estrella Mountains. Cotton, alfalfa, and melon fields stretch for miles. Horses graze lawns. The year's biggest event is a charity barbecue that has been held for more than five decades. Laveen has always been about canals, country roads, and neighbors.

Like South Phoenix, Laveen has been "discovered." Twelve minutes from downtown! Beautiful mountains! About 10,000 people live in Laveen now. That number will double or triple by 2010. A second high school is under construction to relieve crowding at the first high school built only six years ago. With a town center similar to squares in Prescott and Albuquerque and a canalside walkway/bikeway in the works, Laveen has a great location, lots of potential, and plenty of character.

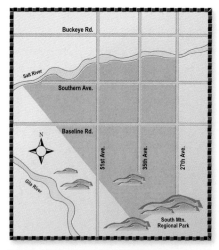

Total Population: 10,000 approx.
Median Age: 32 years
Median Household Income: $39,000 p.a.

## Who Lives There?

Laveen natives – old-Arizona types who wear bola ties and straw cowboy hats and put in for elk hunting permits every year – are plentiful. They drive past the Starbuck's at 51st Avenue where cubicle cowboys pick up caffeine. Farmers still work in the fields. "With the new housing going up, we now have people who work in town," one old-timer points out. The new homes are wildly popular with South Phoenix people both Anglo and Hispanic, who can now upgrade to new homes without having to leave their hometown. The occasional Californian or Midwesterner is only now finding their way to Laveen.

## Homes

New stucco-and-tile homes at starter prices are being built as fast as possible

Most of them cost between $200,000 to $300,000, depending on the number of bedrooms. The new communities are attractive, but they're starter subdivisions; no clubhouses or kids' water parks. Because they're brand-new homes at low prices close to downtown, they sell as fast as they come on the market. There are about 20 subdivisions either under construction or being planned.

Horse properties are extremely rare and pricey. A 1.25-acre horse property listing at $329,000 might come with a trailer, a corral, and the dirt under your feet.

# Amenities

## Schools ★

Historically an agricultural district, the Laveen Elementary District is struggling to emphasize academic achievement and improve standardized test results while building new schools and properly equipping others with essentials like library books and computers. Still, the district has shown some academic improvement and schools that had been "underperforming" are now "performing." The district was among the first in Arizona to implement a mandatory school uniform policy, which it believes has made the schools safer by helping to identify who belongs on campus.

Cesar Chavez High School, currently Laveen's only high school, opened in

1999. The student body is predominantly Hispanic and averages a dismal 65 percent graduation rate. A new high school will open in Fall 2007 at 59th Avenue and Baseline Road, and a third Laveen high school might be built as early as 2011.

## Shopping & Dining ★★

All the shopping in Laveen is new, and all the basic 21st century human needs – Starbuck's coffee, Blockbuster movie rentals, hair, nails, and pizza – are catered for. The Fry's Food & Drug Center at 51st Avenue and Baseline Road hosts all of the above, plus more. A Home Depot and a Wal-Mart are coming soon, as well as another major grocery store. Bottom line: you can get eggs, a haircut, and a brake job in Laveen, but not a book, a set of speakers, or a sweater.

The same rule applies to dining. It's a rural area. You're not going to find a tapas bar or a place with wine tastings. Most of the natives either cook or go to South Phoenix for Mexican food. Two brand-new places

are Applebee's and International House of Pancakes, both of which locals have warmly welcomed.

## Leisure ★★★★

Activities in Laveen suit its rural nature. First of all, it's Arizona farm country bordering wild mountain ranges – for the moment still great horse country. There's a rodeo ground, a dirt-track speedway, and the Laveen Barbecue every February for more than 50 years. "A very nice plate of food," says an old-timer, and it benefits Laveen's local charities.

The Bougainvillea Golf Club and the Aguila Golf Course are both open to the public. Cesar Chavez Park features 25-acre Alvord Lake, stocked with trout, catfish, and bass. The park also has basketball courts, a boat ramp, picnic areas, playgrounds, racquetball and tennis courts, and more.

Plans are in place for the Dobbins Paseo to run along the North Highline Canal, with trails, walkways, benches and restrooms, water features and other amenities. This is top-of-the-line urban design; and will be an excellent addition to Laveen's leisure facilities when completed.

# Real Estate

## Trends

Laveen has some very active and influential citizens' groups, both independent and under the aegis of the city. Mostly old-timers, both Anglo and Hispanic, they've become extraordinarily sophisticated at demanding, and getting, quality development from both the public and private sectors. They know Laveen is going the way of Chandler and Gilbert, but they won't stand for having it ruined, either. General plan development guidelines call for Paradise Valley zoning, i.e. one home per acre. Residents want developers to

preserve that kind of space, and allow for horse privileges. "It's very hard fighting the city because they want to make it as dense as they can," a committee member says. (High home density makes it cheaper for the city to provide services.)

One thoughtful and progressive plan calls for a town center to be built at 59th Avenue and Dobbins. This is the kind of quality planning usually found in private masterplans like Verrado or DC Ranch. It calls for mixed-use retail, commercial, office, and civic buildings surrounding a village green. Land use becomes less dense out from the core, ranging from single-family homes to rural uses like horse properties. The whole town center will be walkable, with a distance from the center of less than 10 minutes. It's only on paper for now, but local willpower and market forces make the Laveen Town Center a good bet to become sticks and bricks.

## Rental & Investment

Rental homes are not scarce in the new developments, and rents are a real bargain: think $1,100 a month for three- or four-bedrooms.

Laveen is an excellent place to put your money. Those vocal residents' groups are working at the right time and in the right way to keep Laveen a quality place to live and invest.

## At a Glance...

## House Prices

### Townhouse
Laveen does not have any town house complexes.

### Family home
| Bedrooms | 🛏 🛏 |
| --- | --- |
| Price | $250,000 - $350,000 |

### Family home
| Bedrooms | 🛏 🛏 🛏 |
| --- | --- |
| Price | $300,000 - $450,000 |

### Family home
| Bedrooms | 🛏 🛏 🛏 🛏 |
| --- | --- |
| Price | $350,000 - $450,000+ |

### Executive home
| Area | Min. 4,000 sq. ft. |
| --- | --- |
| Price | $600,000 - $800,000 |

## Rentals

### Apartment
There are very few apartments in Laveen.

### Townhouse
Laveen does not have any townhouse complexes.

### House
| Bedrooms | 🛏 🛏 🛏 |
| --- | --- |
| Price | $1,000 - $1,200 month |

## Travel Times

Distance to downtown Phoenix: 12 miles

To downtown Phoenix:
| | Peak: 25 minutes |
| --- | --- |
| | Off-peak: 20 minutes |

To the airport:
| | Peak: 30 minutes |
| --- | --- |
| | Off-peak: 25 minutes |

itchfield Park is one of the West Valley's best-kept secrets. It has one of the state's grandest old resorts, a genteel downtown, and attractive, affordable new homes. A Litchfield Park signature is the palm tree-lined streets. It's a sleepy, three square mile town, despite all the growth hoopla; the mayor's name is Woody and his biggest recent problem was an isolated graffiti incident. "At night we don't hear a lot of police sirens out here," according to one resident.

Until five years ago most of Litchfield Park was bean fields and cotton patches. About 4,000 people live here now. About 7,500 are expected to join them in the next decade. "We're no longer the little farm community," one resident says.

New parks, subdivisions, and shopping are high-quality. Many locals have moved from older parts of the Valley and don't want Walmarts following them. City council and planning meetings can get heated, but the end result is a pleasant place to live.

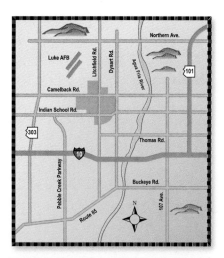

Total Population: 4,800 approx.
Median Age: 45 years
Median Household Income: $72,000 p.a.

## Who Lives There?

The town is mostly families. The master-planned communities are changing the mix from lower-income agricultural to middle/upper middle-class suburban families. Scottsdale imports are also upgrading homes. There are quite a few retired military personnel from nearby Luke Air Force Base. Older, well-to-do families live in the original neighborhoods around the town center.

## Homes

The new production homes are attractive, this is not boring stucco-and-tile. They have a Spanish Colonial Revival influence – turret entryways, for example. Garages have been placed to one side, so the house doesn't look like a garage with a house attached.

At the other end of the spectrum homes top out at around $1.5 million. Some are brand-new 4,000 square-foot, four-bedroom, four-baths with features like three-car garages, pools, gas fireplaces, and central vacuum systems. Lovely older homes near the town center along Old Litchfield Road hit the same price point. They date from the 1960s, with acre-plus lots, pools, mature lawns and trees.

Wigwam Resort

## Amenities

### Schools ★★★

The schools of Litchfield Park are middle-of-the-road. Ranked as "performing," they are academically solid, but they are not the nationally recognized or highly awarded schools of Scottsdale or the Kyrene Elementary District.

Litchfield Elementary District is a mix of old and new schools. Three schools have recently opened and are not yet rated based on their standardized test performances — Dreaming Summit Elementary, Robey Elementary and Wigwam Creek Middle Schools.

There are no high schools in Litchfield Park. Students attend nearby high schools in the Agua Fria Union High School District.

### Shopping & Dining ★★★

Palm Valley has brought stores to the malls on Litchfield Road like Target, Best Buy, Barnes & Noble, Pier 1, Ross, Linens 'N Things, and Banana Republic. Safeway and Albertsons supermarkets also have new stores in the area.

The Wigwam Golf Resort & Spa, one of Arizona's grand old resorts, has sumptuous food at the Terrace Room and the Arizona Kitchen. Across the street, Park Wines is the West Valley's only speciality wine shop, stocking about 350 small-production wines. Sit at the bar or outside and nibble on marinated olives and cheeses.

At the Palm Valley Pavilions, by Interstate 10, you can find Chili's, TGI Friday's, Macaroni Grill, Starbuck's, and other eatery chains.

### Leisure ★★★★

Take the kids to the Wildlife World Zoo on Northern Avenue for their lemur fix. The zoo has about 2,400 scratching, sleeping, and playing critters, including tigers, penguins, and giraffes. Go for a hike in the White Tank Mountains, where petroglyphs cover boulders and waterfalls crash down into hidden tanks during rains.

The Palm Valley Golf Course is a championship standard, mid-length course, with a floodlit pitch-and-putt course and practice facility. Everyone from Erykah Badu to Van Halen plays at the nearby Cricket Pavilion. Litchfield Park also has an annual fall festival of the arts with artists, wine tasting, and food. Lake

Pleasant is a short drive away for water-skiing and sailing.

# Real Estate

## Trends

There are plenty of homes available in the new builds. You'll have to go on waiting lists for one or two builders, but nobody's camping out to get a home here.

"Everyone has a place here," agents say. It's true. A new three-bedroom, two-bath production home in Palm Valley costs about $270,000 to $280,000 for 1,400 to 1,700 square feet. That's $20,000 to $30,000 less than Johnson Ranch in Queen Creek, plus it's 16 miles closer to downtown Phoenix. (Palm Valley sprawls between Litchfield Park and neighboring Goodyear.)

Custom homes and home sites are sold out in Palm Valley, but resales from the $300,000s to the $800,000s are plentiful.

## Rental & Investment

Litchfield Park is chock-full of resort-style apartment complexes: swimming pools, fire pits, fitness centers. Units have washers and dryers, fireplaces, high ceilings, granite counters, and other high-end features. Rents are about $750 a month for a one-bedroom and $1,100 for a three-bedroom.

Investment here will only appreciate as the Glendale Arena is completed and new developments fill the fields. Litchfield Park is convenient to both Interstate 10 and the Loop 303 Freeway.

## At a Glance...

## House Prices

### Townhouse
| Bedrooms | |
|---|---|
| Price | $150,000 - $250,000 |

### Family home
| Bedrooms | |
|---|---|
| Price | $225,000 - $300,000 |

### Family home
| Bedrooms | |
|---|---|
| Price | $300,000 - $500,000 |

### Family home
| Bedrooms | |
|---|---|
| Price | $400,000 - $600,000 |

### Executive home
| Area | Min. 4,000 sq. ft. |
|---|---|
| Price | $700,000 - $900,000 |

## Rentals

### Apartment
| Bedrooms | |
|---|---|
| Price | $950 - $1,100 month |

### Townhouse
| Bedrooms | |
|---|---|
| Price | $900 - $1,200 month |

### House
| Bedrooms | |
|---|---|
| Price | $1,000 - $1,300 month |

## Travel Times

Distance to downtown Phoenix: 20 miles

To downtown Phoenix
Peak: 35 – 45 minutes
Off-peak: 26 minutes

To the airport
Peak: 40 – 50 minutes
Off-peak: 31 minutes

# *West Valley* ★★★★★ Tolleson

Tiny six square-mile Tolleson is a typical dusty white-fly-blown West Valley cotton patch, with one difference.

"The city has a friendly reputation," says state Department of Commerce literature. It's an accurate observation. Native Arizonans from Tolleson tend to be friendly, genteel, and soft-spoken.

Cracks about white flies and dust notwithstanding, Tolleson has some neatly-kept older neighborhoods, horse properties as nice as anything in south Tempe or Chandler, and the affordable new homes creating the West Valley boom are plentiful.

A big, cheap new house, with no frills, in a quiet town. You could do worse.

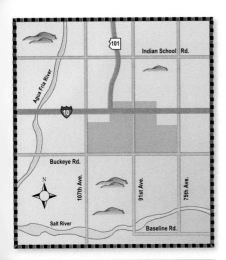

Total Population: 6,000 approx.
Median Age: 29 years
Median Household Income: $39,000 p.a.

## Who Lives There?

The West Valley triumvirate of growers, workers, and fresh-faced families is in full force in Tolleson. The population is 19 percent Anglo, 78 percent Hispanic. Aside from the old timers, the residents are from everywhere: the Midwest, California, the East Valley, and elsewhere.

## Homes

There are a few horse-property sub-divisions with tall trees and backyard corrals. These are nice areas comparable to old Mesa and Chandler horse neighborhoods. There is a pocket of charming old homes downtown, east of the high school. The new production neighborhoods

# Tolleson

## West Valley

are as good as anything in the East Valley, at a much lower price.

# Amenities

## Schools ★

Three districts have schools in Tolleson. Tolleson Elementary District has three kindergarten through eighth grade campuses. Porfirio H. Gonzales Elementary School is a "performing plus" school while the two other schools—Arizona

Desert and Desert Oasis Elementary Schools—are too new to be rated.

Both of Union Elementary District's schools are located in Tolleson. Union Elementary School is an "under performing" school that nonetheless has shown improvement in its Stanford 9 and AIMS test results. A new school, Hurley Ranch Elementary School is currently home to kindergarten through fourth grade students while Union Elementary's campus educates students through the eighth grade.

Tolleson Union High School is the area's high school. It has new fine arts, agricultural and science buildings. Academically, the school struggles. In 2004, the school had a four-year graduation rate of only 70 percent. Tolleson Union High School District's alternative education program for students struggling in their neighborhood schools, James A. Green Continuing Education Academy, is located in Tolleson.

## Shopping, Dining & Leisure ★

Shopping is centered around major intersection corner centers, anchored by grocery stores. That's it. Dining is limited to pizza and Mexican food. Leisure is similarly limited: Tolleson is simply a very small,

very rural town which has only recently had thousands of residents dumped into it. Parks, restaurants, and so on will come with new tax revenues.

# Real Estate

## Trends

A new production three-bedroom, two-bath home will cost around $250,000. For the same dollar, buyers get considerably more house than they would in the East Valley. Horse properties, like those in Tolleson Farms, if you can find them, run from the $300,000s to the $500,000s.

## Smart Buy ✓

You can buy a lot more home here than in the East Valley, with half the commute time (even at peak hours).

## At a Glance...

## House Prices

### Townhouse
Tolleson does not yet have many townhouse complexes.

### Family home
| Bedrooms | 🛏 🛏 |
|---|---|
| Price | $200,000 - $250,000 |

### Family home
| Bedrooms | 🛏 🛏 🛏 |
|---|---|
| Price | $250,000 - $350,000 |

### Family home
| Bedrooms | 🛏 🛏 🛏 🛏 |
|---|---|
| Price | $300,000 - $500,000 |

### Executive home
Tolleson has very few homes larger than 4,000 square feet.

## Rentals

### Apartment
Tolleson has very few apartments. They will be added as the city grows.

### Townhouse
Tolleson does not yet have many townhouse complexes.

### House
| Bedrooms | 🛏 🛏 🛏 |
|---|---|
| Price | $1,000 - $1,100 month |

## Travel Times

Distance to downtown Phoenix: 12 miles

To downtown Phoenix:
Peak 20 – 25 minutes
Off-peak 16 minutes

To the airport:
Peak 23 – 28 minutes
Off-peak 19 minutes

# Northwest Valley

The Northwest Valley is as down to earth as the Northeast is trendy. People in Peoria, Surprise, and the Sun Cities who can afford Hummers drive Ford Explorers instead. They've got their big boats and big RVs parked beside big houses, but they're wearing a company T-shirt, not Hugo Boss.

You're not likely to see people here indoors very much. With the White Tank Mountains glittering five minutes away, critically acclaimed sports complexes, myriad golf courses, and a ten minute drive to Lake Pleasant, there are plenty of places to enjoy the sun.

The area is pool-table flat, with a few bumps on the Valley floor in northern Peoria until it runs into the jagged walls of the White Tanks.

Most of the homes and retail here are new. There's little blight to be redeveloped. The new home communities in the Northwest Valley are fourth- and fifth-generation for some developers. They've ironed out kinks that plague older East Valley master-plans, like M.C. Escher street layouts and identical houses. Builders have also returned to more classic styles, ditching stucco-and-tile for bungalows and Mediterraneans.

## Millions of people will move to this corner of the Valley in the coming years

Not all the new developments are homes. In Surprise's case, it's simply building a town center from scratch. When completed, it will have government offices, businesses, loft-style apartments, restaurants, retail, and entertainment, plus green gathering spaces. (It's bemusing to Phoenicians to realize the hippest small government halls will be in Apache Junction and Surprise, of all places.) The latest urban design trends are applied all over the Northwest, in both public and private projects. Westcor is building an 800-acre multi-use project using new design ideas combining retail and residential.

Millions of people will move to this corner of the Valley in the coming years. Vistancia, Marley Park, Sundial, Sun City Festival, and scores of other masterplans have yet to be built out.

The state Department of Transportation plans to build an outer loop road called the Loop 303 Freeway, but not for quite some time. It will follow the alignment of the Sun Valley Parkway due north from Interstate 10, then bend east at the Beardsley Road alignment and link up with the Loop 101 Freeway. This may not be built for a decade, but it's under nervous government scrutiny.

# El Mirage ★★★★★

*Northwest Valley*

"El Mirage is the little community God forgot," a local businessperson and resident says. "We're the forgotten city. It's a very unknown town." That's from a booster, not a critic.

The best thing the locals can say about 11 square-mile El Mirage (founded by migrant workers in the late 1930s) is that it's right beside Surprise. "They have a lot of nice things there," they say in the tone of a Dickensian slum waif peering in at a steaming dinner from a snowy street. "We have the luxury of living next to Surprise, with all the benefits Surprise has, without Surprise taxes." If you don't have feet you'll save money on shoes, too.

El Mirage doesn't have gas stations or supermarkets, beyond corner places which sell a lot of malt liquor. Businesses don't want to open shop in the town, preferring Surprise. There is one moribund park.

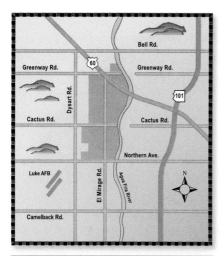

Total Population: 21,000 approx.
Median Age: 25 years
Median Household Income: $34,000 p.a.

## Who Lives There?

Plenty of farm workers live in the old eastern section of El Mirage. Military personnel from Luke Air Force Base like the affordable new homes. Young families from all over the Valley and country live in El Mirage. Almost everyone has kids. The population of about 21,000 is 28 percent Anglo and 67 percent Hispanic. Twenty-four percent of residents are foreign-born (11 percent is the US average).

## Homes

Like an Arab city, El Mirage is divided into an old town and a new town. The new section is between Dysart and Cactus Roads and El Mirage and Thunderbird Roads. These are very nice neighborhoods, with attractive landscaping, kids riding bikes in the street and no blight.

It's a startling contrast to the abysmal old section: down-at-heels dogs barking from chains, couches as lawn furniture, and incomplete but utilized home additions.

Given all this bleakness, let's look at the new subdivisions like Rancho El Mirage and Sundial. These two and the other two major subdivisions in El Mirage offer affordable homes in attractive neighborhoods rivaling anything in Gilbert or Chandler: clean streets with obvious pride of ownership. Go there, drive around, and see for yourself. These really well-kept neighborhoods are the pearl in the oyster.

# Amenities

### Schools ★

El Mirage schools are a part of the Dysart Unified District. Students attend "ele-middle" schools from kindergarten through eighth grade and then move on to Dysart High School. Recent bonds have allowed the district to extensively remodel and rebuild El Mirage schools. At best, these are "performing" schools.

The district's special programs are located in El Mirage. Dysart Preschool has a program for special needs children. Sundown Mountain Alternative Program is a small (under 100 high school students

and 10 middle school students), non-traditional school for students who can't succeed in neighborhood schools. Sundown Mountain's faculty meets every week to discuss each student, and the school offers an internship program that allows students to work either full or part time while earning school credits.

### Shopping, Dining & Leisure ★

A good time in El Mirage is when a pack of coyotes peels out of the riverbed in search of housepets. "The coyotes run by us but they don't do anything," a local mom says. "We don't have too much leisure here. We have to go out. Everything has to be out of El Mirage, which is sad. I have hopes we'll grow and catch up to Surprise."

So you've got to drive to Surprise for movies, meals, and clothes - it's not that far.

# Real Estate

## Trends

New homes sell hotly since they're so affordable. A 1,200-square-foot brand-new home which would cost $1 million in Scottsdale can be bought in El Mirage for $245,000. The same home, or a bit smaller, will cost about $300,000 in neighboring Surprise. Despite all of our comments, appreciation has been very good in El Mirage.

## Rental & Investment

Rentals in the new neighborhoods like Rancho El Mirage are available at about $900 a month for a three-bedroom home. El Mirage itself is slated to remain a bedroom community because of its size.

## At a Glance...

## House Prices

### Townhouse
El Mirage has very few townhouse complexes.

### Family home
| | |
|---|---|
| Bedrooms | 🛏 🛏 |
| Price | $125,000 - $150,000 |

### Family home
| | |
|---|---|
| Bedrooms | 🛏 🛏 🛏 |
| Price | $200,000 - $250,000 |

### Family home
| | |
|---|---|
| Bedrooms | 🛏 🛏 🛏 🛏 |
| Price | $200,000 - $300,000 |

### Executive home
El Mirage has very few homes larger than 4,000 square feet.

## Rentals

### Apartment
El Mirage has very few apartments.

### Townhouse
El Mirage has very few townhouse complexes.

### House
| | |
|---|---|
| Bedrooms | 🛏 🛏 🛏 |
| Price | $850 - $1,000 month |

## Travel Times

| | |
|---|---|
| Distance to downtown Phoenix (via Grand Avenue): | 19 miles |

To downtown Phoenix (via Grand Avenue; take the 101 Freeway and shave off 10 to 15 minutes):
Peak: 45 – 90 minutes
Off-peak: 45 minutes

To the airport (via the 101 Freeway and Interstate 10):
Peak: 45 – 50 minutes
Off-peak: 33 minutes

including Arrowhead Ranch, Historic Glendale & West Glendale

Glendale is perhaps Arizona's only city which didn't begin life as a) a mine, b) a military camp protecting miners, c) a little Gomorrah selling whiskey and women to miners and soldiers, or d) a farm town growing food for miners, soldiers, and prostitutes.

It started in 1891 as a temperance colony for the German Reformed Church. Since then it's borne a pious, conservative reputation – a nice place to raise a family but the sidewalks rolled up at sunset. The city's biggest draw has been the downtown antiques district, 90 speciality and antique stores *USA Today* named as one of the "Top Ten Antique Destinations in the Country." Go to downtown Glendale on a Saturday and you won't see blondes in mini-dresses cruising around in Porsches, but it's a great place to take your grandmother for an afternoon out.

Thirteen miles from Phoenix, Glendale is the educational, financial, and business hub of the West Valley. The schools are good, the neighborhoods are clean, and the people are friendly. It's always been a place you lived, not a place you went. But things are changing – dramatically.

*Total Population: 236,000 approx.*
*Median Age: 31 years*
*Median Household Income: $45,000 p.a.*

## Who Lives There?

The population of Glendale is just over 236,000 according to the most recent statistics, making it Arizona's fourth largest city. Like the rest of the state, Glendale is 65 percent white and 25 percent Hispanic. Median family income is more than $45,000, $3,000 higher than the national median. The average age of the population is 31 but sometimes it feels like 51.

Glendale residents have been described as down-to-earth. They are generally perceived as solid, middle class citizens; more concerned with family values than house values. Recently however, more and more young professionals have recognized the area's lifestyle benefits and easy commuting to downtown

Phoenix which is gradually changing the city's profile and adding heat to its property prices.

## Homes

Glendale is divided into three distinct areas.

## North: Arrowhead Ranch

Arrowhead Ranch brought artificial lakes and luxury housing to Glendale in the 1980s. The 5,000-acre master-planned subdivision stretches from 67th Avenue to 75th Avenue and from Union Hills Road to the Loop 101 Freeway. It's an area with more millionaires than Scottsdale: golf courses, country clubs, and stucco-and-tile palaces with backyard waterfalls, pools, and mature trees. The first home sold for more than $3 million in Glendale changed hands in winter 2004.

Engineering and construction giant Bechtel has its administrative operations center here. Arrowhead Towne Center mall is nearby, with new restaurants and stores opening all the time to catch the locals' dollars.

Thunderbird Park offers miles and miles of desert mountain hiking, biking, and horse-back riding.

## Central: Historic Downtown

Many people say downtown Glendale reminds of them of their hometown. Even if it doesn't actually look like your hometown, it looks like the hometown everyone wishes they'd grown up in: white picket fences, trees arching over the street, flowers on porches.

The downtown historic neighborhood is Catlin Court. It seamlessly runs into an antiques district of homes converted into quaint shops.

Vanguard CityHome LLC is planning a high-end urban community downtown development with 94 townhouses priced to $240,000. The project would also include more than 13,000 square feet of new retail space filled with boutiques, banks, and coffee shops.

## West: Sports & Fun

West Glendale has always been defined by farms and Luke Air Force Base – check out the family farm stands on 75th Avenue – but the arena, the stadium, and the Westgate project will change that in time.

The stadium will host the Fiesta Bowl in 2007 and the Super Bowl in 2008. There is discussion about a white water rafting park and a San Antonio-style river walk south of the stadium along a canal tributary.

Westgate of course will be enormous. New developments are springing up near the arena area every day, almost all stucco-and-tile of varying prices.

Trammel Crow Residential broke ground on the 251-unit Alexan apartments and a 171-unit condominium complex known

as The Quarter in 2005. Ready for residents in fall 2006. Special touches designed to attract the 25-to-35-year-old set are promised.

Due west of downtown, the neighborhoods are older and have larger Hispanic populations. While housing stock is a mixed bag, these are good starter areas.

# Amenities

## Schools ★★★

The Thunderbird Garvin School of International Management, the world's top-rated business school, is in Glendale. (Officials like to say the school is known all around the world but not in its home town.) *U.S. News* and *World Report* recognized Thunderbird as the number one school in the nation for international business for nine years in a row.

In 2005 ratings all Glendale elementary schools rated "performing." In 2006, three boosted up to "performing plus," and one dropped to "underperforming." They offer gifted programs, language immersion programs and special need programs. They also offer free classes for adults in English skills and General Education Diploma (GED) preparation.

There are about 14,000 students in nine high schools with a well-rounded roster of programs including vocational, academic, sports and fine arts. Glendale Union is recognized as a model district for its student performance-based and results-oriented program.

## Shopping & Dining ★★

Arrowhead Towne Center includes five department stores: Dillard's, Robinson's-May, Sears, JCPenney, and Mervyn's, a 24-screen movie theater, two sit-down restaurants, food court, and more than 170 stores.

OK, so celebrity chefs haven't had an urge to move here yet, and the Mastro's at Westgate hasn't been built, but there are a bunch of good Mexican places. Between them and, Erawan Thai on Greenway, and the Indian Maharaja Palace on Bell, your tastebuds won't go unsatisfied. Javelina Springs at the Loop 101 Freeway and 59th Avenue is getting good word-of-mouth recommendations for excellent steaks, bar snacks and comfort food. They don't actually serve javelina. For that, be grateful.

## Leisure ★★★

Tempe, hang on to your Mardi Gras beads and giant foam hands, because Glendale is about to become a fun spot on the national consciousness. Here's what's happening:

- The brand new NHL Coyotes Glendale Arena is open just east of the Loop 101 Freeway.
- Next to the hockey arena the Arizona Cardinals stadium will open in August 2006.
- And now for the biggie. Beside and around both venues the 220-acre Westgate City Center will devour 450,000 square feet of office, retail and entertainment space. That's a fraction of the 6.5 million square feet of an envisioned retail, entertainment, restaurants, office, residential, and hotels megametroplex. Confirmed tenants for the project's first phase include Loew's Cineplex, a Virgin Megastore, a restaurant operated by the steak-and-swank Mastro Group, a Thaifoon restaurant and a Martini Ranch nightclub (the blondes in mini-dresses driving Porsches discover the West Valley).

# Real Estate

## Trends

The West Valley will never have Paradise Valley or north Scottsdale-caliber lots or views, but Arrowhead Ranch is shaping up to be the poshest post-Black Canyon Freeway enclave.

Catlin Court is one of the few historic areas in the Valley with abundant opportunities, i.e. unrestored historic homes with good bones and low prices. There are plenty of bungalows and brick homes from the 1920s and 1940s, just needing a little love. You won't find them any more in Willo or Encanto in Phoenix. Well worth a trip to see what's available and what's going on.

## Rental & Investment

With high hopes for profit windfalls, investors are hunting for properties close to Westgate and the stadium they can rent out during Super Bowl for about $2,000 a week. But beware. That was a huge bust during the Tempe Super Bowl. Turns out CEOs don't want to spend two grand for your average three-bedroom home with Legos on the floor and Spiderman towels.

### Why I live there

### John and Cathy Shrolucke

For the past 16 years, John and Cathy Shrolucke's 1,900 square-foot Glendale home has been the base for friends and family to watch college ball games. Their backyard has three TVs and a barbecue for grilling chicken wings. "We're here to stay," John says. He likes Glendale's down-home attitude on the west side. "It's not snobby like the east side," John laughs.

### Smart Buy ✓

Homes near the coming Westgate City Center will experience collateral benefits from the massive project.

## At a Glance...

## House Prices

### Townhouse
| | |
|---|---|
| Bedrooms | 🛏 🛏 |
| Price | $125,000 - $200,000 |

### Family home
| | |
|---|---|
| Bedrooms | 🛏 🛏 |
| Price | $200,000 - $300,000 |

### Family home
| | |
|---|---|
| Bedrooms | 🛏 🛏 🛏 |
| Price | $250,000 - $350,000 |

### Family home
| | |
|---|---|
| Bedrooms | 🛏 🛏 🛏 🛏 |
| Price | $250,000 - $400,000 |

### Executive home
| | |
|---|---|
| Area | Min. 4,000 sq. ft. |
| Price | $700,000 - $1,000,000 |

## Rentals

### Apartment
| | |
|---|---|
| Bedrooms | 🛏 🛏 |
| Price | $800 - $1,000 month |

### Townhouse
| | |
|---|---|
| Bedrooms | 🛏 🛏 |
| Price | $700 - $900 month |

### House
| | |
|---|---|
| Bedrooms | 🛏 🛏 🛏 |
| Price | $1,000 - $1,500 month |

## Travel Times

Distance to downtown Phoenix: 13 miles

To downtown Phoenix:
Peak: 25 – 40 minutes
Off-peak: 20 – 30 minutes

To the airport:
Peak: 35 – 40 minutes
Off-peak: 30 – 35 minutes

Peoria is not a city with an easily recognizable personality like Scottsdale or Apache Junction. The medium- and high-end neighborhoods in north Peoria are vast expanses of stucco-and-tile. Other Valley cities have miles of tract houses too, but usually there's something else to define those cities' personalities, like a swinging downtown or a couple of miles of orange groves or a mountain peak. Peoria looks like Ahwatukee without mountain views or Chandler without horse properties.

This is not a city of wine bars and independent bookstores, but if living in clean neighborhoods and raising kids with as few worries as possible is what you have in mind, Peoria may be a good choice. The neighborhoods are new, clean, and safe. Enormous Lake Pleasant is in the back yard for sailing, waterskiing, and fishing. Baseball fans can hit spring training with the Seattle Mariners at the lavish Peoria Sports Complex. If you or your children are space fanatics, move near the Challenger Space Center and get up to speed on the shuttle simulator every weekend.

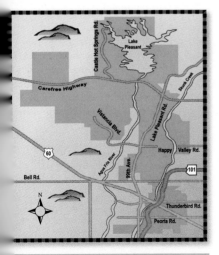

Total Population: 133,000 approx.
Median Age: 35 years
Median Household Income: $52,000 p.a.

## Who Lives There?

Low-key empty-nesters and entrepreneurs like Peoria's lack of drama. Peoria and Glendale share the same demographic chunk of Arrowhead Ranch, which has more millionaires than Scottsdale. Tom Hanks could play Peoria in a movie.

There's a lot of down-to-earth business owners and entrepeneurs who drive Ford Taurus' and Ford Explorers, not BMWs or Mercedes'.

The city has a larger African-American population – 12 percent – than most other Valley cities. Most other demographics are similar to the rest of the Valley.

## Homes

Office condos and luxury apartments start around the Peoria Sports Complex,

and housing becomes progressively more expensive from there on up. These are newer homes, most built in the past five years. At about Deer Valley Road, the stucco-and-tile sea parts. Horse properties appear in low-desert terrain (mesquite trees, creosote bushes, and jumping cholla) – think Paradise Valley countryside with Apache Junction-funky homes and corrals. Past that, the Westwing Mountain master-planned community skirts the bottom slopes of its namesake. The massive master-plan Vistancia is in the distance beyond that.

# Amenities

## Schools ★★★

The Peoria school district is the third largest in the state, with more than 38,000 students in kindergarten through 12th grade. The district was founded in the mid-1800s with a one-room school house. Over the years, and especially during the late 1980s and early 1990s, it's grown to 29 elementary schools and six high schools.

Peoria created an innovative program designed to help teachers work with each student according to his indidivudal needs. The decision support system (DSS) contains information on each student's strengths and weaknesses, based on AIMS test results. Teachers use the information to provide individual attention and learning support.

All of Peoria's schools are rated as performing and about a third are highly performing. Copperwood Elementary is rated as excelling.

## Shopping & Dining ★★

It used to be the East Valley had all the perks. That's changing. Arrowhead Towne Center is owned by Westcor, the same company which runs Scottsdale Fashion Square and Chandler Fashion Center, and it has most of the stores the other malls have. The center has five department stores – Dillard's, Robinson's-May, Sears, JC Penney, and Mervyn's, a 14-screen movie theater, two sit-down restaurants, a food court, about 170 stores, and an outdoor amphitheater.

It has all the Westcor touches: manicured landscaping, lots of palm trees, and a high-end feel. You still need to go to Scottsdale for Crane stationery or Tiffany's silver, though. The mall is across the street from the Peoria Sports Complex.

More amenities are on the way to Peoria, too. A $250 million development is being planned for the northwest corner of the Loop 101 and Northern Avenue. The mixed-use project is slated to include 350,000 square feet of entertainment and retail space; 100,000 square feet of office space; and 215 multifamily residential units. A mega-plex movie theater is also planned for the project. It'll look something like Desert Ridge when complete.

## Leisure ★★

The Peoria Sports Complex is the spring training venue for baseball's San Diego Padres and Seattle Mariners. Fans and critics rave about the complex because it has lawn seating, a barbecue pit, and generally intelligent design. Connoisseurs argue about whether it's the nicest spring training stadium in the Valley.

Lake Pleasant offers about 10,000 acres of water for water-skiing, bass fishing, boat camping, sailing regattas, or anything else aquatic. There is a full-service marina with a bar, restaurant, and store, ten- and four-lane boat ramps. Dry storage is also available. Park entrance fees are $5 per vehicle and $2 per watercraft.

At the Challenger Space Center you can fly simulated space flight missions as flight crew, mission controller, or scientist. There's also stargazing, an indoor planetarium, space camps, lectures, and telescope classes.

A fun San Gennaro Feast is held annually at the Peoria Sports Complex with live Italian entertainment, Italian sausage and peppers, calzones, scampi, linguine and clams, Italian pastry, cannoli, tiramisu, zeppoli ... yummm.

# Real Estate

## Trends

WestWing Mountain has some (for now) vacant space between it and the rest of the city. A low-density master-plan, it slumps down off the side of its namesake mountain like a pancake. It's a bit like a small McDowell Mountain Ranch. At build-out, the community will have more than 2,000 homes, built by six builders, with Mediterranean themes and styles. A third of the neighborhood is untouched desert with 341 acres of hillside and wash corridors, and trails and nature paths for walking, jogging, biking and skating. Multiple parks include a 20-acre park behemoth and a 3,300-square-foot community center, with meeting rooms, homeowners' association offices, a kitchen, a children's play area, and a kiddies water-play feature.

North of Happy Valley Road, Vistancia is well under way. One of the new breed of super master-planned communities, Vistancia is an Insta-City with a high school, a fire station, and shopping centers. Eventually 45,000 will live

there. If these things start coming out of the ground any bigger, they're going to need Congressmen.

Vistancia covers 7,100 acres, nearly 1,700 of which will be preserved as natural desert. There will be four elementary schools in addition to the high school, a 15,000-square-foot community center with pools, water slides, a tennis complex, game lawn, gym; golf courses and a golf clubhouse with a grill; seven parks; and more than six million square feet of commercial space. There are three areas: an 11-neighborhood family community; a 55-plus community; and a country club neighborhood with custom home sites and its own golf course. Homes run from $500,000 to $700,000.

South Peoria is where the only starter-affordable homes in the city are located: a 1972 1,400-square-foot three-bedroom, two-bathroom, asking $120,000 (with swamp cooler, not air conditioning), for instance.

North from where Peoria originated, homes jump in size and price. Between Grand Avenue and the sports complex you'll find a 1984 1,200 to 1,400-square-foot three bedroom, two bath asking $225,000.

## Rental and Investment

Rentals in Peoria are mostly townhouses and houses, not apartment complexes. Monthly rent for most units ranges from about $800 to $1,000 a month.

## At a Glance...

## House Prices

### Townhouse
| Bedrooms | 🛏 🛏 |
|---|---|
| Price | $200,000 - $300,000 |

### Family home
| Bedrooms | 🛏 🛏 |
|---|---|
| Price | $200,000 - $400,000 |

### Family home
| Bedrooms | 🛏 🛏 🛏 |
|---|---|
| Price | $250,000 - $350,000 |

### Family home
| Bedrooms | 🛏 🛏 🛏 🛏 |
|---|---|
| Price | $300,000 - $450,000 |

### Executive home
| Area | Min. 4,000 sq. ft. |
|---|---|
| Price | $700,000 - $900,000 |

## Rentals

### Apartment
| Bedrooms | 🛏 🛏 |
|---|---|
| Price | $1,100 - $1,300 month |

### Townhouse
| Bedrooms | 🛏 🛏 |
|---|---|
| Price | $1,000 - $1,300 month |

### House
| Bedrooms | 🛏 🛏 🛏 |
|---|---|
| Price | $800 - $1,400 month |

## Travel Times

Distance to downtown Phoenix: 13 miles

To downtown Phoenix:
Peak: 30 minutes
Off-peak: 25 minutes

To the airport:
Peak: 35 minutes
Off-peak: 30 minutes

Sun City opened in 1960. Visiting the country's first master-planned retirement community is like stepping into a time capsule holding Kennedy-era homes, miles and miles of palm trees, citrus with whitewashed trunks, golf carts, green gravel lawns and the occasional beehive hairdo. You wouldn't be surprised to step into a house and hear Walter Cronkite reporting that John Glenn just orbited the earth.

It's amazingly well kept. There is not a single eyesore to be found. No fountain cups lie in gutters, not a blade of grass dares to rise above its fellows, and palms are trimmed like Marine recruits. Most people get around by golf cart. In the winter it's not uncommon to see them outnumber cars on streets.

Sun City has been called a sterile Geritol ghetto, but there's plenty of life in the 14-square-mile northwest Valley enclave. In 2001 police reported more than two dozen sightings of people having sex in public: on golf courses, in parks, in spas, in golf carts, at the dog run ... One resident told CNN, "Sex in Sun City isn't a sin; it's a miracle."

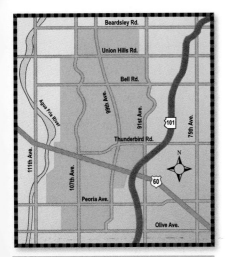

*Total Population: 65,000 approx.*
*Median Age: 74 years*
*Median Household Income: $37,000 p.a.*

## Who Lives There?

Sun City is 98 percent Anglo, according to the U.S. Census. Twenty percent of residents have bachelor's degrees and 29 percent are veterans.

Deed restrictions require at least one member of each household to be 55 or older. Kids can visit; but only for two weeks. That's still a big draw for many people. You don't have loud music playing and kids zipping up and down the street.

It's not a city of people who want to eat the young. It's just that, like most of the rest of the world, they'd rather not deal with teenagers who want to get into a little mischief. After years of raising kids, they figure it's time to take it easy.

## Homes

Housing runs the gamut in Sun City: single family homes, duplexes, condominiums,

independent living centers, assisted living centers, life care communities and apartment complexes. There is an upscale area called Ranch Estates with acre properties and horse and RV parking privileges: high-priced homes, for people who want a little more room.

Sun City is a good bargain. The annual $330 homeowners' fee covers the golf courses, tennis courts, swimming pools, and recreation centers. RV storage rates are dirt cheap – about $220 per year, compared to $600 per year elsewhere. (RVs are not allowed to be parked beside homes.)

# Amenities

## Schools – No stars

There are no schools within Sun City. In a community where most residents are 55 plus, that seems reasonable. Sun City residents don't pay school taxes. This occasionally causes a ruffle with neighboring communities when the local school district is trying to get a capital improvement project approved. But there's immediate

concern this will change. Sun City is not incorporated into Maricopa County. The county maintains the street, provides police and other services, but no schools.

## Shopping & Dining ★★

Local shopping is limited to drug stores and patio furniture stores.

For serious shopping, Arrowhead Towne Center is less than five miles east on Bell Road. The newly renovated mall provides 1.3 million square feet of shopping bliss. It has the usual cast of mall shops and anchor department stores. It boasts a 14-screen theatre, a rejuvenated food court and all the merchandise your credit card can bear. Within easy driving distance of Arrowhead are a Costco, a Home Depot and all the other smaller stores that set up nearby to catch the traffic generated by these retail giants.

Sun City does not have destination dining. It has cafeterias. The best joint in town is Lou's Tivoli Gardens on Del Webb Boulevard. It's been around forever, the food's great, and half the clientele look like extras from "The Sopranos." If you're visiting your parents, take them there. If you are parents, insist you be taken there. Other reliable old timers include Little Bite of Italy and Bobby's Café.

## Leisure ★★★★

The marketing tag "active adult" is taken seriously in Sun City. There are 11 golf courses, more than 130 clubs for every interest from dogs to computers, a community college, symphony and

chamber music and big bands. Seven recreation centers offer arts and crafts, lawn bowling, jewelry making, swimming, tennis, dance, handball, music, woodwork, and other diversions. On Dawn Lake, members can fish for bass, tilapia and blue gill. Viewpoint Lake is open to all residents. Both are man-made. There are 11 golf courses, eight for residents and three private.

The Sundome Center for the Performing Arts in Sun City West hosts numerous professional shows and theater productions appealing to an age-appropriate crowd. The Symphony of the West Valley's 85-piece orchestra plays six classical concerts a year in the Sundome and is the world's only symphony orchestra located in an over-55 community.

# Real Estate

## Trends

Sun City homes hold their value because of their condition and the area's popularity. (An ad last year in a retirement magazine drew 3,000 responses.)

Even that Sputnik-era look is joining the 21st-century. In the past few years, people with a younger mentality have begun fixing them up.

A new generation is gradually moving in as the original residents die or move into assisted living. Since 2000, more than 24,000 new members have joined the recreation center association. Sun

City expects about half the population to change in the next five years.

What's also changing are the homes. Buyers and investors are totally revamping many homes, tearing out popcorn ceilings, rounding corners, and replacing cabinets and lighting. Interior walls aren't load-bearing, so renovation options are wide open.

## Sun City West & Sun City Grand

Del Webb took one look at the wild success of Sun City, improved on the formula, and repeated it with Sun City West in 1978 and Sun City Grand in 1996. Both have the same basic idea behind them: age-restricted living with lots of fun in the sun. The same market forces drive real estate in both Sun City West and Grand: well-maintained homes holding their value and guaranteed winter rentals.

About 31,000 people live in Sun City West. It's mostly single-family homes ranging from 920 square feet to 3,500 square feet, although there are duplexes, garden apartments, condos, and casitas as well.

## Local Hero: The Sun City Poms

The Sun City Poms are a group of 10 cheerleaders from Sun City ranging in age from 61 to 81. They are world famous (Japanese TV crews seem to film them on a monthly basis) and appear at conventions, sporting events, fund-raisers and parades. If you ever see the Poms in action, you'll be amazed. These ladies can give any squad of 16-year-olds a run for their money. They perform headstands, handstands, leglifts, pyramids and splits as well as modern jazz, tap and their famous "Pom Routine."

Homeowners' annual fees to use golf courses, recreation, and fitness centers are $414 per couple.

Sun City Grand is the newest and most pricey of the trio. Officially located in the city of Surprise, Sun City Grand will have 9,800 homes on about 4,000 acres when completed. It has four 18-hole golf courses and two recreational "villages" with swimming pools, fitness centers, indoor tennis courts, a fishing lake, spas, and scads of other diversions. Homeowners' yearly fees are the highest in the Sun Cities: $855 per couple.

Another chapter is about to begin farther up the road. Del Webb is planning the 3,100-acre Sun City Festival at the foot of the White Tank Mountains. Interested buyers can put their name on a list on Del Webb's Web site for updates as Festival nears opening day.

## At a Glance...

## House Prices

### Townhouse
| Bedrooms | 🛏 🛏 |
|---|---|
| Price | $120,000 - $160,000 |

### Family home
| Bedrooms | 🛏 🛏 |
|---|---|
| Price | $200,000 - $300,000 |

### Family home
| Bedrooms | 🛏 🛏 🛏 |
|---|---|
| Price | $250,000 - $350,000 |

### Family home
| Bedrooms | 🛏 🛏 🛏 🛏 |
|---|---|
| Price | $400,000 - $500,000 |

### Executive home
| Area | Min. 4,000 sq. ft. |
|---|---|
| Price | $450,000 - $550,000 |

## Rentals

### Apartment
| Bedrooms | 🛏 🛏 |
|---|---|
| Price | $700 - $900 month |

### Townhouse
Townhouses are not common in Sun City. If you can find one, you'll pay about $650 to $750 a month.

### House
| Bedrooms | 🛏 🛏 🛏 |
|---|---|
| Price | $1,000 - $2,000 month |

## Travel Times

Distance to downtown Phoenix: 16 miles

To downtown Phoenix:
  Peak: 35 to 40 min. on surface streets;
                  25 – 30 minutes freeway
  Off-peak: 20 – 25 minutes on
                          surface streets;
                  10 – 15 minutes freeway

To the airport:
                  Peak: 50 minutes
                  Off-peak: 30 minutes

U ntil the 1990s Surprise was a sleepy burg of about 11,000. Now 96,000 people live in what's shaping up to be the Northwest Valley's version of south Tempe: big parks, young families, baseball, and a dense but fun downtown.

City officials point out there were more than 7,000 new home starts in 2004: a new home completed almost every hour and 50 new residents a day. Surprise has one of the lowest property tax rates in Arizona ($0.91 per $100), but the city is wallowing in money and lavishing it on its citizens. A 200-acre megapark including a spring training stadium, a library, an aquatic center and other features, will eventually be part of a square-mile city center with new government buildings, offices, movie theaters, retail, and restaurants.

Production homes are at the high end of affordable in Surprise. An interesting new master-plan is being built there in the styles of Phoenix's historic neighborhoods by the same company that built DC Ranch in Scottsdale.

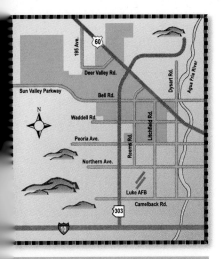

Total Population: 96,000 approx.
Median Age: 46 years
Median Household Income: $44,000 p.a.

## Who Lives There?

Retirees live in Sun City Grand and another development, called Arizona Traditions. Surprise consists mainly of young families. Like the area, all of them are so new no one can pin any common denominators on them.

## Homes

Surprise is strictly new production single-family homes. In general in the West Valley the big builders have learned from the mistakes they made in East Valley master-plans. For instance, instead of one big park (usually a field which must look like the Great Plains to a five year-old), there are now several smaller, human-scale parks.

They're not all stucco-and-tile, however. One of the Valley's most interesting master-

plans is being built in Surprise. Marley Park will be a re-creation of the historic neighborhoods of central Phoenix with tree-lined streets and Craftsman, Bungalow, and Spanish Colonial styles.

# Amenities

### Schools ★★

It's hard to talk about schools in Surprise without talking about construction. Almost all the schools are less than five years old, and even older schools like Kingswood Elementary School (rated "performing plus") have undergone extensive remodeling. Because the schools are so new, it remains to be seen how they will perform academically in the long run. These schools educate kindergarten through eighth graders on the same campus.

Like the primary schools, Willow Canyon High School is part of the Dysart Unified District. Built in 2002, Willow Canyon has earned a "performing plus" rating and will graduate its first senior class in 2006. High School #3 is scheduled to open at 15550 N. Parkview Place in 2006.

### Shopping & Dining ★★★

Surprise has two mega shopping centers across the street from each other. A huge Home Depot, a Lowe's Home Improvement Center and Target anchor more than 50 local and national retailers including Bed, Bath & Beyond, Barnes & Noble, Pier One Imports, Linens 'N Things, Red Lobster, Olive Garden and Starbuck's.

Westcor is developing an enormous multi-use project called Prasada that will include 800 acres of shopping, dining, and entertainment, including a multiplex.

More gas stations, drug, and grocery stores are opening up around the city for dads making the midnight Pampers run.

### Leisure ★★★

As the name suggests, the 200-acre Surprise Recreation Campus is more than just a park. The centerpiece of the complex is a 10,500-seat multi-use stadium, training facility and practice fields where the

Kansas City Royals and Texas Rangers play in spring training games. The campus also includes a regional library, aquatic center, recreation center, and a 37-acre park featuring a 5-acre urban fishing lake and a large playground. Surprise is also building Dream Catcher Park, a multi-use sports park for physically and mentally challenged children.

There is a brand-new second aquatic center as well as smaller new parks. A $1.7 million recreation center and $1.5 million youth softball complex are under construction.

The Heard Museum is building a branch to display part of its 32,000-piece collection of Native American art and artifacts. Surprise is already home to a small but sophisticated art museum.

If you want to get your wild on, the White Tank Mountains are full of beauty, snakes, and prehistoric secrets.

# Real Estate

## Trends

Marley Park will eventually cover more than 950 acres with more than 3,700 homes inspired by the architecture of historic Phoenix. (Models are even named Coronado, Brentwood, and Alvarado.) They really are very attractive, with modern amenities and without the endless headaches of a home built in 1926. The 1,700 to 3,700 square-foot homes are priced around $260,000 to the $500,000s.

There are parks and gathering places with shade trees and play areas, front porches overlooking leafy streets, and a neighborhood school. All of it linked by 16 miles of pedestrian friendly, tree-lined paths and trails. Production home builders are constantly abused by architecture snobs; here they really deserve a cheer. Marley Park is a classic and will never go out of style.

## Rental & Investment

Whether bought as residences or investments, Surprise homes look likely to appreciate. Good government, wise planning, quality projects, and a great location will keep Surprise in demand.

Surprise Stadium

## Smart Buy ✓

Surprise is shaping up to be one of the most desirable West Valley cities, with progressive government, excellent amenities, and thoughtful planning.

## Look Out! ⚠

Grand Avenue is a time-devouring gauntlet of six-way stoplights, medicated drivers in Buick Skylarks, and towering construction vehicles. Do anything to avoid it, even though on a map it looks like the most direct route to downtown. Maps should be marked with the skeletons of drivers who died waiting for Grand Avenue lights to change. Bell Road is also the Devil's Road for heavy traffic, at any time of day.

## At a Glance...

### House Prices

**Townhouse**

| | |
|---|---|
| Bedrooms | 🛏 🛏 |
| Price | $150,000 - $200,000 |

**Family home**

| | |
|---|---|
| Bedrooms | 🛏 🛏 |
| Price | $200,000 - $300,000 |

**Family home**

| | |
|---|---|
| Bedrooms | 🛏 🛏 🛏 |
| Price | $300,000 - $350,000 |

**Family home**

| | |
|---|---|
| Bedrooms | 🛏 🛏 🛏 🛏 |
| Price | $300,000 - $400,000 |

**Executive home**

| | |
|---|---|
| Area | Min. 4,000 sq. ft. |
| Price | $500,000 - $700,000 |

### Rentals

**Apartment**

| | |
|---|---|
| Bedrooms | 🛏 🛏 |
| Price | $1,000 - $1,500 month |

**Townhouse**

| | |
|---|---|
| Bedrooms | 🛏 🛏 |
| Price | $950 - $1,000 month |

**House**

| | |
|---|---|
| Bedrooms | 🛏 🛏 🛏 |
| Price | $900 - $1,200 month |

### Travel Times

| | |
|---|---|
| Distance to downtown Phoenix (via Grand Avenue): | 20 miles |

To downtown Phoenix (via Grand Avenue):
Peak: 35 – 50 minutes
Off-peak: 35 minutes

To the airport (via the Loop 101 and Interstate 10):
Peak: 48 minutes – 1 hour
Off-peak: 38 minutes

# *Northwest Valley* ★★★★★ Youngtown

Youngtown was the nation's first retirement community, built in 1954. (What other year but 1954 could come up with a name like Youngtown for a retirement community?)

Like a wrinkly fairy princess, Youngtown slumbered for decades in the land of gravel and cactus gardens, her subjects toodling off each day to bocce in their golf carts. Then, in the late 1990s, a 17-year-old prince arrived under less than fortunate circumstances. He moved in with an aunt or grandmother, having lost the rest of his family to tragedy.

After the two-week kid-guest deadline expired, the neighbors went berserk. Everybody reached for their lawyers and drew. It turns out you can't be an incorporated town and discriminate, too. When the dust settled, the age restriction was dead. Home prices shot up about 35 percent immediately.

The younger residents love the place, saying it's affordable, quiet, well-kept, and safe. The original residents say it's become anarchy: kids, dogs, it's just not the same, I need to lie down . . .

Trust the former perception.

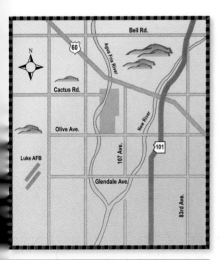

Total Population: 4,000 approx.
Median Age: 65 years
Median Household Income: $23,000 p.a.

## Who Lives There?

Young people and old people, and not many of either: about 4,000.

## Homes

The earliest style of ranch, the Traditional Ranch, is represented here in full force. Residents pour care into their homes and landscaping is at its best. Youngtown is a very attractive neighborhood. One can easily envision the retro/hipster crowd buying here for its vintage value.

# Amenities

## Schools ★★

Youngtown itself does not have any public schools. There is one charter school,

Youngtown Public Charter School. Opened in 2002, this school is "under performing" and most of its teachers have less than three years experience.

Youngtown's students attend schools in the Dysart Unified District. These schools are mostly "performing" schools except for El Mirage Elementary School. Most Youngtown students, though, attend Luke or Dysart Elementary Schools.

Dysart High School is the local high school. Also a "performing" school, it has had an internationally recognized Key Club since 1990.

## Shopping, Dining & Leisure ★

Youngtown has grocery stores – small ones – and little shops selling antique dolls and assorted paraphernalia. For a good meal, try the Heidelberg Inn: German and American, seafood, chicken, and ribs. No one leaves hungry.

There's a nice little park and cactus garden in the center of town, also a lake, both pleasant places to push a stroller. For racecars, football games, opera, rock concerts, and celebrity-studded resorts, go east. Far east.

# Real Estate

## Trends

Youngtown doesn't have property, elementary school, or high school taxes. New homes built on teardown lots can hit the low $300,000s; that's top of the line in Youngtown. Original Youngtown homes were extremely well built. They're solid, spacious, and surrounded by neighborhoods in excellent condition. Where else can you get a three- bedroom, two- bath, 1,200 square foot home on a big lot for $200,000?

## Rental & Investment

With an average age of 65, Youngtown rentals have on-site chaplains and water aerobics instead of volleyball courts and video game rooms. Baptist Village offers retirement garden apartments with utilities, shuttle service, cable TV, and free laundry. Rates range from $922 per month for a studio (not including a $480 "service fee") or $1,305 for a two bedroom with a $590 service fee. If you're not planning to live in a nursing home, three-bedroom homes rent for about $1,000 a month.

## At a Glance...

### House Prices

**Townhouse**

| Bedrooms | 🛏 🛏 |
|---|---|
| Price | $70,000 - $90,000 |

**Family home**

| Bedrooms | 🛏 🛏 |
|---|---|
| Price | $150,000 - $160,000 |

**Family home**

| Bedrooms | 🛏 🛏 🛏 |
|---|---|
| Price | $200,000 - $300,000 |

**Family home**

| Bedrooms | 🛏 🛏 🛏 🛏 |
|---|---|
| Price | $200,000 - $300,000 |

**Executive home**

There are currently no 4,000 square foot homes in Youngtown.

### Rentals

**Apartment**

| Bedrooms | 🛏 🛏 |
|---|---|
| Price | $900 - $1,100 month |

**Townhouse**

| Bedrooms | 🛏 🛏 |
|---|---|
| Price | $600 - $700 month |

**House**

| Bedrooms | 🛏 🛏 🛏 |
|---|---|
| Price | $900 - $1,000 month |

### Travel Times

Distance to downtown Phoenix: 18.5 miles

To downtown Phoenix (via Grand Avenue; see Look Out! in Surprise):

Peak: 40 – 50 minutes

Off-peak: 31 minutes

To the airport (via the Loop 101 and Interstate 10):

Peak: 45 minutes – 1 hour

Off-peak: 36 minutes

## where to live in
# PHOENIX
### and the Valley of the Sun

# Facts & Figures

*You will sincerely appreciate the natural beauty, the overall commitment to quality, and the sense of community that I enjoy each day as a resident of the "Valley of the Sun". Whether you're moving to the area or seeking investment properties. Let me be your guide.*

Shawn Stagg
480-797-3217
E-mail sstagg@cableaz.com
Web: Shawnstagg.com

# Focus on...

## Summer Heat

Arizona's legendary summer heat can be startling, but it's also survivable. Some people even like it. Here's what you need to know, including the facts to end all disputes at bars and dinner parties.

The state's heat record belongs to Lake Havasu City: 128 degrees fahrenheit on June 29, 1994. Phoenix's record is 122°, set on June 26, 1990. The world record is 136.4° at Al Azizyah in Libya on September 13, 1922. (Phoenix's coldest temperature ever recorded was 16° on January 7, 1913.)

The average number of 100°or higher days in Phoenix is 89. The fewest number of 100° or higher days ever recorded was 48, in 1913. The greatest number of 100° or higher days ever recorded in Phoenix was 143 in 1989.

The heat is not to be ignored even if you're dashing from air-conditioned house to car to mall and back again. You're dehydrating all day long when it's scorching, so you still need to drink a lot of water. If you're playing golf or working in the yard for the afternoon, you'll need to drink a MINIMUM of a gallon, probably more. Without water, you will die in five hours here during the summer. The human brain doesn't have much more stamina than a tropical fish. The survival record goes to a Mexican miner lost in the desert southeast of Yuma in 1905.

Pablo Valencia was lost for almost seven days. He was found by a scientist studying local summer meteorology and biology. If you're squeamish, skip the following paragraph.

His "lips had disappeared as if amputated, leaving low edges of blackened tissue; his teeth and gums projected like those of a skinned animal, but the flesh was black and dry as a hank of jerky; his nose was withered and shrunken to half its length... the freshest cuts were as so many scratches in dry leather, without trace of blood or scrum...We found him deaf to all but loud sounds, and so blind as to distinguish nothing save light and dark."

That's an extreme example. Most of us will simply blow off getting a drink while you're running errands and come home with a headache feeling wiped-out.

## Beat the Heat

1. Do not lie in the sun and fall asleep. (In the late 1990s a woman from out of state visiting friends in Tempe had too many vodka and tonics. She passed out by the pool wearing a bikini. By the time someone checked on her after sundown, she was dead. She literally cooked to death.)

2. Do not leave children or pets in your car. Not even for a minute. Not even with the window partially open.

3. Do not walk your pet on the pavement after the sun has heated it up. The pads of its feet will burn.

4. Do not leave your car outside with the windows completely shut. Leave them cracked open half-inch; your car will cool down a lot faster when you turn on the AC.

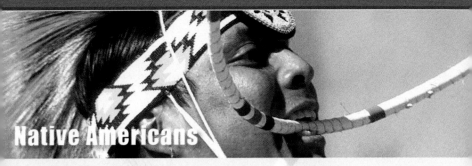

# Native Americans

When Europeans were busy painting their behinds blue and throwing rocks at Romans, the Hohokam Indians lived a sophisticated existence in the Salt River Valley. They built a 200-mile gravity-fed canal system, more than 20 towns, scores of ball courts, and traded pottery and jewelry with tribes hundreds of miles away.

Four tribes live in metro Phoenix: the Fort McDowell Yavapai, the Gila River, the Salt River Pima-Maricopa, and the Ak Chin. Each tribe has casinos. The Gila River tribe has built an elaborate resort rivaling anything in Phoenix with golf, spa, fine dining, and gambling. Gaming has been a huge boon to the tribes, vastly improving their quality of life and political power.

Few Native Americans permanently live in the cities. They usually come to the city to work for periods of time, become homesick, and return to the reservation. East Phoenix has the largest native population in the Valley due to the federal Indian hospital at 16th Street and Indian School Road. Indians come from all over the state for surgery and treatments which can't be dealt with in reservation clinics. Across the street is a Native American music and crafts store which occasionally has a frybread cookout in the parking lot.

Most Indians don't use banks. They deal in cash or jewelry. It's common for Native Americans to pawn jewelry and claim it later. Pawn stores like the Jewel Box on Central Avenue downtown are the best places to buy authentic high quality turquoise and silver.

Indian arts like blankets, baskets, jewelry, and pottery are extraordinarily expensive. A Navajo blanket about a foot square can easily cost more than $100. Don't drive up to the Navajo and Hopi nations expecting to get great deals by the side of the road. That little old lady with the two dogs sitting in a windswept lean-to charges just as much as any gallery in Santa Fe. Spend some time with an Indian artist and you'll find out why; the process for making blankets or pots starts with collecting plants and other materials from the wild. Hundreds of hours can go into a kachina or a basket. Some Pima women can weave baskets which are so tight they hold water.

The best place to begin learning about the Southwest's original peoples is the Heard Museum. The private museum has about 35,000 artifacts in its collection and hosts powwows, hoop dance competitions, and art fairs all year round.

There's no substitute for a visit to Indian country, however. Camping, hunting, and fishing are allowed on most reservations by permit. A few offer rafting, skiing, and canyoneering with guides. Shungopavi on the Hopi Second Mesa is the oldest continuously-occupied town in north America. The tiny Havasupai tribe live in the Grand Canyon by a creek flowing with Caribbean-blue water and gorgeous waterfalls. The enormous Navajo reservation covers some of Arizona's most spectacular scenery. All are well worth a trip.

# Focus on...

# Desert Storms

There are two ways to die in the desert: by thirst, and by drowning. Massive thunderstorms explode over the desert in July, dumping tons of water on to dry, hard ground. Flash flooding can be lethal. Roofs can collapse under the water's weight. Cars are swept away like paper boats.

This annual six-week period of intense afternoon weather is called the monsoon season. Properly called "monsoon thunderstorms" according to the National Weather Service, they build during the day and burst in late afternoon. They're almost always over by midnight. Sometimes the rain is preceded by immense walls of dust called "haboobs" which fill every open car, home, and nostril with grit when they pass over. Warning signs are wind gusts picking up and the air turning a funny shade of pink.

Monsoon winds can be powerful. Lawn furniture gets tossed around, tree limbs snapped, and anything like an awning or a carport that's not well-attached will be ripped away. In August 1996, a wind gust of 115 mph was recorded at the Deer Valley airport.

Arizona oldtimers call monsoon storms "gullywashers." Washes and dry crossings throughout the city – mainly in southwest Phoenix, Paradise Valley, and Indian Bend Wash in the middle of Scottsdale – overflow their banks, running fast with debris and water the color of chocolate milk.

Driving around the Valley, you'll notice depressed grassy areas used as parks and soccer fields. They are retention basins. There are hundreds of them in the new subdivisions because there aren't any rivers to handle floods. Subdivisions are designed so that streets drain into these common areas. The water either dissipates through a storm drain or percolates into the ground.

If you come across a "closed-road" sign, turn around, even if the water only looks ankle-deep. Six inches of fast-moving flood waters can knock you off your feet. Two feet will float your big bad SUV. In 1995 the legislature passed the Stupid Motorist Law. If you or your vehicle have to be rescued, you'll repay the state for the cost. (Two rescuers and a helicopter for one hour can top $800.)

**NO COMMISSION!**
**NO KIDDING!**

**The Best way to**
**Buy & Sell a Home**

**buyowner.com**

**800-771-7777**

Golf in the Valley of the Sun is the best in the country. Foreign tourists come to the state for natural wonders, but Americans come to Arizona for golf. From Clark Gable playing at the Biltmore to Saudi sheikhs on the back nine at the Phoenician to Tiger Woods in the Phoenix Open at the Tournament Players Club, the Valley has more game in its Game than Palm Springs or Florida. Golf is as woven into the Arizona experience as the Grand Canyon.

The weather is the biggest asset. If there's a little bit of a breeze, some people consider it a bad day.

Course conditions are superior to anywhere else in the country. An average course here is better than anything in California or Nevada. Phoenix has traditional courses and desert vista courses. To have the best of golf in most places, you have to join a private club. Most of the Valley's 200 links are public access. Opportunities and course varieties in design, conditioning, and location offer something for every golfer in any part of the Valley.

Phil Mickelson, John Daly, Vijay Singh, all golf's top luminaries play in the FBR (formerly the Phoenix) Open in Scottsdale. The LPGA Safeway Classic is held in Apache Junction in March. More than 100 PGA and LPGA pros live in the Valley year-round.

Municipal courses are adequate. Because cities have so much growth to contend with, infrastructure rather than recreation has been their focus. The city of Phoenix is looking at renovating their courses.

Golf has been a $1 billion industry for the past 15 years, according to the Arizona Golf Association, but future growth is in question. Land and water are both expensive, and access to effluent water is an issue. Plastic irrigation pipes made from petroleum are also costly.

Green fees on the best courses during peak season can easily soar past $100 per round. Population growth has outpaced course development during the past five years, when 39 courses were built, according to a recent ASU study.

Rattlesnakes on the fairways? Hype, snort leathery Phoenix oldtimers. "I've seen one once in 20 years," one says. Even the snakes are scared by the bill for a January Saturday afternoon at Troon.

# Simplify Your Life

## *e*verything's *i*ncluded

Ranked among the nation's leading builders, Greystone Homes has helped thousands of families make the dream of home ownership come true. Greystone Homes offers the most generous list of standard features found in the marketplace. Features like a built-in GE Microwave oven, front yard desert landscaping, 12 Seer air conditioning unit, raised panel doors, covered patio, garage door opener, rounded corners and much, much more. Tour our exciting homes and simplify your life with Greystone Homes, where "everything's included."

To learn more about Greystone Homes and our "everything's included" homes, visit:

## www.greystoneaz.com

or call us at:

## 1.800.864.1055

## Swamp Coolers

If you're not from the Southwest, you may never have heard of a swamp cooler. Swamp, or evaporative, coolers were invented in the late 1930s. As water evaporates, it absorbs heat. If you've ever stood in front of a fan wearing a wet T-shirt, you've witnessed this principle. Until the late 1930s, Arizonans slept inside huge wood or metal frames with wet sheets draped over them.

Swamp coolers are big boxes. The sides of the box are frames holding thick pads made from porous materials. Water pours down over the pads, keeping them saturated with water. A fan pulls air from the outside through the wet pads and pumps it into your house. The dampened air passes through the house and cools it anywhere from 20 to 25 degrees.

Why should you care about evaporative cooling? Because you'll damn near be able to buy a car for what you'll save in electric bills. Power bill for 1,000 square feet in June with air: about $225, depending on a lot of factors. Power bill for 1,000 square feet in June with swamp: about $45.

Why does anyone have air conditioning at all if these magical, wonderful devices exist? They don't work very well when the dew point rises above 57 or 58. (The dew point is announced on local news weather broadcasts.) Hence, when Arizona's monsoon season (see Desert Storms, p. 218) occurs from late July to mid-September, swamp-cooled houses feel like swamps. Summer with a swamp cooler is survivable with floor fans pointed everywhere, but it's not easy living. Underwear and sarongs become your wardrobe. Only 13 percent of Phoenix homes have swamp coolers as their sole source of summer comfort.

They're cheap to buy. They blow all the dust and cigarette smoke and food smells out of the nearest window. The air has a wonderfully refreshing quality, like air after a summer storm. It smells slightly earthy, a real old-Arizona smell.

If you rent storage space, question the manager carefully about how the place is cooled. "Air-cooled" is a fairly ambiguous term for swamp cooling. If you'll be storing vintage albums or mounted butterflies or a colonial highboy that cannot tolerate any moisture, you need to know this. You should not be charged the same rate for swamp-cooled space as air conditioned space.

**YOUR DREAM HOME.
OUR EXPERTS.
YOUR INSTANT EQUITY.**

ubuildit.com

- Custom Homes, Additions, or Major Remodels
- Expert Help Every Step of the Way
- Build Instant Equity into Your Dream Home
- 100% Financing Available for Owner-occupied Dwellings

## BY INVESTING A LITTLE BIT OF TIME, YOU TOO CAN

# BUILD YOUR FUTURE

## BY BUILDING YOUR OWN DREAM HOME!

dIt, the nation's leading owner-builder consultant company, can help you build your own dream home that will sell for thousands more then it cost to build. Contact your nearest UBuildIt office for a FREE Planning Session and find out how you, too can maximize your equity by building your own custom built home.

**4 OFFICES TO SERVE YOU**

| | | | |
|---|---|---|---|
| AVONDALE | 623-932-9797 | CHANDLER | 480-403-0000 |
| ER VALLEY | 623-869-8887 | SCOTTSDALE | 480-477-1112 |

Franchises available nationwide. Independently owned & operated.

## Tubing

Riding an inner tube down the Salt River is a Phoenix summer institution. All manner of mankind joins together, united by a desire to drink a lot of beer and effortlessly float through the sun-baked desert with their butts in a cool river. There are people who tube every weekend (you can recognize them by their bronzed complexions and powerful custom-made waterborne stereos). Teenagers and twenty-somethings are the biggest groups out there, but it's not uncommon to see entire Vietnamese families with granny tucked in an inflatable kayak, bikers in black jeans and boots, and the occasional Scottsdale glamour girl fulfilling a guilty pleasure.

Complaints revolve around the facts the river gets crowded and there are a million rusty beer cans on the riverbed. (If you want pristine wilderness, go to the North Kaibab.) Tubing is a rock concert, not a chamber music recital. You invariably run across a fisherman trying to have a mystical fly-fishing experience while the rest of the river is cranking "Heatseeker" by AC/DC, whipping beer cans at each other, and dropping their bikini tops. (Uptight fishermen should follow the wildlife's example. It's common to spot great and little blue herons and snowy egrets feeding ten yards away from a car stereo cranking Ozzy Osbourne out of a plywood pyramid mounted in a tube.)

Here's how it works: drive to the parking lot (see Web site or call number below for directions) with a cooler full of drinks and snacks and rent a tube for everyone in the party plus one for your cooler ($13 each). Get on an ancient school bus blasting classic rock, get off at the put-in, hop in the river, open a beer, and enjoy cool water whisking you downstream for about four to five hours.

Insider advice: since the drought started in the mid-1990s, flows have been slow. The whole trip from Points One to Four can take five hours. In other words, a roast beef sandwich is worth its weight in gold. Salt River Tubing recommends taking the same stuff your Mom would: sunscreen, bottled water, and a hat. We recommend potato chips, a party-hearty attitude, and a trustworthy pal to be the designated driver on the long trip home.

Salt River Tubing
480-984-3305
www.saltrivertubing.com

# #1 Property Manager
# Company in Arizona

- We do Guarantee our ~~tenants~~
- Low Monthly Management Fee for High Quality Service.
- Our World Class Maintenance Dept. handles all maintenance calls quickly with 24 hour Emergency Service.
- Access detailed owner statements online anytime with our top rated website.

Our agents make certain that your property meets the 3 top priorities to be rented quickly.

1. The property is rent ready for immediate move in.
2. Your property has maximum exposure in the market
3. The property will be listed at the right rental price.

...t us help you get the
...ost out of one of the
...ottest Housing Markets
...the Country.

Need Help selling your Home?
...Sell your Home Fast through
Brewer - Caldwell
for Top Dollar!

...all Now: (480) 834-9200 or visit us
...nline at http://ahouseisbetter.com
...r more information on our unique
...ome sales sysyem, visit us online at
...tp://itsalreadysold.com

### Brewer Caldwell
Property Management, Inc.

# Pink In Phoenix

Phoenix's gay and lesbian community is not like most others, in the sense that it's not a physical community. It's not like West Hollywood or the Castro or the Village in New York, with gay businesses and homes.

Arizona has a stereotyped reputation of being an intolerant place, but lifelong gay residents say they've never witnessed it. Sure, Arizona is a conservative place, but it's Barry Goldwater-conservative: live and let live.

The closest place Phoenix has to a West Hollywood is central and east Phoenix. ZIP code 85012 has the biggest gay population in Arizona, according to a study by the Greater Phoenix Gay & Lesbian Chamber of Commerce. There's a lot going on in terms of night life and arts events in central and east Phoenix, and that's where most of the gay and lesbian bars are located. The Denny's at 7th Street and Camelback Road has been the gay Denny's for decades. The Bally's gym on east Indian School Road is nicknamed Sally's by its well-toned habitués.

Many new lofts and high rises have large gay populations, as do all the historic neighborhoods; Roosevelt, Coronado and Willo are three of the biggest.

Tempe has always been the most progressive city in the Valley. It has a sizeable gay and lesbian population but no bars. (The East Valley's only gay and lesbian bar is Wild Card at 801 N Arizona Avenue in Chandler.) Scottsdale also has a substantial gay and lesbian population, with a handful of mixed gay and straight hotspots.

The Roadrunner Regional Rodeo has moved to Laveen for its annual mid January roping and riding competitions It's a serious rodeo, not a livestock pageant. Gay Pride in Phoenix is usually celebrated the first weekend of April It's held at Steele Indian School Park at the northeast corner of Central Avenue and Indian School Road. More than 18,000 people went to Phoenix Pride in 2005.

# Focus on...

# Pinal County Expansion

Valley development has followed the path of a tennis ball, bouncing from Phoenix to the East Valley to the West Valley. Now it's headed east again to Pinal County, bringing fake lakes and insta-cities to ranching and mining country.

Fifteen years ago, commerce in Gold Canyon consisted of the resort, livery stables, a saloon that was closed most of the time, and two genial hippies who sold pizza out on the highway by the trailer park. AJ – and beer – was a long way away by ten p.m. Farther down the road the shuttered mining town of Superior was another sleepy outpost in the saguaros.

That's rapidly changing. More than a third of all new homes in the area are predicted to be built in Pinal County in the next few years. Zoning has been approved southeast of Queen Creek for enough homes for more than 420,000 residents, a population equal to a city the size of Mesa.

South of Queen Creek Del Webb is building another "do-it-all-here lifestyle" Anthem development on 3,200 acres near prison town Florence, 30 miles southwest of Phoenix. Plans call for 9,000 homes. That translates into about 25,000 people. About 5,000 people have already expressed interest in the community.

The company behind the swanky Esplanade Place condo tower is building an 11,000-home master plan on 3,200 acres in Coolidge 26 miles south of Queen Creek. In Sandia (named after watermelon fields it's replacing), homes are slated to be in Mexican contemporary style architecture. Prices will range from $150,000 to $350,000.

As well as schools and parks, Sandia will have a 35-acre mixed-use town center with an 8-acre community lake, sports fields, tennis courts, volleyball pits, a recreation center, library, outdoor cafes and special retail stores. Buildout will take 16 years.

When Magma Copper blew the whistle on mining in Superior in 1982, the town promptly went dormant. Most able-bodied people moved away to find jobs elsewhere. Businesses vanished. However, a British copper company recently announced plans to spend about $1 billion to develop a new mine in Superior. That operation could mean as many as 1,400 jobs – 1,000 for construction and another 400 permanent high-quality mining positions after the high-tech operation is built out. Company estimates also project three service jobs for every full time mine employee, totaling about 1,500 permanent jobs for the 3,200-population town. What effect new mining and nearby development will have on Superior remains to be seen.

Some housing is trickling in. One company is building a three-phase subdivision with 140 two-story units on a beautiful spot on the mountains. It's geared towards first time homebuyers. One major Superior investor predicts that town to begin turnaround in three to five years.

Expect traffic to worsen as Pinal's population booms. As of now, no freeways have been planned to serve that part of Pinal County. However, the State Department of Transportation is looking at one major east-west corridor and one major north south corridor.

www.summitcoppersquare.com
602-252-1118

**THE SUMMIT AT COPPER SQUARE**

NOW UNDER CONSTRUCTION

FOCUS O

## WHO SAYS YOU CAN'T BE ABOVE IT ALL?

If you enjoy the finer things in life and crave the excitement of a vibrant metropolitan locale, **The Summit at Copper Square** beckons you.

Located directly across from Bank One Ballpark, **The Summit at Copper Square** boasts 22 stories of urban loft-style residences complete with granite countertops, stainless steel appliances, marble master baths, and some of the best views *above* downtown this Valley has to offer.

### OVER 80% SOLD
For availability: Anthony Trakas 602-252-1118 or atrakas@summitcoppersquare.com.

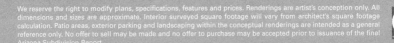

# Homeowners Associations

Homeowners associations (HOA) govern hundreds of neighborhoods in the Valley. If you buy a home in the area, you automatically agree to pay dues and abide by a list of rules governing upkeep and aesthetics. A board of residents runs the association.

Tin foil in the windows, weeds in the yard, shade tree mechanics; HOAs outlaw all that. Many don't allow basketball hoops in driveways. Rules often include where boats may be parked. No pink paint or front yard whirligigs or tomato patches. The list of rules is called the CC&Rs, for codes, covenants and restrictions.

Dues range anywhere from $50 per month in a townhouse complex to thousands in gated North Scottsdale Xanadus. (Don't worry; in an average starter master-plan, dues will be minimal. Often they're wrapped into mortgage payments with property taxes.) These pay for landscaping entryways and common areas, pool maintenance, guard gates, fitness centers, or any number of features.

The advantages of homeowners associations are that they maintain property values and neighborhood quality. You'll never have to put up with the neighbor's teenager cannibalizing three trucks in the street. They also worry about keeping the complex painted, if it's multifamily, and other headaches. Studies show growth in the median and average values of HOA-governed community homes has topped the growth in value of single-family homes not governed by HOAs.

The disadvantages have led to some spectacular news stories. A veteran in a posh North Scottsdale neighborhood flew an enormous American flag and got into a bitter fight with the HOA. Boards have cut down trees and been sued by residents. A Northwest Valley woman was kicked out of her home after her HOA sued her for a judgment she couldn't afford to pay. She was in her eighties and refused to trim her landscaping. One man charged into an HOA meeting in Peoria with a rifle and a pistol and shot five of the board members, killing two. That originated with landscaping, too.

HOA boards can be packed by cronies or run by mouth breathers, and there's no government oversight or outside appeal process available in a dispute. HOA boards are judge, jury, and executioner.

These are the horrors which make headlines, however. The vast majority more than 70 percent - of HOA community residents are happy, according to the Community Associations Institute. Only four percent reported a bad relationship with their HOA. Fifty-five percent also felt they received good value for their dues. Association communities didn't appear to be rife with people with binoculars spying on each other; only 23 percent said they'd complained about a neighbor.

# Focus on...

## Buying a Brand New Home

### Demanding Supply - Buying a Brand New Home

Most people buy production homes in master-planned communities from a builder who's designed several home models to choose from. This is the least expensive option for a new home. Most homes are "stick built" though production builders are using more factory components and getting better quality as a result. The buyers then select the personal touches like cabinets, countertops and appliances.

Other buyers prefer semi-custom homes. Working with the builder, they customize a standard plan and are involved with more than the finishing touches. Leaders in the semi-custom market are companies like Pulte (Del Webb), Lennar and their semi-custom home unit Greystone, Meritage and Scott Communities.

The most upscale option is to build a custom home designed by an architect and built by a general contractor to the buyers' specifications.

### Turning Their House Into Your Home

After selecting a location, the lot and model are chosen. This is the process that turns a production house plan into a semi-custom home.

The builder seeks and receives permits, breaks ground, pours the slab and begins to erect the framing. Next comes "roughing in" the electrical and plumbing. The city or county inspections follow. Upon inspection approvals, the insulation, interior dry wall, exterior stucco and roofing are completed. Completing and personalizing the structure to make the house a home is next. This includes installing the cabinets and countertops the homeowner has selected. Electric fixtures and plumbing accessories are installed followed by flooring and carpet. The task is completed with a final inspection, review of final items (walkthrough and punch list) and final contract closing and taking possession.

### Urban, Suburban and Exurban

Locations of these communities have moved further away from the core business districts as builders have followed available land from the suburbs into exurbia. The latest builder trend is to reconfigure their businesses to exploit in-fill housing. Meritage, Toll Brothers and Engle Homes have all taken positions in urban builders with infill plans.

### Demanding Supply

Production builders are really good at building homes in most price ranges. They have put up about 100 new homes a day in the Valley since the 1990s. If this pace continues til 2020, they will only just match expected demand. This bodes well for builders and buyers alike as any home purchase will remain consistent with Arizona's history of uninterrupted appreciation.

# Focus on...

## Living Vertical

### How to Buy a High-Rise Home

Steel cranes are set up all over the Valley of the Sun, piling on steel and concrete as fast as possible to meet the new lust for living in the sky. Ranging from basic lofts to multimillion-dollar luxury condominiums, high-rise dwelling is in demand. New projects are announced every week. Entire buildings sell out in days.

If you're thinking about high-rise living, what should you consider as you choose which building and which location is best for you? At the end of the article, you'll find a list to help you clearly define what's most important to you.

### The Buildings & the Dwelling Units

Almost without exception, the buildings — completed, under construction or planned — are spectacular. Even newly renovated mid-century rental apartment high-rises boast upscale features. They are generally well built and well appointed. Most have great views and are tastefully decorated.

Most of the buildings offer nearly identical luxury amenities:

- A generous entrance, some with the option of valet parking
- An attractive lobby
- Reception and concierge services, lobby to receive guests and deliveries
- Extensive electronic security systems with monitoring local or remote
- Clubrooms with fireplaces, large screen TV, bar and kitchen for private events for residents
- Business center with conference room, computer, copy and fax services for resident use
- Fitness center with men's and women's locker rooms, steam rooms and massage room
- Swimming pools, spas and sundecks
- Private secured storage room in the parking garage
- Secured underground parking garage providing two parking spaces for each residence with ample parking for guests

The individual dwelling unit typically includes:

- Stone, marble or tile flooring in foyer and kitchen
- Carpet
- Non-standard ceilings heights
- Integrated window coverings
- Stereo pre-wiring in selected rooms
- Upgraded doors (interior and hallway)
- Custom door casings and baseboards
- Upgraded hinge and lock hardware
- Optional fireplace and mantle
- Central heating and air conditioning system
- Professionally designed electrical and lighting plan
- Wiring to digital video, voice and data systems
- Home theater pre-wiring in selected rooms
- Spacious walk-in closets adjustable closet systems
- Front door chime and individual security system with entry keypad

### Location, Location, Location

The Valley has five natural village cores that have reached critical mass that can successfully support the street life high-rise communities require: Downtown Phoenix, Mid-Central Phoenix, Camelback corridor (around 24th Street), downtown Scottsdale and Tempe at Mill Avenue and at the Lake. Kierland Commons in North Phoenix and Chandler Mall are on plan to build the critical mass necessary to support a high-rise village lifestyle.

Experts say that what is around a building is more important than what is in it. High-rise living is about convenience. If you have to get in your car to mail a letter, your convenience level is minimal. If you can walk every place you go, you've hit the convenience jackpot. Since high-rise living is new in the Valley, you'll probably have to compromise on what you can walk to and where you must drive. It's important to know your priorities when you make your selection.

## What's Important to You?
### Location

- Does the area around the building have all the amenities you want and need? Are they under construction? How long before they are completed? Do you mind waiting?
- How many places you go are within walking distance? Do you have to drive your car every day?
- Are you near to family and friends? Will the new location put you closer or farther away?
- How will the new location affect your ease in getting to the places you visit frequently?
- Who lives in your new building? Will you be comfortable with your new neighbors?
- Who lives in your new community around the building?
- Are you moving into a commercial neighborhood?
- A residential neighborhood?
- A lively social and street scene?
- Are these desirable or something you will have to grow into?

### Dwelling Space
- How much will the dwelling unit cost when finished to your specifications?
- If you are downsizing, is there adequate storage space? Is there room for the Manolo Blahnik collection?
- Is there enough living space? When visitors come? For a home office? For a media room?
- What warranties are offered?
- If you use satellite TV today, can you get your same satellite provider in the high-rise? How about a dual TV (TiVo) hook-up?

- Where will you park? Do you pay extra or is it included in the unit price? Who manages the parking? Where will your guests park? How much will they pay?
- Do you want your own private outdoor space? You'll want a patio or balcony.
- What direction do you face? A wall of glass facing west will make it very difficult to keep your unit comfortably cool in the summer months.

### Building
- How important is ambient noise? Is the neighborhood noisy or quiet? Your "convenient to the airport" may also mean listening to jets screaming in for a landing. Watch for trade-offs.
- Does the building match the vision you were sold?
- Who runs the building? Is it a management company? What is the company's reputation? Who will you deal with on everyday issues? Are they on-site? Are they accessible 24/7?
- What residential buildings has the builder built prior to this one?
- Is the number of elevators adequate for the number of floors and residents?
- Will the sophisticated sales process be matched with as sophisticated service and support staff? A cigar-chomping part-time super doesn't cut it.
- Is there a homeowners' association (HOA)? What is included in the fee? What are the terms, conditions, and annual fee escalation? Who runs the HOA?
- Is there a contract with a private security firm? Does each unit have its own security system? Is it wired directly to the security firm?
- How are incidents handled? Are additional security levels available when residents are away for extended periods?
- Does the doorman or concierge accept packages? Any limitations?
- Does the building have emergency power services? How much? Does it run the building or just the emergency exit lights?
- Is there an adequate emergency evacuation plan?
- Are the local city fire services equipped for the number of stories in your building?

## WELCOME TO THE NEIGHBORHOOD.

...ain St. Plaza — Scottsdale now unveils Phase II Condominiums, Penthouse Suites and 10 exclusive ...wn Homes for the most opulent residential living. Designs range from 2,397 to 5,200 square feet and ...will feature private garages and elevators, spacious courtyards with lush landscaping, dual master ...rooms, fitness and home theater rooms. This elite community will boast amenities such as extravagantly ...designed waterfalls, lavishly landscaped courtyard with private poolside cabanas and spa, right in ...ur own backyard. Discover what urban living means — Scottsdale style. From $929,900 to 3.2 Million.

*Main St. Plaza*

SCOTTSDALE

Sales office is located on the corner of Main St. and Goldwater Blvd.

...01 E. MAIN ST., SUITE 2, SCOTTSDALE    480.675.0200    WWW.MAINSTPLAZASCOTTSDALE.COM

# Focus on...

# Putting the House before the (Shopping) Cart

## When there is no "there, there"

There is a quaint story from the dark (early Web) ages about a shopping mall operator who banned his retail mall tenants from advertising on the Web. He feared shoppers would use the Web exclusively and the malls would shut down. If you've tried to find a parking space at a mall lately, you know that didn't happen. In fact, the number of visitors to malls is increasing.

In retail, a physical presence is equally, if not more, important than a cyber presence. "Sticks and bricks" stores serve different markets and different purposes. Malls often become town square-type gathering places that help build a community.

## The Community Effect of Mainstream Retail

Mega mall builders and big box stores are major influences in urban planning. They are essential to the development of smaller peripheral communities that have little or no municipal history or infrastructure. But there are important differences between the two: a big box is about their brand, a mega mall developer is about community. The resistance to Wal-Mart and the welcome given to mall developers is well documented.

As you read through this book, you'll find a number of communities that had little "there, there" until enough "roof tops"

were built to demand retail services. Few companies invest significant money i infrastructure until the market justifies i Major supermarkets are among the las entrants into a community while the are one of the most important. It is on reason why downtown Phoenix's lack c a decent supermarket hurts long term residential development.

## The Role of Major Developers

The balancing act of getting to critica retail mass, while supporting what i already there is a delicate proces: Chandler, Arizona is a textbook example The arrival of an 800-acre mega ma away from the town center moved th retail mass, but dramatically increase commerce, tax receipts, employment an prestige for the city.

## Community Means Value and Residential Appreciation

Understanding where these mega center are going is important to homebuyers a they dramatically improve convenienc and livability. It is no accident residentia value and appreciation rates improve Better transportation access is inevitabl part of this formula.

Primary Retail: Major retail communitie with three or four major anchor tenants and a host (often hundreds) of chains an secondary retail brands.

238

Secondary Retail: These centers normally precede the mega malls and big boxes. They pioneer along "growth paths." These are designed for small retailers, sole proprietorships and tertiary brands that make for the fabric of a community. This is where the first supermarket will land, but later in the development cycle.

Shadow Developers: This is a similar class that shadows the larger secondary developer. Again the tenants are small retailers, sole proprietorships, chef/owner restaurants and tertiary brands. This class of vendors delivers the all-important "street scene" in a high-rise town and local community or "village feel" in a suburb.

## Location and the Development Cycle

The cycle of development for most new communities in the West begins with land availability. Homebuilders have a voracious appetite for the land. Market conditions force them to buy land further and further ahead of community development. It often takes years for mainstream retail to catch up.

Understanding growth paths is an important indicator for any residential purchase, individual homeowner or investor. This is even more important as a community matures.

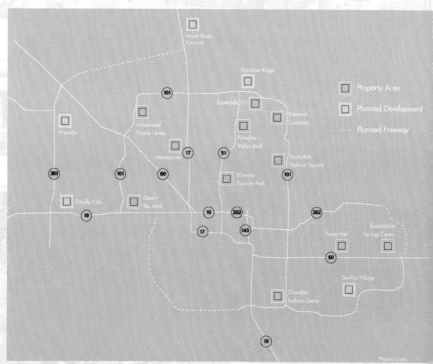

Westcor's existing or planned malls.

*Map: Courtesy of Westcor*

An analysis of recent house sales prices is always a good yardstick on which to base your house buying decisions. None of us wants to over pay for a house, but knowing what is reasonable, especially in a buoyant market, can be difficult to assess. In each of the cities, towns and neighborhoods, in the At a Glance box, we have provided typical prices for a variety of homes based on interviews with real estate agents and the latest MLS data. However, in the following four pages we have graphically illustrated actual latest available (July – September 2005) sales prices according to data provided by Arizona State University, Real Estate Center.

## Which Areas can I Afford?

In the first graph (pages 244 to 245) we show a "snapshot" of median recorded sales by city and neighborhood during the third quarter of 2005. The bar graphs show prices for resale and new single-family homes, and clearly illustrate the comparative desirability of the various areas. If no new home sales were made during the period then no bar graph is included.

Paradise Valley is the most expensive place to live, with an average resale house price of $1,350,000. At the opposite end of the scale, the average price for a

home in Youngtown was $165,000. Using this graph you can quickly identify areas that suit your budget.

## Which Areas are Showing the Greatest Price Appreciation?

The second set of graphs (pages 246 – 247) compare the latest available (July – September 2005) median prices for resale homes with those for the same period in 2004 and record the percentage change for that period. Rio Verde was the stand out performer showing a 96 percent increase, but even the lowest increase was a healthy 20 percent in North Mesa.

This is only a "snapshot" of sales activity during the quarters analysed. All of these prices are averages (medians) of all homes sold, and take no account of the size or condition of the individual properties, but they do give an insight into which areas are increasing in popularity among homebuyers. We recommend you use these graphs in conjunction with the anecdotal price information contained within each city or neighborhood entry.

*Source: Arizona State University, Real Estate Center. Third Quarter Sales 2004 and 2005.*

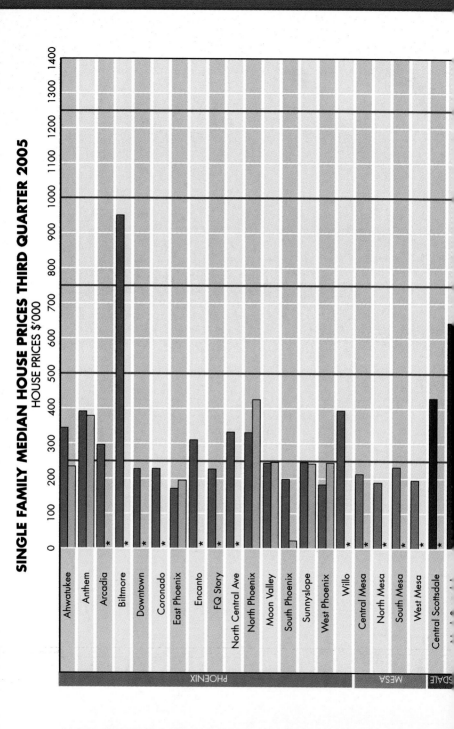

SINGLE FAMILY MEDIAN HOUSE PRICES THIRD QUARTER 2005

HOUSE PRICES $'000

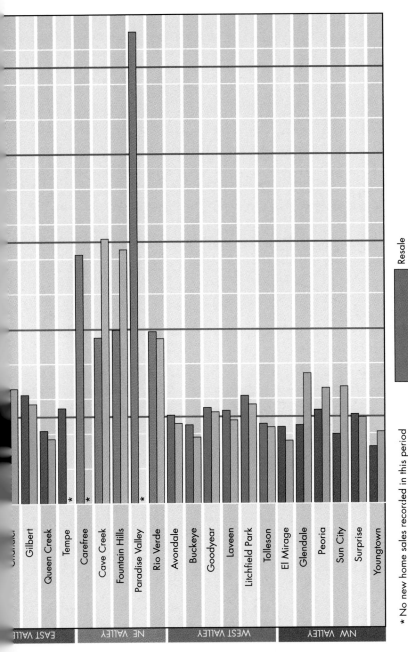

* No new home sales recorded in this period
Source: Arizona Real Estate Centre (AREC)

Resale
New

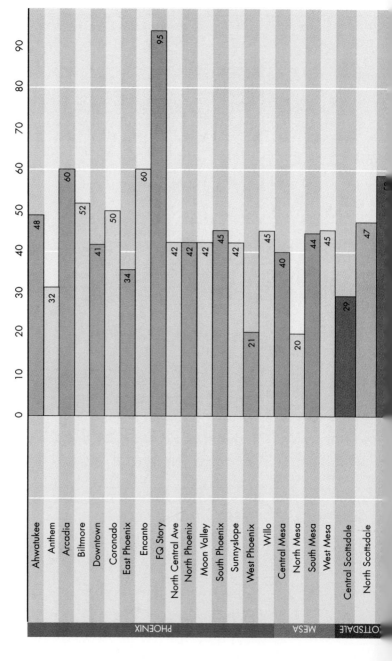

MEDIAN HOUSE PRICE INCREASES THIRD QUARTER 2005 vs 2004
PERCENT DIFFERENCE

| Area | Percent |
|------|---------|
| Ahwatukee | 48 |
| Anthem | 32 |
| Arcadia | 60 |
| Biltmore | 52 |
| Downtown | 41 |
| Coronado | 50 |
| East Phoenix | 34 |
| Encanto | 60 |
| FQ Story | 95 |
| North Central Ave | 42 |
| North Phoenix | 42 |
| Moon Valley | 42 |
| South Phoenix | 45 |
| Sunnyslope | 42 |
| West Phoenix | 21 |
| Willo | 45 |
| Central Mesa | 40 |
| North Mesa | 20 |
| South Mesa | 44 |
| West Mesa | 45 |
| Central Scottsdale | 29 |
| North Scottsdale | 47 |

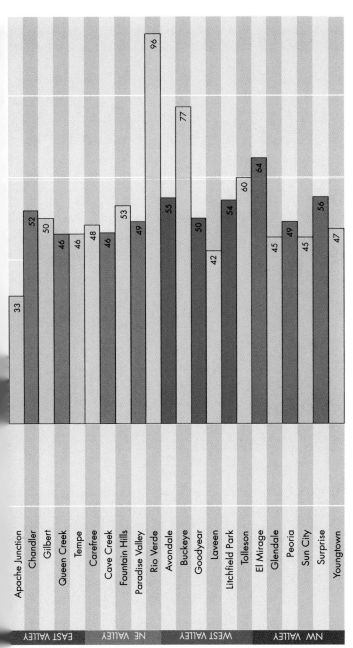

Source: Arizona Real Estate Centre (AREC)

# Facts & Figures

## WHO LIVES WHERE?

| | 2000 Population | % White | % Hispanic /Latino | % Black | % Native American | % Asian | % Other | Median Age | Median $ Household Income | Household <18 | Household >65 |
|---|---|---|---|---|---|---|---|---|---|---|---|
| **PHOENIX** | | | | | | | | | | | |
| Ahwatukee | 76,625 | 80% | 10% | 3% | 1% | 4% | 2% | 35.2 | $72,075 | 38% | 12% |
| Anthem | 8,655 | 84% | 9% | 4% | 1% | 1% | 1% | 37.3 | $66,636 | 40% | 14% |
| Arcadia | 8,775 | 91% | 6% | 1% | 0.3% | 1% | 1% | 39.6 | $75,584 | 34% | 26% |
| Bilmore | 2,374 | 93% | 2% | 1% | 0% | 2% | 1% | 54.5 | $86,825 | 7% | 35% |
| Downtown | 19,297 | 59% | 27% | 8% | 4% | 2% | 2% | 36.2 | $31,182 | 16% | 19% |
| Coronado | 6,801 | 43% | 47% | 5% | 2% | 1% | 2% | 30.8 | $35,470 | 35% | 13% |
| East Phoenix | 77,740 | 56% | 33% | 4% | 3% | 2% | 2% | 33.0 | $36,382 | 30% | 20% |
| Encanto | 1,001 | 71% | 23% | 1% | 2% | 1% | 2% | 37.9 | $77,404 | 30% | 18% |
| FQ Story | 2,770 | 38% | 56% | 3% | 1% | 1% | 1% | 31.9 | $31,142 | 33% | 14% |
| North Central Ave | 12,846 | 81% | 14% | 1% | 1% | 1% | 1% | 41.6 | $65,809 | 30% | 28% |
| North Phoenix | 493,536 | 81% | 12% | 2% | 1% | 2% | 2% | 33.7 | $52,806 | 39% | 15% |
| Moon Valley | 11,372 | 88% | 6% | 2% | 1% | 3% | 1% | 39.6 | $68,538 | 33% | 21% |
| South Phoenix | 83,993 | 16% | 63% | 18% | 1% | 1% | 1% | 26.5 | $33,848 | 52% | 17% |
| Sunnyslope | 49,354 | 55% | 33% | 4% | 3% | 3% | 2% | 30.9 | $34,247 | 30% | 19% |
| West Phoenix | 431,106 | 37% | 52% | 6% | 2% | 2% | 2% | 27.3 | $33,641 | 48% | 17% |
| Willo | 1,983 | 83% | 12% | 2% | 0.5% | 1% | 1% | 39.7 | $58,164 | 18% | 15% |
| **MESA** | | | | | | | | | | | |
| Central Mesa | 91,149 | 60% | 33% | 2% | 2% | 1% | 2% | 28.5 | $40,206 | 43% | 17% |
| North Mesa | 198,327 | 85% | 10% | 1% | 1% | 1% | 1% | 40.3 | $44,964 | 31% | 38% |
| South Mesa | 20,246 | 84% | 11% | 2% | 1% | 1% | 2% | 36.3 | $53,844 | 38% | 33% |
| West Mesa | 90,453 | 64% | 24% | 4% | 3% | 3% | 3% | 29.1 | $41,157 | 35% | 12% |
| **SCOTTSDALE** | | | | | | | | | | | |
| Central Scottsdale | 87,076 | 91% | 4% | 1% | 0.3% | 2% | 1% | 42.7 | $62,743 | 24% | 26% |
| North Scottsdale | 45,296 | 93% | 3% | 1% | 0.2% | 2% | 1% | 43.4 | $98,930 | 28% | 21% |

| Region | City | Population | % | % | % | % | % | % | Age | Median Income | % <18 | % >65 |
|---|---|---|---|---|---|---|---|---|---|---|---|---|
| EAST VALLEY | Apache Junction | 31,814 | 88% | 9% | 1% | 1% | 1% | 1% | 44.1 | $33,170 | 25% | 39% |
| EAST VALLEY | Chandler | 176,581 | 69% | 21% | 3% | 1% | 4% | 2% | 31.2 | $58,416 | 44% | 12% |
| EAST VALLEY | Gilbert | 109,697 | 80% | 12% | 2% | 1% | 4% | 2% | 30.1 | $68,032 | 53% | (8%) |
| EAST VALLEY | Queen Creek | 4,316 | 68% | 30% | 0.3% | 1% | 0.3% | 1% | 30.9 | $63,702 | 56% | 13% |
| EAST VALLEY | Tempe | 158,625 | 70% | 18% | 3% | 2% | (5%) | (3%) | 28.8 | $42,361 | 27% | 13% |
| NORTH EAST VALLEY | Carefree | 2,927 | 96% | 3% | (0%) | 0.4% | 0.4% | 0.5% | 55.2 | $88,702 | 15% | 42% |
| NORTH EAST VALLEY | Cave Creek | 3,728 | 91% | 7% | 0.3% | 0.2% | 0.4% | 1% | 44.7 | $59,938 | 29% | 23% |
| NORTH EAST VALLEY | Fountain Hills | 20,235 | 94% | 3% | 1% | 0.4% | 1% | 1% | 46.4 | $61,619 | 25% | 30% |
| NORTH EAST VALLEY | Paradise Valley | 13,664 | 93% | 3% | 1% | 0.2% | 2% | 1% | 46.3 | ($150,228) | 34% | 30% |
| NORTH EAST VALLEY | Rio Verde | 1,419 | (99%) | (0.3%) | 0% | (0.1%) | (0.1%) | (0.1%) | 68.7 | $86,248 | (0.1%) | (71%) |
| WEST VALLEY | Avondale | 35,883 | 44% | 46% | 5% | 1% | 2% | 2% | 29.0 | $49,193 | 54% | 13% |
| WEST VALLEY | Buckeye | 6,537 | 57% | 37% | 3% | 1% | 0.4% | 1% | 30.0 | $35,383 | 48% | 19% |
| WEST VALLEY | Goodyear | 18,911 | 70% | 21% | 5% | 1% | 2% | 2% | 36.5 | $57,492 | 36% | 21% |
| WEST VALLEY | Laveen | 6,346 | 39% | 23% | 1% | 35% | 0.3% | 2% | 31.5 | $38,514 | 48% | 18% |
| WEST VALLEY | Litchfield Park | 3,810 | 89% | 5% | 1% | 1% | 3% | 1% | 44.7 | $71,875 | 31% | 37% |
| WEST VALLEY | Tolleson | 4,974 | 19% | (78%) | 1% | 1% | 0.3% | 1% | 29.4 | $38,773 | 50% | 26% |
| NORTH WEST VALLEY | El Mirage | 7,609 | 28% | 67% | 3% | 1% | 0.4% | 1% | (24.6) | $33,813 | (57%) | 18% |
| NORTH WEST VALLEY | Glendale | 218,812 | 65% | 25% | 4% | 1% | 3% | 2% | 30.8 | $45,015 | 44% | 15% |
| NORTH WEST VALLEY | Peoria | 108,364 | 78% | 15% | 3% | 1% | 2% | 2% | 35.6 | $52,199 | 40% | 26% |
| NORTH WEST VALLEY | Sun Cities | 64,653 | (98%) | 1% | 0.5% | 0.1% | 0.3% | 0.4% | (74.3) | $36,745 | 0.3% | (89%) |
| NORTH WEST VALLEY | Surprise | 30,848 | 72% | 23% | 2% | 0.3% | 1% | 1% | 46.1 | $44,156 | 24% | 41% |
| NORTH WEST VALLEY | Youngtown | 3,010 | 84% | 13% | 1% | 0.4% | 1% | 1% | 65.3 | ($23,164) | 10% | 64% |

Lowest and highest demographic profiles are highlighted.
Household <18 = % of households with one or more persons under 18.
Household >65 = % of households with one or more persons over 65.
Source: United States Census 2000. US Census Bureau - www.census.gov

# Crime

## How Safe are You?

| | Total Crime | Violent Crime Total | Murder | Rape | Robbery | Assault | Property Crime Total | Burglary | Larceny | Motor Vehicle Theft | Arson |
|---|---|---|---|---|---|---|---|---|---|---|---|
| **CRIME IN PHOENIX AND THE VALLEY OF THE SUN** | | | | | | | | | | | |
| **Reported Crimes per 1000 population** | | | | | | | | | | | |
| Phoenix | 73.62 | 6.68 | 0.14 | 0.35 | 2.63 | 3.57 | 66.94 | 11.65 | 37.46 | 17.56 | 0.27 |
| Mesa | 57.96 | 5.59 | 0.05 | 0.28 | 0.94 | 4.32 | 52.37 | 8.23 | 35.64 | 8.38 | 0.12 |
| Scottsdale | 42.95 | 2.12 | 0.02 | 0.28 | 0.60 | 1.22 | 40.84 | 9.44 | 25.29 | 5.96 | 0.14 |
| Apache Junction | 51.00 | 3.35 | 0.03 | 0.36 | 0.44 | 2.52 | 47.65 | 11.45 | 30.90 | 4.92 | 0.39 |
| Chandler | 46.77 | 3.24 | 0.01 | 0.24 | 0.61 | 2.38 | 43.52 | 6.95 | 29.41 | 6.96 | 0.20 |
| Gilbert | 33.62 | 0.97 | 0.01 | 0.13 | 0.18 | 0.66 | 32.64 | 9.14 | 20.06 | 3.26 | 0.18 |
| Queen Creek | Included in Maricopa County Sheriff's Office statistics | | | | | | | | | | |
| Tempe | 87.41 | 6.09 | 0.05 | 0.53 | 1.63 | 3.87 | 81.32 | 11.15 | 54.96 | 14.99 | 0.22 |
| Carefree | Included in Maricopa County Sheriff's Office statistics | | | | | | | | | | |
| Cave Creek | Included in Maricopa County Sheriff's Office statistics | | | | | | | | | | |
| Fountain Hills | Included in Maricopa County Sheriff's Office statistics | | | | | | | | | | |
| Paradise Valley | 33.45 | 1.18 | 0.07 | 0.28 | 0.28 | 0.56 | 32.27 | 18.81 | 11.17 | 2.29 | 0 |
| Rio Verde | Included in Maricopa County Sheriff's Office statistics | | | | | | | | | | |
| Avondale | N/a | N/a | N/a | N/a | N/a | N/a | N/a | N/a | N/a | N/a | N/a |
| Buckeye | 52.67 | 2.00 | 0 | 0 | 0.83 | 1.17 | 50.67 | 22.61 | 16.34 | 11.31 | 0.4 |
| Goodyear | 51.91 | 2.09 | 0.03 | 0.22 | 0.25 | 1.59 | 49.82 | 27.23 | 16.53 | 5.98 | 0.08 |
| Laveen | Included in Maricopa County Sheriff's Office statistics | | | | | | | | | | |
| Litchfield Park | N/a | N/a | N/a | N/a | N/a | N/a | N/a | N/a | N/a | N/a | N/c |
| Tolleson | 141.78 | 5.33 | 0 | 0.18 | 1.29 | 3.86 | 136.36 | 42.06 | 73.46 | 20.57 | 0.3 |
| El Mirage | 39.84 | 5.76 | 0 | 0.64 | 0.78 | 4.34 | 34.09 | 9.18 | 19.07 | 5.65 | 0.1 |
| Glendale | 64.54 | 6.03 | 0.08 | 0.43 | 1.91 | 3.60 | 58.51 | 11.09 | 31.03 | 16.14 | 0.2 |
| Peoria | 45.37 | 2.32 | 0.07 | 0.38 | 0.52 | 1.35 | 43.05 | 7.84 | 27.03 | 8.05 | 0.1 |
| Sun City | Included in Maricopa County Sheriff's Office statistics | | | | | | | | | | |
| Surprise | 32.07 | 1.45 | 0 | 0.11 | 0.28 | 1.06 | 30.61 | 5.43 | 21.45 | 3.67 | 0.0 |
| Youngtown | 40.55 | 4.28 | 0 | 0.25 | 0.50 | 3.53 | 36.27 | 12.09 | 17.88 | 6.05 | 0.2 |
| Maricopa County SO | 23.72 | 1.98 | 0.04 | 0.08 | 0.25 | 1.61 | 21.74 | 5.61 | 12.36 | 3.67 | 0.1 |

Lowest and highest crime figures are highlighted.
Source - Crime in Arizona 2004 - An Annual Report compiled by Access Integrity Unit of the Arizona Department of Public Safety.

# Schools in the Valley of the Sun

## Choosing the Right School

A unique characteristic of the Valley's schools is "open enrollment." Students do not have to attend school in the district in which they live. They may apply to a school outside their district. If the school has the space, and the parent provides the transportation, the student will be accepted. The key is transportation. If the child lives within the district, the district provides the transportation.

School districts and boundaries do not necessarily follow the city they are named after. For example, kids in Paradise Valley do not attend Paradise Valley district schools. And, there is no city named Kyrene, yet there is a Kyrene school district, which draws kids from Ahwatukee and Chandler.

"Charter schools" are a blend of public and private. They are funded by the state, and owned by a non-profit private corporation. They are not as stringently controlled. Some charter schools offer specialized programs such as arts or alternative programs, in addition to a core curriculum.

Students in public and charter schools must pass the Arizona Instrument to Measure Standards (AIMS) test to graduate from high school. The test is relatively new and somewhat controversial. Teacher's pay raises are determined by students' test scores. One principal quit her job after she was accused of changing test results so teachers could get pay raises. Some educators worry that emphasizing the AIMS test takes away from lessons on critical thinking and problem solving.

Private schools receive no public funding and students are not required to take the AIMS test. Teaching styles run the gamut from traditional text-book centered learning to organic, play-based learning, and everything in between. Often the better private schools are faith-based with amusing results. The education path for a child from a wealthy Jewish family in Phoenix is All Saints Episcopal Day School to Xavier or Brophy (Roman Catholic) College Prep. Expect to pay about $10,000 annual tuition.

The State of Arizona allows taxpayers to take a credit for donations made to public schools or private school tuition organizations to help fund the educational system. In 2006, joint filers will be able to donate up to $1,000 to a tuition organization like the Arizona Christian School Tuition Organization, and then take a $1,000 credit against state taxes owed that year. Joint filers can also donate up to $400 to a public school for its extracurricular activities and take an additional $400 credit against their state taxes. These credits are pursuant to A.R.S. Section 43-1089 and 43-1089.01.

As you look for the district and school where your kids will flourish and learn, do your homework. Go beyond the AIMS test scores and state ratings. Some schools offer surprising programs that may be just the right place for your kids to learn and be happy.

> *KEY TO FOLLOWING PAGES:*
>
> *Schools are listed in the area where they are physically located. Due to space restrictions we have generally only listed schools with a minimum of 350 students.*
>
> *(C) = Charter School*

| Low Grade | High Grade | Achievement Profiles | School Name | District | Street Address | Zip | Phone | Students | Student/Teach Ratio |
|---|---|---|---|---|---|---|---|---|---|
| **CENTRAL PHOENIX** | | | | | | | | | |
| UG | UG | Performing Plus | International Commerce Institute (C) | Humanities & Sciences Academy of The US, Inc. | 5201 N. 7th St | 85014 | 602-650-1116 | 634 | N/a |
| PK | 04 | Excelling | Madison Heights | Madison Elementary | 7150 N. 22nd St | 85020 | 602-664-7800 | 459 | 15.9 |
| PK | 04 | Excelling | Madison Richard Simis | Madison Elementary | 7302 N. 10th St | 85020 | 602-664-7300 | 861 | 18.4 |
| PK | 04 | Performing Plus | Madison Rose Lane | Madison Elementary | 1155 E. Rose Ln | 85014 | 602-664-7400 | 842 | 17.7 |
| PK | 06 | Performing | Augustus H Shaw Jr | Phoenix Elementary | 123 N. 13th St | 85034 | 602-257-3898 | 559 | 14.6 |
| PK | 06 | Performing Plus | Capitol Elementary | Phoenix Elementary | 330 N. 16th Ave | 85007 | 602-257-3835 | 440 | 21 |
| PK | 06 | Performing | Desert View Elementary | Washington Elementary | 8621 N. 3rd St | 85020 | 602-347-4000 | 631 | 16.7 |
| PK | 06 | Performing | Garfield | Phoenix Elementary | 811 N. 13th St | 85006 | 602-257-3863 | 539 | 20 |
| PK | 06 | Performing Plus | Longview Elementary | Osborn Elementary | 1209 E. Indian Rd | 85014 | 602-707-2700 | 595 | 15.1 |
| PK | 06 | Performing | Maie Bartlett Heard | Phoenix Elementary | 2301 W. Thomas Rd | 85015 | 602-257-3880 | 587 | 21 |
| PK | 06 | Performing | Mary Mcleod Bethune | Phoenix Elementary | 1310 S. 15th Ave | 85007 | 602-257-3830 | 581 | 21.5 |
| PK | 06 | Performing | Maryland Elementary | Washington Elementary | 6503 N. 21st Ave | 85015 | 602-347-2300 | 643 | 17.9 |
| PK | 06 | Performing | Montecito Community | Osborn Elementary | 715 E. Montecito Ave | 85014 | 602-707-2500 | 563 | 15.6 |
| PK | 06 | Performing | Orangewood Elementary | Washington Elementary | 7337 N. 19th Ave | 85021 | 602-347-2900 | 729 | 19 |
| PK | 06 | Performing Plus | Ralph Waldo Emerson | Phoenix Elementary | 915 E. Palm Ln | 85006 | 602-257-3853 | 609 | 18.5 |
| PK | 06 | Performing | Solano | Osborn Elementary | 1526 W. Missouri Ave | 85015 | 602-707-2600 | 742 | 17.9 |
| PK | 06 | Performing | Thomas A Edison | Phoenix Elementary | 804 N. 18th St | 85006 | 602-257-3848 | 512 | 18.4 |
| PK | 06 | Performing Plus | Whittier Elementary | Phoenix Elementary | 2000 N. 16th St | 85006 | 602-257-2890 | 457 | 21.8 |
| PK | 08 | Performing | Kenilworth Elementary | Phoenix Elementary | 1210 N. 5th Ave | 85003 | 602-257-3889 | 552 | 13.6 |
| PK | 08 | Performing Plus | Lowell | Phoenix Elementary | 1121 S. 3rd Ave | 85003 | 602-257-3902 | 625 | 17.3 |
| PK | 08 | Performing | William T Machan Elementary | Creighton Elementary | 2140 E. Virginia Ave | 85006 | 602-381-6120 | 826 | 15.7 |
| KG | 06 | Performing Plus | Mountain View Elementary | Washington Elementary | 1502 W. Mountain View Rd | 85021 | 602-347-4100 | 1067 | 17.2 |
| KG | 06 | Performing | Richard E Miller | Washington Elementary | 2021 W. Alice | 85021 | 602-347-3000 | 735 | 20.9 |
| KG | 03 | Performing Plus | Encanto | Osborn Elementary | 1426 W. Osborn Rd | 85013 | 602-707-2300 | 646 | 15 |
| KG | 03 | Performing Plus | Westwood Primary | Alhambra Elementary | 4711 N. 23rd | 85015 | 602-242-2442 | 1040 | 18.9 |
| KG | 05 | N/a | Phoenix Thomas J Pappas | Maricopa County Regional | 355 N. 5th Ave | 85003 | 602-452-4750 | 453 | 20.6 |
| KG | 08 | Performing Plus | Excelencia | Creighton Elementary | 2181 E. Mcdowell Rd | 85006 | 602-381-4670 | 957 | 19.7 |
| KG | 08 | Performing | Silvestre S Herrera | Phoenix Elementary | 1350 S. 11th St | 85034 | 602-257-3885 | 527 | 16.1 |
| | | | | | 1431 E. Campbell | 85014 | 602-664-7500 | 899 | 15.4 |

| | | | | | | | | /49 | 13.4 |
|---|---|---|---|---|---|---|---|---|---|

| | | | | | | Zip | Phone | Enroll | Ratio |
|---|---|---|---|---|---|---|---|---|---|
| 04 | 08 | Performing | R E Simpson | Alhambra Elementary | 5330 N. 23rd Ave | 85015 | 602-246-0699 | 1105 | 20.1 |
| 04 | 06 | Performing Plus | Clarendon | Osborn Elementary | 1225 W. Clarendon | 85013 | 602-707-2200 | 438 | 13.3 |
| 07 | 08 | Performing Plus | Osborn Middle | Osborn Elementary | 1102 W. Highland St | 85013 | 602-707-2400 | 731 | 16.6 |
| 07 | 08 | Pending | Phoenix Prep Academy | Phoenix Elementary | 735 E. Fillmore | 85006 | 602-257-4843 | 1050 | 15.5 |
| 09 | 12 | Performing | Central High | Phoenix Union High | 4525 N. Central Ave | 85012 | 602.764.7500 | 2178 | 17.1 |
| 09 | 12 | Performing | Metro Tech High | Phoenix Union High | 1900 W. Thomas Rd | 85015 | 602.764.8008 | 2399 | 20.4 |
| 09 | 12 | Performing | North High | Phoenix Union High | 1101 E. Thomas Rd | 85014 | 602.764.6500 | 2358 | 16.7 |
| 09 | 12 | N/a | Summit High (C) | Summit Public Charter High | 728 E. Mcdowell Rd | 85006 | 602.258.8959 | 467 | N/a |
| 09 | 12 | Highly Performing | Washington High | Glendale Union High | 2217 W. Glendale Ave | 85021 | 623-915-8400 | 1511 | 20.6 |

## EAST PHOENIX

| | | | | | | | | | |
|---|---|---|---|---|---|---|---|---|---|
| PK | 02 | Performing | Madison Camelview Elementary | Madison Elementary | 2002 E. Campbell | 85016 | 602-664-7200 | 556 | 14.7 |
| PK | 03 | Performing Plus | Wilson Primary | Wilson Elementary | 415 N. 30th St | 85008 | 602-683-2500 | 658 | 15.7 |
| PK | 05 | Highly Performing | Tavan Elementary | Scottsdale Unified | 4610 E. Osborn | 85018 | 480-484-3500 | 700 | 18.4 |
| PK | 08 | Performing Plus | Loma Linda Elementary | Creighton Elementary | 2002 E. Clarendon | 85016 | 602-381-6080 | 1002 | 18.2 |
| PK | 08 | Performing | Papago | Creighton Elementary | 2013 N. 36th St | 85008 | 602-381-6100 | 1045 | 19 |
| KG | 05 | Performing | Brunson-lee Elementary | Balsz Elementary | 1350 N. 48th St | 85008 | 602-629-6900 | 512 | 20.5 |
| KG | 05 | Excelling | Hopi Elementary | Scottsdale Unified | 5110 E. Lafayette Blvd | 85018 | 480-484-2000 | 720 | 20.5 |
| KG | 05 | Performing Plus | Monte Vista Elementary | Creighton Elementary | 3501 E. Osborn | 85018 | 602-381-6140 | 873 | 16.5 |
| KG | 08 | Performing Plus | Balsz | Balsz Elementary | 4309 E. Belleview St | 85008 | 602-629-6500 | 784 | 18.6 |
| KG | 08 | Performing | Creighton Elementary | Creighton Elementary | 2802 E. Mcdowell Rd | 85008 | 602-381-6060 | 1073 | 18.8 |
| KG | 08 | Performing Plus | David Crockett | Balsz Elementary | 501 N. 36th St | 85008 | 602-629-6600 | 686 | 16.7 |
| KG | 08 | Performing Plus | Gateway | Creighton Elementary | 1100 N. 35th St | 85008 | 602-552-1000 | 816 | 15.5 |
| KG | 08 | Performing Plus | Griffith Elementary | Balsz Elementary | 4505 E. Palm Ln | 85008 | 602-629-6700 | 727 | 19.5 |
| KG | 08 | Performing Plus | Larry C Kennedy | Creighton Elementary | 2702 E. Osborn | 85016 | 602-381-6180 | 950 | 18.7 |
| KG | 08 | Performing Plus | Orangedale Elementary | Balsz Elementary | 5048 E. Oak St | 85008 | 602-629-6800 | 723 | 18.4 |
| KG | 08 | Performing Plus | Phoenix Advantage Charter (C) | Phoenix Advantage Charter, Inc. | 3738 N. 16th St | 85016 | 602-263-8777 | 854 | N/a |
| KG | 08 | Performing Plus | Squaw Peak Elementary | Creighton Elementary | 4601 N. 34th St | 85018 | 602-381-6160 | 840 | 16.8 |
| KG | 08 | Highly Performing | Villa Montessori - Phoenix Campus (C) | Villa Montessori Charter | 4535 N. 28th St | 85016 | 602-955-2210 | 493 | N/a |
| 04 | 08 | Performing Plus | Wilson Elementary | Wilson Elementary | 2929 E. Fillmore St | 85008 | 602-683-2400 | 738 | 18.9 |
| 05 | 08 | Highly Performing | Madison #1 Elementary | Madison Elementary | 5525 N. 16th St | 85016 | 602-664-7100 | 887 | 19.8 |
| 06 | 08 | Highly Performing | Ingleside Middle | Scottsdale Unified | 5402 E. Osborn Rd | 85018 | 480-484-4900 | 789 | 20.1 |

PHOENIX

# Schools

| Low Grade | High Grade | Achievement Profiles | School Name | District | Street Address | Zip | Phone | Students | Student/Teach Ratio |
|---|---|---|---|---|---|---|---|---|---|
| 08 | 12 | Excelling | Arcadia High | Scottsdale Unified | 4703 E. Indian Rd | 85018 | 480-484-6300 | 1242 | 20.6 |
| 09 | 12 | Performing | Camelback High | Phoenix Union High | 4612 N. 28th St | 85016 | 602-764-7000 | 2274 | 18.2 |
| **WEST PHOENIX** | | | | | | | | | |
| PK | 04 | Performing | Westwind Primary | Pendergast Elementary | 9040 W. Campbell Ave | 85037 | 623-772-2700 | 930 | 20.9 |
| PK | 05 | Performing Plus | Sun Canyon | Fowler Elementary | 8150 W. Durango St | 85043 | 623-707-2000 | 553 | 17.8 |
| PK | 05 | Performing | Sunridge Elementary | Fowler Elementary | 6244 W. Roosevelt | 85043 | 623-707-4600 | 602 | 19.2 |
| PK | 05 | Performing | Western Valley Elementary | Fowler Elementary | 6250 W. Durango St | 85043 | 623-707-2100 | 423 | 17.6 |
| PK | 06 | Performing Plus | Acacia Elementary | Washington Elementary | 3021 W. Evans Dr | 85051 | 602-896-5000 | 687 | 20.5 |
| PK | 06 | Performing Plus | Alta Vista Elementary | Washington Elementary | 8710 N. 31st Ave | 85051 | 602-347-2000 | 705 | 22.9 |
| PK | 06 | Performing | Manzanita Elementary | Washington Elementary | 8430 N. 39th Ave | 85051 | 602-347-2200 | 751 | 18.2 |
| PK | 06 | Performing | Roadrunner Elementary | Washington Elementary | 7702 N. 39th Ave | 85051 | 602-347-3100 | 800 | 21.1 |
| PK | 06 | Performing | Washington Elementary | Washington Elementary | 8033 N. 27th Ave | 85051 | 602-347-3400 | 1072 | 19 |
| PK | 08 | Performing | Alfred F Garcia | Murphy Elementary | 1441 S. 27th Ave | 85009 | 602-353-5110 | 757 | 18.9 |
| PK | 08 | Underperforming | Arthur M Hamilton | Murphy Elementary | 2020 W. Durango St | 85009 | 602-353-5330 | 460 | 15.8 |
| PK | 08 | Performing | Copper King Elementary | Pendergast Elementary | 10730 W. Campbell Ave | 85037 | 623-772-2580 | 1034 | 17.8 |
| PK | 08 | Performing Plus | Desert Horizon Elementary | Pendergast Elementary | 8525 W. Osborn Rd | 85037 | 623-772-2430 | 1324 | 19.6 |
| PK | 08 | Performing Plus | Pendergast Elementary | Pendergast Elementary | 3802 N. 91st Ave | 85037 | 623-772-2400 | 895 | 18.3 |
| PK | 08 | Performing | Riverside Elementary | Riverside Elementary | 1414 S. 51st Ave | 85043 | 602-272-1339 | 559 | 21.5 |
| PK | 08 | Performing | Villa De Paz Elementary | Pendergast Elementary | 4940 N. 103rd Ave | 85037 | 623-772-2490 | 788 | 18.1 |
| PK | 08 | Performing Plus | Westwind Intermediate | Pendergast Elementary | 9040a W. Campbell Ave | 85037 | 623-772-2460 | 675 | 20.5 |
| KG | 03 | Performing | Andalucia Primary | Alhambra Elementary | 4530 W. Campbell Ave | 85031 | 623-848-8420 | 1019 | 19.4 |
| KG | 03 | Performing Plus | Cordova Primary | Alhambra Elementary | 5631 N. 35th Ave | 85017 | 602-242-5828 | 758 | 21.5 |
| KG | 03 | Performing | Granada Primary | Alhambra Elementary | 3232 W. Campbell Ave | 85017 | 602-841-1403 | 1144 | 20.5 |
| KG | 04 | Performing Plus | Sevilla Primary | Alhambra Elementary | 3801 W. Missouri | 85019 | 602-242-0281 | 905 | 19.9 |
| KG | 05 | Underperforming | Alta E Butler | Isaac Elementary | 3843 W. Roosevelt | 85009 | 602-442-2300 | 559 | 16.4 |
| KG | 05 | Performing Plus | Cortez Park Charter Elementary | Pathfinder Charter Fdn | 3535 W. Dunlap | 85051 | 602-589-9840 | 579 | N/a |
| KG | 05 | Performing | Esperanza Elementary | Isaac Elementary | 3025 W. Mcdowell Rd | 85009 | 602-442-2800 | 431 | 18.7 |
| KG | 05 | Underperforming | Fowler Elementary | Fowler Elementary | 6707 W. Van Buren | 85043 | 623-707-2500 | 658 | 19.1 |
| KG | 05 | Performing Plus | J B Sutton Elementary | Isaac Elementary | 1001 N. 31st Ave | 85009 | 602-442-3200 | 834 | 19.9 |

| Grade | | Rating | School | District | Address | Zip | Phone | Enrollment | % |
|---|---|---|---|---|---|---|---|---|---|
| KG | 05 | *(cut)* | *(cut)* | *(cut)* | 406 N. 41st Ave | 85009 | 602-442-2600 | *(cut)* | 19.3 |
| KG | 05 | Performing Plus | Moya Elementary | Isaac Elementary | 3801 W. Roanoke | 85009 | 602-442-3100 | 574 | 19.8 |
| KG | 05 | Performing Plus | P T Coe Elementary | Isaac Elementary | 4301 N. 51st Ave | 85009 | 602-442-2400 | 1011 | 19.1 |
| KG | 06 | Performing Plus | Bret Tarver Elementary | Cartwright Elementary | 2533 N. 60th Ave | 85031 | 623-691-1900 | 782 | 19.8 |
| KG | 06 | Performing Plus | Byron A Barry Elementary | Cartwright Elementary | 9650 N. 39th Ave | 85035 | 623-691-5700 | 767 | 20.5 |
| KG | 06 | Performing | Cactus Wren Elementary | Washington Elementary | 5833 W. Thomas Rd | 85051 | 602-347-2100 | 420 | 13.2 |
| KG | 06 | Performing | Cartwright Elementary | Cartwright Elementary | 2252 N. 55th Ave | 85031 | 623-691-4100 | 1077 | 23.1 |
| KG | 06 | Performing | Charles W Harris Elementary | Cartwright Elementary | 6935 W. Osborn | 85035 | 623-691-4800 | 1095 | 20.7 |
| KG | 06 | Performing | G Frank Davidson | Cartwright Elementary | 3611 N. 47th Ave | 85033 | 623-691-1500 | 1064 | 21.7 |
| KG | 06 | Performing | Glenn L Downs | Cartwright Elementary | 7070 W. Heatherbrae | 85031 | 623-691-4200 | 672 | 18.8 |
| KG | 06 | Performing | Heatherbrae Elementary | Cartwright Elementary | 4417 N. 66th Ave | 85033 | 623-691-5200 | 1004 | 21.5 |
| KG | 06 | Performing | Holiday Park Elementary | Cartwright Elementary | 4407 N. 55th Ave | 85033 | 623-691-4500 | 1003 | 20.5 |
| KG | 06 | Performing | John F Long | Cartwright Elementary | 3201 N. 46th Dr | 85031 | 623-691-4300 | 1034 | 22.2 |
| KG | 06 | Performing Plus | Justine Spitalny Elementary | Cartwright Elementary | 2550 N. 79th Ave | 85031 | 623-691-4400 | 792 | 20.6 |
| KG | 06 | Performing Plus | Manuel Pena Jr. Elementary | Cartwright Elementary | 2043 N. 64th Dr | 85035 | 623-691-3100 | 946 | 21.4 |
| KG | 06 | Performing Plus | Palm Lane Elementary | Cartwright Elementary | 7125 W. Encanto | 85035 | 623-691-5500 | 956 | 20.5 |
| KG | 06 | Performing Plus | Peralta Elementary | Cartwright Elementary | 7960 W. Osborn Rd | 85035 | 623-691-5600 | 1177 | 23.1 |
| KG | 06 | Performing Plus | Starlight Park | Cartwright Elementary | 6602 W. Osborn Rd | 85033 | 623-691-4700 | 1102 | 20.8 |
| KG | 06 | Performing | Sunset | Cartwright Elementary | 7820 W. Turney Ave | 85033 | 623-691-4600 | 856 | 18.5 |
| KG | 06 | Performing | Tomahawk Elementary | Cartwright Elementary | 10444 N. 39th Ave | 85033 | 623-691-5800 | 1212 | 22 |
| KG | 06 | Excelling | Abraham Lincoln Traditional | Washington Elementary | 5350 W. Indian Rd | 85051 | 602-896-6300 | 566 | 21.1 |
| KG | 08 | Performing | Acclaim Charter | Acclaim Charter | 3736 W. Osborn Rd | 85031 | 623-691-0919 | 332 | N/a |
| KG | 08 | Excelling | Alhambra Traditional | Alhambra Elementary | 6331 W. 39th Ave | 85019 | 602-484-8816 | 641 | 22.1 |
| KG | 08 | Performing | Catalina Ventura | Alhambra Elementary | 5631 N. 35th Ave | 85019 | 602-841-7445 | 1376 | 22.2 |
| KG | 08 | Performing | Cordova Middle | Alhambra Elementary | 3201 W. Sherman St | 85017 | 602-841-0704 | 808 | 19.7 |
| KG | 08 | Performing Plus | Jack L Kuban Elementary | Murphy Elementary | 4027 N. 45th Ave | 85009 | 602-353-5440 | 488 | 17.7 |
| KG | 08 | Performing | Liberty Traditional Charter (C) | Liberty Traditional Charter | 2602 N. 23rd Ave | 85031 | 602-442-8791 | 360 | N/a |
| KG | 08 | Highly Performing | Magnet Traditional | Phoenix Elementary | 5725 W. 27th Ave | 85009 | 602-257-6281 | 505 | 25.3 |
| KG | 08 | Performing | Montebello | Alhambra Elementary | 3715 W. Roosevelt St | 85017 | 602-336-2000 | 1185 | 20.4 |
| KG | 08 | Performing Plus | Morris K. Udall Escuela De Bellas Artes | Isaac Elementary | 2 N. 31 Ave | 85009 | 602-442-2700 | 656 | 17.7 |
| KG | 08 | Performing Plus | William R Sullivan Elementary | Murphy Elementary | 9450 W. Encanto | 85009 | 602-353-5220 | 882 | 18.1 |
| 01 | 08 | Performing Plus | Sheely Farms Elementary | Tolleson Elementary | | 85037 | 623-907-5270 | 799 | 18.8 |

**PHOENIX**

| Low Grade | High Grade | Achievement Profiles | School Name | District | Street Address | Zip | Phone | Students | Student/Teach Ratio |
|---|---|---|---|---|---|---|---|---|---|
| 02 | 08 | Performing | Sevilla West | Alhambra Elementary | 3851 W. Missouri Ave | 85019 | 602-347-0232 | 607 | 17.6 |
| 03 | 08 | Underperforming | Andalucia Middle | Alhambra Elementary | 4730 W. Campbell Ave | 85031 | 623-848-8646 | 1173 | 20.7 |
| 04 | 08 | Performing | Granada East | Alhambra Elementary | 3022 W Campbell Ave | 85017 | 602-589-0110 | 1328 | 23.2 |
| 06 | 08 | Performing | Isaac Middle | Isaac Elementary | 3402 W. Mcdowell Rd | 85009 | 602-455-6800 | 1045 | 19.4 |
| 06 | 08 | Performing Plus | Pueblo Del Sol Middle | Isaac Elementary | 3449 N. 39th Ave | 85019 | 602-455-6900 | 1036 | 18.8 |
| 06 | 08 | Performing Plus | Santa Maria Middle | Fowler Elementary | 7250 W. Lower Buckeye Rd | 85043 | 623-707-1100 | 504 | 16.6 |
| 06 | 08 | Underperforming | Western Valley Middle | Fowler Elementary | 6250 W. Durango | 85043 | 623-707-2200 | 386 | 17.5 |
| 07 | 08 | Performing Plus | Atkinson Middle | Cartwright Elementary | 4315 N. Maryvale Pkwy | 85031 | 623-691-1700 | 981 | 21.8 |
| 07 | 08 | Performing Plus | Desert Sands Middle | Cartwright Elementary | 6308 W. Campbell Ave | 85033 | 623-691-4900 | 946 | 20.3 |
| 07 | 08 | Performing Plus | Estrella Middle | Cartwright Elementary | 3733 N. 75th Ave | 85033 | 623-691-5400 | 1121 | 20.4 |
| 07 | 08 | Performing | Frank Borman Middle | Cartwright Elementary | 3637 N. 55th Ave | 85033 | 623-691-5000 | 1025 | 22.3 |
| 07 | 08 | Performing | Polo Verde Middle | Washington Elementary | 7502 N. 39th Ave | 85051 | 602-347-2500 | 1275 | 15.3 |
| 07 | 12 | Performing Plus | North Pointe Preparatory | Pointe Educational Services | 10215 N. 43 Ave | 85051 | 623-209-0017 | 385 | N/a |
| 09 | 12 | Performing | Alhambra High | Phoenix Union High | 3839 W. Camelback Rd | 85019 | 602-764-6022 | 2597 | 19.9 |
| 09 | 12 | Performing | Carl Hayden High | Phoenix Union High | 3333 W. Roosevelt | 85009 | 602-764-3000 | 2209 | 18.5 |
| 09 | 12 | Highly Performing | Cortez High | Glendale Union High | 8828 N. 31st Ave | 85051 | 623-915-8200 | 1224 | 19.2 |
| 09 | 12 | Performing Plus | Maryvale High | Phoenix Union High | 3415 N. 59th Ave | 85033 | 602-764-2009 | 2393 | 19.9 |
| 09 | 12 | N/a | Maya High (C) | Maya Public Charter High | 3660 W. Glendale Ave | 85051 | 602-242-3442 | 598 | N/a |
| 09 | 12 | Performing Plus | Trevor Browne High | Phoenix Union High | 7402 W. Catalina | 85033 | 602-764-8500 | 2592 | 20.5 |
| 09 | 12 | N/a | West Phoenix High (C) | West Phoenix Public Charter High | 3835 W. Thomas Rd | 85019 | 602-269-1110 | 743 | N/a |
| **NORTH PHOENIX** | | | | | | | | | |
| PK | 03 | Performing Plus | Echo Mountain Primary | Paradise Valley Unified | 1811 E. Michigan Ave 3 | 85022 | 602-493-6110 | 654 | 16.7 |
| PK | 03 | Performing | Palomino Primary | Paradise Valley Unified | 15833 N. 29th St | 85032 | 602-493-6190 | 707 | 19.1 |
| PK | 06 | Performing Plus | Arrowhead Elementary | Paradise Valley Unified | 3820 E. Nisbet | 85032 | 602-493-6050 | 539 | 15.2 |
| PK | 06 | Highly Performing | Cactus View Elementary | Paradise Valley Unified | 17602 N. Central Ave | 85022 | 602-493-6280 | 825 | 22 |
| PK | 06 | Performing Plus | Campo Bello Elementary | Paradise Valley Unified | 2650 E. Contention Mine Ln | 85032 | 602-493-6060 | 543 | 15.1 |
| PK | 06 | Performing Plus | Chaparral Elementary | Washington Elementary | 3808 W. Joan D'arc | 85029 | 602-896-5300 | 551 | 18.4 |
| PK | 06 | Performing | Constitution Elementary | Deer Valley Unified | 18440 N. 15th Ave | 85023 | 602-467-6100 | 763 | 16.1 |
| PK | 06 | Performing | Desert Winds Elementary | Deer Valley Unified | 19825 N. 15th Ave | 85027 | 623-445-3900 | 633 | 16.4 |

| | | Performance | School | District | Address | Phone | Zip | | |
|---|---|---|---|---|---|---|---|---|---|
| PK | 06 | Highly Performing | Hidden Hills Elementary | Paradise Valley Unified | 1919 E. Sharon Dr | 602-493-6270 | 85022 | 683 | 19.5 |
| PK | 06 | Performing Plus | Indian Bend Elementary | Paradise Valley Unified | 3633 E. Thunderbird Rd | 602-493-6140 | 85032 | 795 | 17.6 |
| PK | 06 | Performing Plus | Ironwood Elementary | Washington Elementary | 14850 N. 39th Ave | 602-896-5600 | 85053 | 638 | 19 |
| PK | 06 | Performing Plus | John Jacobs Elementary | Washington Elementary | 14421 N. 23rd Ave | 602-896-5700 | 85023 | 589 | 17.6 |
| PK | 06 | Excelling | Larkspur Elementary | Paradise Valley Unified | 2430 E. Larkspur | 602-493-6150 | 85032 | 572 | 15.9 |
| PK | 06 | Pending | Mercury Mine Elementary | Paradise Valley Unified | 9640 N. 28th St | 602-493-6170 | 85028 | 641 | 20.5 |
| PK | 06 | Performing Plus | Moon Mountain | Washington Elementary | 13425 N. 19th Ave | 602-896-6000 | 85029 | 693 | 19.3 |
| PK | 06 | Performing | Sahuaro | Washington Elementary | 12835 N. 33rd Ave | 602-896-6200 | 85029 | 652 | 19.5 |
| PK | 06 | Performing Plus | Shaw Butte | Washington Elementary | 12202 N. 21st Ave | 602-347-4200 | 85029 | 1142 | 22.3 |
| PK | 06 | Excelling | Sunset Canyon | Paradise Valley Unified | 2727 E. Siesta Ln | 602-493-6430 | 85050 | 634 | 19.8 |
| PK | 06 | Performing | Tumbleweed Elementary | Washington Elementary | 4001 W. Laurel Ln | 602-896-6600 | 85029 | 620 | 20.5 |
| PK | 08 | Highly Performing | Anthem | Deer Valley Unified | 41020 N. Freedom Way | 623-376-3700 | 85086 | 890 | 19.6 |
| KG | 06 | Performing Plus | Aire Libre Elementary | Paradise Valley Unified | 16428 N. 21st St | 602-493-6040 | 85022 | 545 | 18.6 |
| KG | 06 | Performing | Bell Canyon Charter (C) | Bell Canyon Charter, Inc | 18052 N. Black Canyon Hwy | 602-547-7920 | 85053 | 542 | N/a |
| KG | 06 | Excelling | Boulder Creek Elementary | Paradise Valley Unified | 22801 N. 22nd St | 480-419-5640 | 85024 | 604 | 18.3 |
| KG | 06 | Highly Performing | Desert Cove Elementary | Paradise Valley Unified | 11020 N. 28th St | 602-493-6070 | 85028 | 657 | 15.1 |
| KG | 06 | Excelling | Desert Trails Elementary | Paradise Valley Unified | 4315 E. Cashman Dr | 480-419-5630 | 85050 | 898 | 21.5 |
| KG | 06 | Performing Plus | Esperanza Elementary | Deer Valley Unified | 251 W. Mohawk | 623-445-3700 | 85027 | 664 | 17.7 |
| KG | 06 | Performing | Lakeview Elementary | Washington Elementary | 3040 W. Yucca St | 602-896-5800 | 85029 | 677 | 22.1 |
| KG | 06 | Excelling | Lookout Mountain | Washington Elementary | 15 W. Coral Gables Dr | 602-896-5900 | 85023 | 973 | 21.9 |
| KG | 06 | Excelling | Quail Run Elementary | Paradise Valley Unified | 3303 E. Utopia | 602-493-6240 | 85050 | 612 | 19.4 |
| KG | 06 | Performing | Sunnyslope Elementary | Washington Elementary | 801 W. Peoria | 602-347-4300 | 85029 | 758 | 17 |
| KG | 06 | N/a | Sunrise Elementary | Deer Valley Unified | 17624 N. 31st Ave | 602-467-5900 | 85053 | 751 | 18.2 |
| KG | 06 | Performing | Village Meadows Elementary | Deer Valley Unified | 2020 W. Morningside Dr | 602-467-6300 | 85023 | 724 | 16.1 |
| KG | 06 | Highly Performing | Village Vista Elementary | Paradise Valley Unified | 4215 E. Andora Dr | 602-493-6230 | 85032 | 533 | 19 |
| KG | 06 | Highly Performing | Whispering Wind | Paradise Valley Unified | 15844 N. 43rd St | 602-493-6360 | 85032 | 588 | 17 |
| KG | 08 | Highly Performing | Gavilan Peak Elementary | Deer Valley Unified | 2701 W. Memorial Dr | 623-445-7400 | 85086 | 1220 | 21.7 |
| KG | 08 | Performing | Hearn Academy, The - A Ball Charter (C) | Ball Charter (Hearn) | 17606 N. 7th Ave | 602-896-9160 | 85022 | 513 | N/a |
| KG | 08 | Performing Plus | Paseo Hills Elementary | Deer Valley Unified | 3302 W. Louise | 623-445-4500 | 85027 | 1188 | 20.4 |
| KG | 08 | Excelling | Valley Academy (C) | Valley Academy, Inc. | 1520 W. Rose Garden Ln | 623-516-7747 | 85027 | 654 | N/a |
| 04 | 06 | Performing | Echo Mountain Intermediate | Paradise Valley Unified | 1811 E. Michigan 3 | 602-485-7040 | 85022 | 483 | 16.7 |

| Low Grade | High Grade | Achievement Profiles | School Name | District | Street Address | Zip | Phone | Students | Student/Teach Ratio |
|---|---|---|---|---|---|---|---|---|---|
| 04 | 06 | Performing | Palomino Intermediate | Paradise Valley Unified | 15815 N. 29th St | 85032 | 602-494-8000 | 474 | 16.3 |
| 07 | 08 | Performing | Cholla Middle | Washington Elementary | 3120 W. Cholla | 85029 | 602-896-5400 | 870 | 16.9 |
| 07 | 08 | Performing Plus | Deer Valley Middle | Deer Valley Unified | 21100 N. 27th Ave | 85027 | 623-445-3300 | 1024 | 19.8 |
| 07 | 08 | Performing Plus | Desert Foothills Middle | Washington Elementary | 3333 W. Banff | 85053 | 602-896-5500 | 901 | 22.8 |
| 07 | 08 | Highly Performing | Explorer Middle | Paradise Valley Unified | 22401 N. 40th St | 85050 | 480-419-5600 | 595 | 19.6 |
| 07 | 08 | Performing Plus | Greenway Middle | Paradise Valley Unified | 3002 E. Nisbet | 85032 | 602-493-6300 | 760 | 15.4 |
| 07 | 08 | Highly Performing | Mountain Sky Middle | Washington Elementary | 16225 N. 7th Ave | 85023 | 602-896-6100 | 889 | 22.3 |
| 07 | 08 | Excelling | Mountain Trail Middle | Paradise Valley Unified | 2323 E. Mountain Gate Pass | 85024 | 480-538-7100 | 875 | 22.3 |
| 07 | 08 | Performing Plus | Royal Palm Middle | Washington Elementary | 8520 N. 19th Ave | 85021 | 602-347-3200 | 1172 | 18.6 |
| 07 | 08 | Highly Performing | Shea Middle | Paradise Valley Unified | 2728 E. Shea Blvd | 85028 | 602-493-6440 | 908 | 20.3 |
| 07 | 08 | Performing | Vista Verde Middle | Paradise Valley Unified | 2826 E. Grovers | 85032 | 602-493-6013 | 933 | 18.3 |
| 09 | 12 | Highly Performing | Barry Goldwater High | Deer Valley Unified | 2820 W. Rose Garden Ln | 85027 | 623-445-3000 | 2188 | 20.6 |
| 09 | 12 | Highly Performing | Greenway High | Glendale Union High | 3930 W. Greenway Rd | 85053 | 623-915-8500 | 1676 | 22.2 |
| 09 | 12 | Highly Performing | Moon Valley High | Glendale Union High | 3625 W. Cactus Rd | 85029 | 623-915-8000 | 1688 | 22 |
| 09 | 12 | Highly Performing | North Canyon High | Paradise Valley Unified | 1700 E. Union Hills Dr | 85022 | 623-780-4200 | 2367 | 24.7 |
| 09 | 12 | N/a | Ocotillo High (C) | Ocotillo Public Charter High | 2616 E. Greenway Rd | 85032 | 602-765-8470 | 427 | N/a |
| 09 | 12 | Performing Plus | Paradise Valley High | Paradise Valley Unified | 3950 E. Bell Rd | 85032 | 602-867-5505 | 1986 | 21.7 |
| 09 | 12 | Excelling | Pinnacle High | Paradise Valley Unified | 3535 E. Mayo Blvd | 85050 | 480-419-4400 | 1863 | 25.9 |
| 09 | 12 | Highly Performing | Shadow Mountain High | Paradise Valley Unified | 2902 E. Shea Blvd | 85028 | 602-867-5326 | 1886 | 23.8 |
| 09 | 12 | Pending | Sunnyslope High | Glendale Union High | 35 W. Dunlap | 85021 | 623-915-8760 | 1602 | 22.3 |
| 09 | 12 | Highly Performing | Thunderbird High | Glendale Union High | 1750 W. Thunderbird | 85023 | 623-915-8900 | 1694 | 21.9 |
| **SOUTH PHOENIX** | | | | | | | | | |
| PK | 03 | Performing | Santa Rosa Elementary | Maricopa Unified | 45012 W. Honeycutt Ave | 85239 | 520-568-6151 | 510 | 20.8 |
| PK | 05 | Excelling | Kyrene De La Estrella Elementary | Kyrene Elementary | 2620 E. Liberty Ln | 85048 | 480-783-1800 | 624 | 17.9 |
| PK | 05 | Highly Performing | Kyrene De Las Lomas | Kyrene Elementary | 11820 S. Warner Elliot Loop | 85044 | 480-783-2800 | 730 | 17.8 |
| PK | 05 | Excelling | Kyrene De Los Cerritos | Kyrene Elementary | 14620 S. Desert Foothills Pkwy | 85048 | 480-783-1200 | 738 | 18.7 |
| PK | 05 | Highly Performing | Highly Performing | Kyrene Elementary | 4630 E. Frye Rd | 85048 | 480-783-3400 | 535 | 17.1 |
| PK | 05 | Excelling | Kyrene Monte Vista | Kyrene Elementary | 15221 S. Ray Rd | 85048 | 480-783-1500 | 613 | 19.6 |
| PK | 05 | Performing Plus | Palo Verde | Casa Grande Elementary | 40 N. Roosevelt | 85222 | 520-421-1650 | 470 | 17 |

| KG | | | | | | | | | |
|---|---|---|---|---|---|---|---|---|---|
| KG | 03 | Underperforming | John F Kennedy Elementary | Roosevelt Elementary | 6825 S. 10th St | 85042 | 602-232-4220 | 661 | 19.4 |
| KG | 05 | Performing Plus | Cottonwood Elementary | Casa Grande Elementary | 1667 N. Kadota | 85222 | 520-836-5601 | 483 | 19.6 |
| KG | 05 | Performing | Ironwood | Casa Grande Elementary | 1460 N. Pinal Ave | 85222 | 520-836-5086 | 503 | 18.7 |
| KG | 05 | Excelling | Kyrene De La Colina | Kyrene Elementary | 13612 S. 36th St | 85044 | 480-783-2600 | 708 | 18.6 |
| KG | 05 | Excelling | Kyrene De La Esperanza | Kyrene Elementary | 14841 S. 41st Pl | 85044 | 480-783-1700 | 641 | 18.4 |
| KG | 05 | Excelling | Kyrene De La Sierra | Kyrene Elementary | 1122 E. Liberty Ln | 85048 | 480-783-1100 | 671 | 19.7 |
| KG | 05 | Highly Performing | Kyrene De Los Lagos | Kyrene Elementary | 17001 S. 34th Wy | 85048 | 480-783-1400 | 522 | 18.1 |
| KG | 05 | Performing Plus | Nevitt Elementary | Tempe Elementary | 4525 E. St Anne | 85042 | 602-431-6640 | 790 | 18.8 |
| KG | 05 | Performing Plus | Saguaro Elementary | Casa Grande Elementary | 1501 N. Center Ave | 85222 | 520-836-7661 | 573 | 19.2 |
| KG | 06 | N/a | C. I. Wilson Academy (C) | C. I. Wilson Academy | 2033 E. Southern Ave | 85040 | 602-268-0275 | 403 | N/a |
| KG | 06 | Performing | Cholla Elementary | Casa Grande Elementary | 1180 E. Kortsen Rd | 85222 | 520-836-4719 | 537 | 23.2 |
| KG | 06 | Performing | Evergreen Elementary | Casa Grande Elementary | 1000 N. Amarillo | 85222 | 520-836-6694 | 513 | 18.4 |
| KG | 08 | Underperforming | Brooks Academy | Roosevelt Elementary | 3146 E. Wier Ave | 85040 | 602-232-4200 | 602 | 18.2 |
| KG | 08 | Underperforming | C J Jorgensen | Roosevelt Elementary | 1701 W. Roeser Rd | 85041 | 602-232-4990 | 671 | 19.7 |
| KG | 08 | Underperforming | Cesar E Chavez Community | Roosevelt Elementary | 4001 S. Third St | 85040 | 602-232-4940 | 627 | 18.4 |
| KG | 08 | Underperforming | Cloves C Campbell Sr | Roosevelt Elementary | 2624 E. South Mountain Ave | 85040 | 602-304-3170 | 641 | 20 |
| KG | 08 | Performing | Ed & Verma Pastor Elementary | Roosevelt Elementary | 2101 W. Alta Vista | 85041 | 602-304-3160 | 627 | 19 |
| KG | 08 | Failing To Meet Academic Standards | Ignacio Conchos | Roosevelt Elementary | 1718 W. Vineyard Rd | 85041 | 602-232-4250 | 604 | 20.1 |
| KG | 08 | Underperforming | John R Davis | Roosevelt Elementary | 6209 S. 15th Ave | 85041 | 602-232-4930 | 649 | 17.5 |
| KG | 08 | Underperforming | Maxine O Bush Elementary | Roosevelt Elementary | 602 E. Siesta Dr | 85042 | 602-232-4260 | 660 | 18.3 |
| KG | 08 | Performing | Rose Linda | Roosevelt Elementary | 4610 S. 12th St | 85040 | 602-232-4920 | 698 | 19.1 |
| KG | 08 | Underperforming | Sierra Vista Elementary | Roosevelt Elementary | 6401 S. 16th St | 85040 | 602-232-4970 | 511 | 17 |
| KG | 08 | Performing | Southwest Elementary | Roosevelt Elementary | 1111 W. Dobbins | 85041 | 602-232-4270 | 743 | 19.3 |
| KG | 08 | Performing | Sunland Elementary | Roosevelt Elementary | 5401 S. 7th Ave | 85041 | 602-232-4960 | 585 | 17.7 |
| KG | 08 | Underperforming | T G Barr | Roosevelt Elementary | 2041 E. Vineyard | 85042 | 602-232-4900 | 419 | 16.8 |
| KG | 08 | Performing | V H Lassen Elementary | Roosevelt Elementary | 909 W. Vineyard | 85041 | 602-232-4210 | 530 | 16.1 |
| KG | 08 | Performing | Valley View | Roosevelt Elementary | 8220 S. 7th Ave | 85041 | 602-232-4980 | 748 | 20.8 |
| KG | 10 | Performing Plus | Sabis International (C) | Phoenix Education Management, LLC | 1903 E. Roeser Rd | 85040 | 612-941-3500 | 690 | N/a |
| KG | 12 | Pending | Horizon Community Learning Center (C) | Horizon Community Learning Center, Inc. | 16233 S. 48th St | 85048 | 480-659-3000 | 1378 | N/a |
| KG | 12 | Performing Plus | NFL Yet Academy | Espiritu Com. Dev. Cnt. | 4848 S. 2nd St | 85040 | 602-305-7788 | 671 | N/a |

| Low Grade | High Grade | Achievement Profiles | School Name | District | Street Address | Zip | Phone | Students | Student/Teach Ratio |
|---|---|---|---|---|---|---|---|---|---|
| 04 | 08 | Performing | C O Greenfield | Roosevelt Elementary | 7009 S. 10th St | 85042 | 602-232-4240 | 743 | 17.7 |
| 04 | 08 | Performing | Percy L Julian | Roosevelt Elementary | 2149 E. Carver Dr | 85040 | 602-232-4950 | 412 | 15.8 |
| 06 | 08 | Performing Plus | Cactus Middle | Casa Grande Elementary | 1220 E. Kortsen Rd | 85222 | 520-421-3330 | 928 | 20.4 |
| 06 | 08 | Performing | Casa Grande Middle | Casa Grande Elementary | 300 W. Mc Murray Blvd | 85222 | 520-836-7310 | 1042 | 20.1 |
| 06 | 08 | Excelling | Kyrene Akimel A-al Middle | Kyrene Elementary | 2720 E. Liberty Ln | 85048 | 480-783-1600 | 1074 | 19.9 |
| 06 | 08 | Excelling | Kyrene Altadena Middle | Kyrene Elementary | 14620 S. Desert Foothills Blvd | 85048 | 480-783-1300 | 1220 | 19.7 |
| 06 | 08 | Excelling | Kyrene Centennial Middle | Kyrene Elementary | 13808 S. 36th St | 85044 | 480-783-2500 | 1190 | 18.4 |
| 09 | 12 | Performing Plus | Casa Grande Union High | Casa Grande Union High | 2730 N. Trekell Rd | 85222 | 520-836-8500 | 2299 | 17.5 |
| 09 | 12 | Excelling | Desert Vista High | Tempe Union High | 16440 S. 32nd St | 85044 | 480-706-7900 | 2836 | 22.4 |
| 09 | 12 | Excelling | Mountain Pointe High | Tempe Union High | 4201 E. Knox Rd | 85044 | 480-759-8449 | 2270 | 22.1 |
| 09 | 12 | Performing | Precision Academy System (C) | Precision Academy Systems, Inc. | 3906 E. Broadway | 85040 | 602-453-3661 | 709 | N/a |
| 09 | 12 | Performing | South Mountain High | Phoenix Union High (C) | 5401 S. 7th St | 85040 | 602-764-5000 | 2114 | 16 |
| 09 | 12 | N/a | South Pointe High | South Pointe Public Charter | 8325 S. Central Ave | 85042 | 602-243-0600 | 484 | N/a |

## CENTRAL MESA

| Low Grade | High Grade | Achievement Profiles | School Name | District | Street Address | Zip | Phone | Students | Student/Teach Ratio |
|---|---|---|---|---|---|---|---|---|---|
| PK | 06 | Performing Plus | Eisenhower Elementary | Mesa Unified | 848 N. Mesa Dr | 85201 | 480-472-5200 | 825 | 22.1 |
| PK | 06 | Highly Performing | Harris Elementary | Gilbert Unified | 1820 S. Harris Dr | 85204 | 480-545-7060 | 678 | 15.8 |
| PK | 06 | Performing | Hawthorne Elementary | Mesa Unified | 630 N. Hunt Dr | 85203 | 480-472-7500 | 847 | 21.6 |
| PK | 06 | Performing | Holmes Elementary | Mesa Uwnified | 948 S. Horne | 85204 | 480-472-5600 | 793 | 19.8 |
| PK | 06 | Performing Plus | Keller Elementary | Mesa Unified | 1445 E. Hilton Ave | 85204 | 480-472-6200 | 792 | 17.4 |
| PK | 06 | Performing | Lehi Elementary | Mesa Unified | 2555 N. Stapley Dr | 85203 | 480-472-5500 | 576 | 18 |
| PK | 06 | Performing Plus | Lincoln Elementary | Mesa Unified | 930 S. Sirrine | 85210 | 480-472-6400 | 757 | 19 |
| PK | 06 | Performing Plus | Lindbergh Elementary | Mesa Unified | 930 S. Lazona | 85204 | 480-472-6300 | 764 | 20.7 |
| PK | 06 | Performing | Longfellow Elementary | Mesa Unified | 345 S. Hall St | 85204 | 480-472-6550 | 902 | 22.3 |
| PK | 06 | Underperforming | Lowell Elementary | Mesa Unified | 920 E. Broadway | 85204 | 480-472-1400 | 839 | 19.6 |
| KG | 06 | Performing | Edison Elementary | Mesa Unified | 545 N. Horne | 85203 | 480-472-5300 | 731 | 23.4 |
| KG | 06 | Excelling | Franklin Elementary | Mesa Unified | 1753 E. 8th Ave | 85204 | 480-472-6500 | 788 | 22.5 |
| KG | 06 | Highly Performing | Macarthur Elementary | Mesa Unified | 1435 E. Mclellan | 85203 | 480-472-7800 | 623 | 18.7 |
| KG | 06 | Performing | Sequoia Charter Elementary (C) | Sequoia Charter, Inc. | 1460 S. Horne | 85204 | 480-649-7737 | 378 | N/a |
| KG | 08 | Performing | Burke Basic (C) | American Basic Schools LLC | 131 E. Southern Ave | 85210 | 480-964-4602 | 601 | N/a |

PHOENIX

MESA

| Grade Low | Grade High | Status | School | District | Address | Zip | Phone | Enrollment | Ratio |
|---|---|---|---|---|---|---|---|---|---|
| 07 | 09 | Performing Plus | Mesa Junior High | Mesa Unified | 828 E. Broadway Rd | 85204 | 480-472-1300 | 1095 | 17.9 |
| 07 | 09 | Performing | Powell Junior High | Mesa Unified | 855 W. 8th Ave | 85210 | 480-472-1100 | 1345 | 18.9 |
| 07 | 12 | Excelling | Heritage Academy, Inc. | Heritage Academy, Inc. | 32 S. Center | 85210 | 480-969-5641 | 391 | N/a |
| 07 | 12 | Performing Plus | Sequoia Charter (C) | Sequoia Charter, Inc. | 1460 S. Horne | 85204 | 480-649-7737 | 388 | N/a |
| 09 | 12 | Highly Performing | Mesa High | Mesa Unified | 1630 E. Southern Ave | 85204 | 480-472-5900 | 2707 | 20.7 |

## NORTH MESA

| Grade Low | Grade High | Status | School | District | Address | Zip | Phone | Enrollment | Ratio |
|---|---|---|---|---|---|---|---|---|---|
| PK | 06 | Performing Plus | Dilworth Brinton | Mesa Unified | 11455 E. Sunland Ave | 85208 | 480-472-4081 | 837 | 21.4 |
| PK | 06 | Excelling | Entz Elementary | Mesa Unified | 4132 E. Adobe | 85205 | 480-472-7300 | 696 | 19.7 |
| PK | 06 | Excelling | Hermosa Vista Elementary | Mesa Unified | 2626 N. 24th St | 85213 | 480-472-7550 | 726 | 19.7 |
| PK | 06 | Performing | Irving Elementary | Mesa Unified | 3220 E. Pueblo | 85204 | 480-472-1700 | 645 | 19.7 |
| PK | 06 | Excelling | Ishikawa Elementary | Mesa Unified | 2635 N. 32nd St | 85213 | 480-472-7700 | 832 | 21.8 |
| PK | 06 | Performing | Jefferson Elementary | Mesa Unified | 120 S. Jefferson | 85208 | 480-472-8700 | 835 | 20.7 |
| PK | 06 | Highly Performing | Johnson Elementary | Mesa Unified | 3807 E. Pueblo | 85206 | 480-472-6800 | 808 | 20.3 |
| PK | 06 | Highly Performing | Madison Elementary | Mesa Unified | 849 S. Sunnyvale | 85206 | 480-472-8800 | 638 | 20.6 |
| PK | 06 | Highly Performing | Mendoza Elementary | Mesa Unified | 5831 E. Mclellan Rd | 85205 | 480-472-2000 | 827 | 19.3 |
| PK | 06 | Highly Performing | O'Connor Elementary | Mesa Unified | 4840 E. Adobe Rd | 85205 | 480-472-7850 | 716 | 18.3 |
| PK | 06 | Performing | Salk Elementary | Mesa Unified | 7029 E. Brown Rd | 85207 | 480-472-8400 | 948 | 20.9 |
| PK | 06 | Highly Performing | Sousa Elementary | Mesa Unified | 616 N. Mountain | 85207 | 480-472-8900 | 702 | 21.1 |
| PK | 06 | Performing Plus | Stevenson Elementary | Mesa Unified | 638 S. 96th St | 85208 | 480-472-9000 | 957 | 22.9 |
| PK | 06 | Highly Performing | Superstition Springs Elementary | Gilbert Unified | 7125 E. Monterey Ave | 85208 | 480-641-6413 | 929 | 20.7 |
| PK | 06 | Performing | Taft Elementary | Mesa Unified | 9800 E. Quarterline Rd | 85207 | 480-472-9100 | 750 | 19.3 |
| KG | 06 | Excelling | Barbara Bush Elementary | Mesa Unified | 4925 N. Ingram | 85205 | 480-472-8500 | 710 | 19.4 |
| KG | 06 | Highly Performing | Dwight Patterson Elementary | Mesa Unified | 615 S. Cheshire | 85208 | 480-472-9700 | 1017 | 22.9 |
| KG | 06 | Excelling | Falcon Hill Elementary | Mesa Unified | 1645 N. Sterling St | 85207 | 480-472-8600 | 625 | 19.7 |
| KG | 06 | Highly Performing | Field Elementary | Mesa Unified | 2325 E. Adobe St | 85213 | 480-472-9800 | 874 | 20.7 |
| KG | 06 | Excelling | Franklin South | Mesa Unified | 5005 E. Southern Ave | 85206 | 480-472-2240 | 372 | 26.6 |
| KG | 06 | Excelling | Hale Elementary | Mesa Unified | 1425 N. 23rd St | 85213 | 480-472-7400 | 631 | 18.5 |
| KG | 06 | Highly Performing | Highland Elementary | Mesa Unified | 3042 E. Adobe Rd | 85213 | 480-472-7600 | 669 | 22.2 |
| KG | 06 | Excelling | Las Sendas Elementary | Mesa Unified | 3120 N. Red Mountain Rd | 85207 | 480-472-8750 | 884 | 22 |
| KG | 06 | Highly Performing | Marilyn Thiele Wilson | Mesa Unified | 5619 E. Glade Ave | 85206 | 480-472-9250 | 893 | 22.9 |
| KG | 06 | Highly Performing | Noah Webster Basic (C) | Noah Webster Basic | 8350 E. Baseline Rd | 85208 | 480-986-2335 | 1004 | N/a |

MESA

## MESA

| Low Grade | High Grade | Achievement Profiles | School Name | District | Street Address | Zip | Phone | Students | Student/Teach Ratio |
|---|---|---|---|---|---|---|---|---|---|
| KG | 06 | Performing | Porter Elementary | Mesa Unified | 1350 S. Lindsay St | 85204 | 480-472-6700 | 729 | 19.5 |
| KG | 06 | Highly Performing | Red Mountain Ranch Elementary | Mesa Unified | 6650 E. Raftriver Rd | 85215 | 480-472-7900 | 786 | 21.3 |
| KG | 06 | Highly Performing | Robson Elementary | Mesa Unified | 2122 E. Pueblo Ave | 85204 | 480-472-6600 | 667 | 18.9 |
| KG | 08 | Excelling | Franklin Northeast | Mesa Unified | 7042 E. Adobe Rd | 85207 | 480-472-9300 | 506 | 26.2 |
| KG | 12 | N/a | Life College Preparatory - Gold | Life College Preparatory, Inc. | 2929 E. Mckellips Rd | 85213 | 480-924-1500 | 381 | N/a |
| 07 | 09 | Highly Performing | Brimhall Junior High | Mesa Unified | 4949 E. Southern Ave | 85206 | 480-472-2600 | 1355 | 18.4 |
| 07 | 09 | Highly Performing | Fremont Junior High | Mesa Unified | 1001 N. Power Rd | 85205 | 480-472-8300 | 1488 | 20.6 |
| 07 | 09 | Excelling | George Smith | Mesa Unified | 10100 E. Adobe Rd | 85207 | 480-472-9900 | 1456 | 20.3 |
| 07 | 09 | Excelling | Poston Junior High | Mesa Unified | 2433 E. Adobe Rd | 85213 | 480-472-2100 | 1415 | 21.1 |
| 07 | 09 | Highly Performing | Shepherd Junior High | Mesa Unified | 1407 N. Alta Mesa Dr | 85205 | 480-472-1800 | 1543 | 20.1 |
| 07 | 09 | Highly Performing | Stapley Junior High | Mesa Unified | 3250 E. Hermosa Vista Dr | 85213 | 480-472-2700 | 1403 | 20.5 |
| 07 | 09 | Highly Performing | Taylor Junior High | Mesa Unified | 705 S. 32nd St | 85204 | 480-472-1500 | 1231 | 19.8 |
| 07 | 12 | Performing | Skyline High | Mesa Unified | 845 S. Crismon | 85208 | 480-472-9400 | 1658 | 21.8 |
| 09 | 12 | Excelling | Red Mountain High | Mesa Unified | 7301 E. Brown Rd | 85207 | 480-472-8000 | 2421 | 22.8 |
| 09 | 12 | N/a | Sun Valley High (C) | Sun Valley Public Charter High | 1143 S. Lindsay Rd | 85204 | 480-497-4800 | 956 | N/a |
| 10 | 12 | Excelling | Mountain View High | Mesa Unified | 2700 E. Brown Rd | 85213 | 480-472-6900 | 2707 | 21.6 |

### SOUTH MESA

| Low Grade | High Grade | Achievement Profiles | School Name | District | Street Address | Zip | Phone | Students | Student/Teach Ratio |
|---|---|---|---|---|---|---|---|---|---|
| PK | 06 | Highly Performing | Superstition Springs Elementary | Gilbert Unified | 7125 E. Monterey Ave | 85208 | 480-641-6413 | 929 | 20.7 |
| PK | 06 | Highly Performing | Boulder Creek Elementary | Gilbert Unified | 8045 S. Portobello Ave | 85212 | 480-507-1404 | 856 | 19.2 |
| PK | 06 | Highly Performing | Canyon Rim | Gilbert Unified | 3045 S. Canyon Rim | 85212 | 480-984-3216 | 998 | 20 |
| KG | 06 | Highly Performing | Augusta Ranch Elementary | Gilbert Unified | 9430 E. Neville Ave | 85212 | 480-635-2011 | 1253 | 21.4 |
| KG | 12 | N/a | Life Liberty (C) | Life College Preparatory, Inc. | 3015 S. Power Rd | 85212 | 480-830-3444 | 460 | N/a |
| 07 | 08 | Highly Performing | Desert Ridge Jr High | Gilbert Unified | 10211 E. Madero Ave | 85212 | 480-635-2025 | 848 | 20.6 |
| 07 | 08 | Excelling | Highland Jr High | Gilbert Unified | 6915 E. Guadalupe Rd | 85212 | 480-632-4739 | 1260 | 20 |
| 09 | 12 | Excelling | Desert Ridge High | Gilbert Unified | 10045 E. Madero Ave | 85212 | 480-984-8947 | 1465 | 18.1 |

### WEST MESA

| Low Grade | High Grade | Achievement Profiles | School Name | District | Street Address | Zip | Phone | Students | Student/Teach Ratio |
|---|---|---|---|---|---|---|---|---|---|
| PK | 06 | Performing | Adams Elementary | Mesa Unified | 738 S. Longmore | 85202 | 480-472-4300 | 982 | 20.6 |
| PK | 06 | Performing | Alma Elementary | Mesa Unified | 1313 W. Medina | 85202 | 480-472-3900 | 768 | 20.7 |
| PK | 06 | Highly Performing | Crismon Elementary | Mesa Unified | 825 W. Medina | 85210 | 480-472-4000 | 758 | 19.9 |

## MESA

| | | Rating | School | District | Address | Zip | Phone | | |
|---|---|---|---|---|---|---|---|---|---|
| PK | 06 | Performing | Pedro Guerrero | Mesa Unified | 463 S. Alma Rd | 85210 | 480-472-9200 | 753 | 21 |
| PK | 06 | Performing Plus | Redbird Elementary | Mesa Unified | 1020 S. Extension | 85210 | 480-472-1200 | 670 | 20.9 |
| PK | 06 | Performing Plus | Roosevelt Elementary | Mesa Unified | 828 S. Valencia | 85202 | 480-472-4200 | 654 | 20.2 |
| PK | 06 | Performing Plus | Webster Elementary | Mesa Unified | 202 N. Sycamore | 85201 | 480-472-4800 | 879 | 20.1 |
| PK | 06 | Performing Plus | Whitman Elementary | Mesa Unified | 1829 N. Grand | 85201 | 480-472-5000 | 730 | 17.5 |
| KG | 06 | Highly Performing | Washington Elementary | Mesa Unified | 2260 W. Isabella Ave | 85202 | 480-472-4100 | 618 | 21.3 |
| KG | 06 | Performing Plus | Whittier Elementary | Mesa Unified | 733 N. Longmore | 85201 | 480-472-4900 | 652 | 18.8 |
| KG | 09 | N/a | Eagleridge Enrichment Program | Mesa Unified | 737 W. Guadalupe | 85210 | 480-472-3685 | 512 | 1024 |
| 07 | 09 | Performing | Carson Junior High | Mesa Unified | 525 N. Westwood | 85201 | 480-472-2900 | 1294 | 19.1 |
| 07 | 09 | Highly Performing | Rhodes Junior High | Mesa Unified | 1860 S. Longmore St | 85202 | 480-472-2300 | 1224 | 21.2 |
| 09 | 12 | N/a | East Valley Institute of Tech | East Valley Institute of Tech | 1601 W. Main St | 85201 | 480-461-4173 | 2266 | 37.3 |
| 09 | 12 | Performing | Westwood High | Mesa Unified | 945 W. 8th St | 85201 | 480-472-4400 | 2351 | 20.8 |
| 10 | 12 | Excelling | East Valley Academy | East Valley Academy | 1727 West Main | 85201 | 480-472-9350 | 337 | 30.6 |
| 10 | 12 | Pending | Dobson High | Mesa Unified | 1501 W. Guadalupe | 85202 | 480-472-3000 | 2452 | 21.4 |

## CENTRAL SCOTTSDALE

| | | Rating | School | District | Address | Zip | Phone | | |
|---|---|---|---|---|---|---|---|---|---|
| PK | 05 | Excelling | Aztec Elementary | Scottsdale Unified | 13636 N. 100th St | 85260 | 480-484-7700 | 586 | 17.7 |
| PK | 05 | Excelling | Laguna Elementary | Scottsdale Unified | 10475 E. Lakeview Dr | 85258 | 480-484-2400 | 671 | 18.4 |
| PK | 05 | Excelling | Zuni Elementary | Scottsdale Unified | 9181 E. Redfield Rd | 85260 | 480-484-4000 | 602 | 19.7 |
| PK | 06 | Highly Performing | Desert Shadows Elementary | Paradise Valley Unified | 5902 E. Sweetwater | 85254 | 602-493-6080 | 591 | 17.9 |
| PK | 06 | Excelling | Desert Springs Elementary | Paradise Valley Unified | 6010 E. Acoma Rd | 85254 | 602-493-6090 | 467 | 16.3 |
| PK | 06 | Excelling | Liberty Elementary | Paradise Valley Unified | 5125 E. Marilyn Rd | 85254 | 602-493-6160 | 606 | 19.9 |
| PK | 06 | Excelling | Sandpiper Elementary | Paradise Valley Unified | 6724 E. Hearn Rd | 85254 | 480-367-5800 | 466 | 17.6 |
| PK | 06 | Excelling | Sonoran Sky Elementary | Paradise Valley Unified | 12990 N. 75th St | 85260 | 480-367-5820 | 486 | 17.1 |
| KG | 05 | Excelling | Cochise Elementary | Scottsdale Unified | 9451 N. 84th St | 85258 | 480-484-1100 | 551 | 17.3 |
| KG | 05 | Excelling | Sequoya Elementary | Scottsdale Unified | 11808 N. 64th St | 85254 | 480-484-3200 | 662 | 19.4 |
| KG | 06 | Excelling | Copper Canyon Elementary | Paradise Valley Unified | 17650 N. 54th St | 85254 | 602-493-6310 | 699 | 20.5 |
| KG | 06 | Excelling | North Ranch Elementary | Paradise Valley Unified | 16406 N. 61st Pl | 85254 | 480-367-5810 | 534 | 17 |
| KG | 06 | Performing Plus | Pueblo Elementary | Scottsdale Unified | 6320 N. 82nd St | 85250 | 480-484-3100 | 568 | 18.4 |
| KG | 08 | Excelling | Cheyenne Traditional Elementary | Scottsdale Unified | 11130 E. Cholla St | 85259 | 480-484-5600 | 929 | 19.1 |
| 06 | 08 | Excelling | Cocopah Middle | Scottsdale Unified | 6615 E. Cholla St | 85254 | 480-484-4400 | 1111 | 19.9 |
| 07 | 08 | Excelling | Desert Shadows Middle | Paradise Valley Unified | 5858 E. Sweetwater | 85254 | 602-493-6000 | 832 | 21.5 |

| Low Grade | High Grade | Achievement Profiles | School Name | District | Street Address | Zip | Phone | Students | Student/Teach Ratio |
|---|---|---|---|---|---|---|---|---|---|
| 07 | 08 | Highly Performing | Mohave Middle | Scottsdale Unified | 5520 N. 86th St | 85250 | 480-484-5200 | 681 | 11.6 |
| 07 | 08 | Performing Plus | Sunrise Middle | Paradise Valley Unified | 4960 E. Acoma Dr | 85254 | 602-493-6030 | 753 | 19.9 |
| 08 | 12 | Excelling | Saguaro High | Scottsdale Unified | 6250 N. 82nd St | 85250 | 480-484-7100 | 1685 | 21.6 |
| 09 | 12 | Excelling | Horizon High | Paradise Valley Unified | 5601 E. Greenway Rd | 85254 | 602-953-4104 | 2395 | 24.6 |
| **NORTH SCOTTSDALE** | | | | | | | | | |
| PK | 06 | Excelling | Grayhawk Elementary | Paradise Valley Unified | 7525 E. Grayhawk Dr | 85255 | 480-419-5620 | 617 | 18.4 |
| PK | 08 | Excelling | Desert Canyon Elementary | Scottsdale Unified | 10203 E. McDowell Mtn | 85255 | 480-484-1700 | 725 | 19.1 |
| KG | 05 | Excelling | Anasazi Elementary | Scottsdale Unified | 12121 N. 124th St | 85259 | 480-484-7300 | 618 | 19.1 |
| KG | 05 | Excelling | Copper Ridge Elementary | Scottsdale Unified | 10101 E. Thompson Peak Pwy | 85255 | 480-484-1400 | 375 | 17.5 |
| KG | 06 | Excelling | Pinnacle Peak Elementary | Paradise Valley Unified | 7690 E. Williams Dr | 85255 | 480-538-7120 | 793 | 22.7 |
| 01 | 08 | Excelling | Desert Canyon Middle | Scottsdale Unified | 10203 E. McDowell Mtn | 85259 | 480-484-4600 | 803 | 19.6 |
| 06 | 08 | Excelling | Copper Ridge Middle | Scottsdale Unified | 10101 E. Thompson Peak Pwy | 85255 | 480-484-1500 | 529 | 22.8 |
| 06 | 08 | Excelling | Mountainside Middle | Scottsdale Unified | 11256 N. 128th St | 85259 | 480-484-5500 | 1000 | 21 |
| 08 | 12 | Excelling | Desert Mountain High | Scottsdale Unified | 12575 E. Via Linda | 85259 | 480-484-7000 | 2417 | 22.4 |
| **SOUTH SCOTTSDALE** | | | | | | | | | |
| PK | 06 | Performing Plus | Navajo Elementary | Scottsdale Unified | 4525 N Granite Reef Rd | 85251 | 480-484-2600 | 563 | 16.7 |
| PK | 06 | Performing Plus | Yavapai Elementary | Scottsdale Unified | 701 N. Miller Rd | 85257 | 480-484-3800 | 712 | 15.5 |
| KG | 06 | Performing | Hohokam Elementary | Scottsdale Unified | 8451 E. Oak St | 85257 | 480-484-1800 | 574 | 18 |
| KG | 06 | Excelling | Pima Elementary | Scottsdale Unified | 8330 E. Osborn Rd | 85251 | 480-484-2800 | 560 | 17.5 |
| KG | 06 | Performing Plus | Tonalea Elementary | Scottsdale Unified | 6801 E. Oak St | 85257 | 480-484-3600 | 540 | 16.8 |
| KG | 08 | Highly Performing | Arcadia Neighborhood Learning Center | Scottsdale Unified | 5301 E. Mitchell Dr | 85251 | 480-484-7500 | 523 | 18.9 |
| 07 | 08 | Performing Plus | Supai Middle | Scottsdale Unified | 6720 E. Continental | 85257 | 480-484-5800 | 671 | 16.9 |
| 09 | 12 | Performing Plus | Coronado High | Scottsdale Unified | 2501 N. 74th St | 85257 | 480-484-6800 | 1249 | 19.1 |
| **APACHE JUNCTION** | | | | | | | | | |
| PK | 05 | Performing Plus | Superstition Mountain Elementary | Apache Junction Unified | 550 S. Ironwood | 85220 | 480-982-1110 | 699 | 17 |
| KG | 05 | Performing Plus | Desert Vista Elementary | Apache Junction Unified | 3701 E. Broadway | 85219 | 480-982-1110 | 730 | 21.2 |
| KG | 05 | Performing | Four Peaks Elementary | Apache Junction Unified | 1755 N. Idaho Rd | 85219 | 480-982-1110 | 392 | 15.7 |
| KG | 05 | Performing Plus | Gold Canyon Elementary | Apache Junction Unified | 5810 S. Alameda Rd | 85218 | 480-982-1110 | 519 | 19.2 |
| KG | 05 | Performing Plus | Peralta Trail Elementary | Apache Junction Unified | 10965 E. Peralta Rd | 85218 | 480-982-1110 | 470 | 20 |

SCOTTSDALE

EAST VALLEY

| Low | High | Rating | School | District | Address | Zip | Phone | Enroll. | Ratio |
|---|---|---|---|---|---|---|---|---|---|
| 09 | 12 | Performing Plus | Apache Junction High | Apache Junction Unified | 2525 S. Ironwood Rd | 85220 | 480-982-1110 | 1466 | 19.5 |

## CHANDLER

*EAST VALLEY*

| Low | High | Rating | School | District | Address | Zip | Phone | Enroll. | Ratio |
|---|---|---|---|---|---|---|---|---|---|
| PK | 05 | Excelling | Kyrene De Las Brisas | Kyrene Elementary | 777 N. Desert Breeze Blvd | 85226 | 480-783-2300 | 675 | 19.2 |
| PK | 05 | Excelling | Kyrene Del Cielo | Kyrene Elementary | 1350 N. Lakeshore Dr | 85226 | 480-783-2100 | 717 | 16.8 |
| PK | 06 | Performing Plus | Clifford J Goodman Elementary | Chandler Unified | 2600 W. Knox | 85224 | 480-812-6900 | 623 | 24.8 |
| PK | 06 | Performing | Frye Elementary | Chandler Unified | 801 E. Frye Rd | 85225 | 480-812-6400 | 831 | 22.8 |
| PK | 06 | Highly Performing | Jordan Elementary | Mesa Unified | 3320 N. Carriage Ln | 85224 | 480-472-3800 | 604 | 18.8 |
| PK | 06 | Performing Plus | Pomeroy Elementary | Mesa Unified | 1507 W. Shawnee Dr | 85224 | 480-472-3700 | 570 | 19.1 |
| PK | 06 | Performing Plus | San Marcos Elementary | Chandler Unified | 451 W. Frye Rd | 85225 | 480-883-4200 | 614 | 23.9 |
| PK | 06 | Highly Performing | Sirrine Elementary | Mesa Unified | 591 Mesquite St | 85224 | 480-472-3600 | 683 | 20.7 |
| PK | 08 | Performing | Erie Elementary | Chandler Unified | 1150 W. Erie St | 85224 | 480-812-6300 | 681 | 23.8 |
| PK | 08 | Excelling | Jane D. Hull Elementary | Chandler Unified | 2424 E. Maren Dr | 85249 | 480-883-4500 | 1046 | 23.2 |
| PK | 08 | Excelling | Santan K-8 | Chandler Unified | 1550 E. Chandler Heights Rd | 85249 | 480-883-4600 | 1619 | 22.8 |
| PK | 12 | Excelling | Basha High | Chandler Unified | 5990 S. Val Vista Dr | 85249 | 480-224-2100 | 1041 | 23.1 |
| KG | 05 | Excelling | Kyrene De La Mirada | Kyrene Elementary | 5500 W. Galveston St | 85226 | 480-783-2900 | 673 | 17.4 |
| KG | 05 | Excelling | Kyrene De La Paloma | Kyrene Elementary | 5000 W. Whitten | 85226 | 480-783-2700 | 622 | 18 |
| KG | 05 | Highly Performing | Kyrene Del Sureno | Kyrene Elementary | 3375 W. Galveston Rd | 85226 | 480-783-3000 | 539 | 17.7 |
| KG | 06 | Excelling | Anna Marie Jacobson Elementary | Chandler Unified | 1515 NW. Jacaranda Pkwy | 85248 | 480-883-4100 | 1030 | 24.4 |
| KG | 06 | Excelling | Chandler Traditional Academy - Liberty Campus | Chandler Unified | 550 N. Emmett | 85225 | 480-883-4900 | 506 | 24.9 |
| KG | 06 | Highly Performing | Dr Howard K Conley Elementary | Chandler Unified | 500 S. Arrowhead Dr | 85224 | 480-812-6200 | 897 | 23.2 |
| KG | 06 | Highly Performing | Frost Elementary | Mesa Unified | 1560 W. Summit Pl | 85224 | 480-472-3500 | 574 | 22.5 |
| KG | 06 | Performing Plus | Galveston Elementary | Chandler Unified | 661 E. Galveston St | 85225 | 480-812-6500 | 965 | 20.4 |
| KG | 06 | Performing Plus | Hartford Elementary | Chandler Unified | 700 N. Hartford St | 85224 | 480-812-6700 | 673 | 23.9 |
| KG | 06 | Excelling | John M Andersen Elementary | Chandler Unified | 1350 N. Pennington Dr | 85224 | 480-812-6000 | 537 | 19.5 |
| KG | 06 | Performing Plus | Knox Elementary | Chandler Unified | 700 W. Orchid Ln | 85225 | 480-812-6100 | 644 | 22.5 |
| KG | 06 | Performing Plus | Marshall Humphrey Ii Elementary | Chandler Unified | 125 S. 132nd St | 85225 | 480-812-6800 | 766 | 23.3 |
| KG | 06 | Excelling | Robert And Danell Tarwater Elementary | Chandler Unified | 2300 S. Gardner Dr | 85248 | 480-883-4300 | 865 | 21.1 |
| KG | 06 | Performing Plus | Rudy G Bologna Elementary | Chandler Unified | 1625 E. Frye Rd | 85225 | 480-883-4000 | 805 | 20.2 |
| KG | 06 | Excelling | Sanborn Elementary | Chandler Unified | 700 N. Superstition Blvd | 85225 | 480-812-7300 | 818 | 22.7 |
| KG | 06 | Excelling | Shumway Elementary | Chandler Unified | 1325 N. Shumway Ave | 85225 | 480-812-7400 | 729 | 23.7 |

# Schools

| Low Grade | High Grade | Achievement Profiles | School Name | District | Street Address | Zip | Phone | Students | Student/Teach Ratio |
|---|---|---|---|---|---|---|---|---|---|
| KG | 06 | Highly Performing | Weinberg Elementary | Chandler Unified | 21221 S. Val Vista Rd | 85249 | 480-812-7500 | 854 | 23.5 |
| KG | 08 | Excelling | Bright Beginnings #1 (C) | Bright Beginnings, Inc. | 400 N. Andersen Blvd | 85224 | 480-821-1404 | 405 | N/a |
| KG | 08 | Pending | Dobson Academy, The - A Ball Charter (C) | Ball Charter Schools | 2207 N. Dobson Rd | 85224 | 480-855-6325 | 572 | N/a |
| KG | 12 | Excelling | Basha Elementary | Chandler Unified | 3535 S. Basha Rd | 85248 | 480-883-4400 | 999 | 23.4 |
| 06 | 08 | Excelling | Kyrene Aprende Middle | Kyrene Elementary | 777 N. Desert Breeze Blvd | 85226 | 480-783-2200 | 1158 | 17.6 |
| 06 | 08 | Excelling | Kyrene Del Pueblo Middle | Kyrene Elementary | 360 S. Twelve Oaks Blvd | 85226 | 480-783-2400 | 1073 | 18.8 |
| 07 | 08 | Highly Performing | Bogle Junior High | Chandler Unified | 1600 W. Queen Creek Rd | 85248 | 480-883-5500 | 965 | 21.4 |
| 07 | 09 | Highly Performing | Hendrix Junior High | Mesa Unified | 1550 W. Summit Pl | 85224 | 480-472-3300 | 985 | 20.2 |
| 07 | 08 | Highly Performing | John M Andersen Jr High | Chandler Unified | 1255 N. Dobson Rd | 85224 | 480-883-5300 | 1175 | 21.8 |
| 07 | 08 | Performing Plus | Willis Junior High | Chandler Unified | 401 S. Mcqueen Rd | 85225 | 480-883-5700 | 1139 | 20.5 |
| 09 | 12 | Pending | Chandler High | Chandler Unified | 350 N. Arizona Ave | 85225 | 480-812-7700 | 2612 | 20.1 |
| 09 | 12 | N/a | Evit Basha High | East Valley Institute Of Technology | 550 E. Chandler Heights Rd | 85249 | 480-883-4600 | 428 | N/a |
| 09 | 12 | N/a | Evit Chandler High | East Valley Institute Of Technology | 350 N. Arizona Ave | 85224 | 480-461-4101 | 1352 | N/a |
| 09 | 12 | Excelling | Hamilton High | Chandler Unified | 3700 S. Arizona Ave | 85248 | 480-883-5000 | 3156 | 21.2 |
| **GILBERT** | | | | | | | | | |
| PK | 06 | Excelling | Ashland Elementary | Gilbert Unified | 1945 S. Ashland Ranch Rd | 85296 | 480-917-9900 | 862 | 20.4 |
| PK | 06 | Performing | Burk Elementary | Gilbert Unified | 545 N. Burk St | 85234 | 480-926-3816 | 673 | 17.4 |
| PK | 06 | Excelling | Carol Rae Ranch Elementary | Gilbert Unified | 3777 E. Houston Ave | 85234 | 480-507-1359 | 968 | 21.1 |
| PK | 06 | Highly Performing | Gilbert Elementary | Gilbert Unified | 175 W. Elliott | 85233 | 480-892-8624 | 950 | 16.5 |
| PK | 06 | Excelling | Gps Traditional Academy | Gilbert Unified | 321 W. Juniper Ave | 85233 | 480-892-2805 | 552 | 17.3 |
| PK | 06 | Highly Performing | Houston Elementary | Gilbert Unified | 500 E. Houston Ave | 85234 | 480-497-9790 | 626 | 15.1 |
| PK | 06 | Excelling | Islands Elementary | Gilbert Unified | 245 S. Mcqueen Rd | 85233 | 480-497-0742 | 721 | 18.5 |
| PK | 06 | Highly Performing | Oak Tree Elementary | Gilbert Unified | 140 S. Gilbert Rd | 85294 | 480-632-4785 | 786 | 18.1 |
| PK | 06 | Excelling | Patterson Elementary | Gilbert Unified | 1211 E. Guadalupe Rd | 85234 | 480-892-2803 | 624 | 18.2 |
| PK | 06 | Excelling | Playa Del Rey Elementary | Gilbert Unified | 550 N. Horne St | 85233 | 480-892-7810 | 862 | 19.3 |
| PK | 06 | Excelling | Sonoma Ranch Elementary | Gilbert Unified | 601 N. Key Biscayne | 85234 | 480-497-9343 | 792 | 19.5 |
| PK | 06 | Excelling | Spectrum Elementary | Gilbert Unified | 2846 S. Spectrum Way | 85296 | 480-917-0117 | 521 | 16 |
| PK | 06 | Excelling | Val Vista Lakes Elementary | Gilbert Unified | 1030 N. Blue Grotto | 85234 | 480-926-6301 | 753 | 19.1 |
| PK | 08 | Highly Performing | Pioneer Elementary | Gilbert Unified | 1535 N. Greenfield Rd | 85234 | 480-892-2022 | 673 | 15.8 |

*EAST VALLEY*

**EAST VALLEY**

| Grade | | Rating | School | District | Address | Zip | Phone | Enroll. | Ratio |
|---|---|---|---|---|---|---|---|---|---|
| | | | | ...ngley Unified | 3445 E. Calistoga | 85297 | 480-279-7000 | 1185 | 19.6 |
| KG | 05 | Excelling | West Gilbert Charter Elementary (C) | West Gilbert Charter Elementary, Inc. | 14919 S. Gilbert Rd | 85296 | 480-855-2700 | 423 | N/a |
| KG | 06 | Excelling | Benjamin Franklin Charter - Gilbert (C) | Benjamin Franklin Charter | 13732 E. Warner Rd | 85296 | 480-632-0722 | 500 | N/a |
| KG | 06 | Excelling | Finley Farms Elementary | Gilbert Unified | 375 S. Columbus Dr | 85296 | 480-507-1624 | 989 | 19.7 |
| KG | 06 | Highly Performing | Greenfield Elementary | Gilbert Unified | 2550 E. Elliot | 85234 | 480-892-2801 | 851 | 20.2 |
| KG | 06 | Highly Performing | Mesquite Elementary | Gilbert Unified | 1000 E. Mesquite St | 85296 | 480-813-1240 | 756 | 17.4 |
| KG | 06 | Highly Performing | Settlers Point Elementary | Gilbert Unified | 423 E. Settler's Point Dr | 85296 | 480-507-1481 | 900 | 19 |
| KG | 08 | Performing Plus | Coronado Elementary | Higley Unified | 4333 S. Deanza Blvd | 85297 | 480-279-6900 | 872 | 19.8 |
| KG | 08 | Excelling | Edu-prize, Inc. (C) | Edu-prize, Inc. | 580 W. Melody Ave | 85233 | 480-813-9537 | 1128 | n/a |
| 07 | 08 | Highly Performing | Gilbert Junior High | Gilbert Unified | 1016 N. Burk | 85234 | 480-892-6908 | 1002 | 19.3 |
| 07 | 08 | Excelling | Greenfield Junior High | Gilbert Unified | 101 S. Greenfield Rd | 85296 | 480-813-1770 | 1472 | 18.6 |
| 07 | 08 | Highly Performing | Mesquite Jr High | Gilbert Unified | 140 S. Gilbert Rd | 85296 | 480-926-1433 | 1034 | 17.8 |
| 09 | 12 | N/a | Desert Hills High (C) | Desert Hills Public Charter High | 1515 S. Val Vista Dr | 85296 | 480-813-1151 | 384 | N/a |
| 09 | 12 | Excelling | Gilbert High | Gilbert Unified | 1101 E. Elliot Rd | 85296 | 480-497-0177 | 2996 | 18.2 |
| 09 | 12 | Excelling | Highland High | Gilbert Unified | 140 S. Gilbert Rd | 85296 | 480-813-0051 | 2347 | 18.2 |
| 09 | 12 | Highly Performing | Higley High | Higley Unified | 4068 E. Pecos Rd | 85296 | 480-279-7300 | 1126 | 21.4 |
| 09 | 12 | Highly Performing | Mesquite High | Gilbert Unified | 500 S. Mcqueen Rd | 85233 | 480-632-4750 | 3034 | 17.5 |
| **QUEEN CREEK** | | | | | | | | | |
| PK | 05 | Highly Performing | Desert Mountain Elementary | Queen Creek Unified | 22301 S. Hawes | 85242 | 480-987-5912 | 356 | 16.6 |
| PK | 05 | Excelling | Jack Barnes Elementary | Queen Creek Unified | 20750 S. 214th St | 85242 | 480-987-7400 | 425 | 19.1 |
| PK | 05 | Highly Performing | Queen Creek Elementary | Queen Creek Unified | 23636 S. 204th St | 85242 | 480-987-5920 | 373 | 15.7 |
| PK | 08 | Performing | Kathryn Sue Simonton Elementary | J O Combs Elementary | 40300 N. Simonton Blvd | 85242 | 480-987-5330 | 607 | 19.9 |
| KG | 08 | Highly Performing | Benjamin Franklin Charter (C) | Benjamin Franklin Charter | 21151 Crisman Rd | 85242 | 480-987-0722 | 504 | N/a |
| 06 | 08 | Highly Performing | Queen Creek Middle | Queen Creek Unified | 20435 S. Ellsworth Rd | 85242 | 480-987-5940 | 577 | 17 |
| 09 | 12 | Performing Plus | Queen Creek High | Queen Creek Unified | 22149 E. Ocotillo | 85242 | 480-987-5973 | 785 | 18 |
| **TEMPE** | | | | | | | | | |
| PK | 05 | Excelling | Kyrene De Las Manitas | Kyrene Elementary | 1201 W Courtney Ln | 85284 | 480-783-2000 | 594 | 16.1 |
| PK | 05 | Highly Performing | Kyrene De Los Ninos | Kyrene Elementary | 1330 E. Dava Dr | 85283 | 480-783-3100 | 462 | 17.1 |
| KG | 05 | Performing Plus | Aguilar | Tempe Elementary | 5800 S. Forest Ave | 85283 | 480-897-2544 | 512 | 15.4 |
| KG | 05 | Performing | Arredondo Elementary | Tempe Elementary | 1330 E. Carson Dr | 85282 | 480-897-2744 | 427 | 17.1 |
| KG | 05 | Highly Performing | Broadmor Elementary | Tempe Elementary | 311 Aepli Dr | 85282 | 480-967-6599 | 532 | 18.9 |
| KG | 05 | Highly Performing | Bustoz School | Tempe Elementary | 2020 E. Carson Dr | 85282 | 480-897-2955 | 347 | 16 |

| Low Grade | High Grade | Achievement Profiles | School Name | District | Street Address | Zip | Phone | Students | Student/Teach Ratio |
|---|---|---|---|---|---|---|---|---|---|
| KG | 05 | Excelling | C I Waggoner | Kyrene Elementary | 1050 E. Carver Rd | 85284 | 480-783-1900 | 624 | 17.9 |
| KG | 05 | Performing Plus | Carminati | Tempe Elementary | 4001 S. Mcallister Ave | 85282 | 480-784-4484 | 452 | 16.4 |
| KG | 05 | Performing Plus | Curry Elementary | Tempe Elementary | 1974 E. Meadow Dr | 85282 | 480-967-8336 | 583 | 16.3 |
| KG | 05 | Performing | Evans Elementary | Tempe Elementary | 4525 S. College Ave | 85282 | 480-839-8489 | 448 | 15.7 |
| KG | 05 | Performing | Flora Thew Elementary | Tempe Elementary | 2130 E. Howe Ave | 85281 | 480-894-4574 | 608 | 15.4 |
| KG | 05 | Performing | Fuller Elementary | Tempe Elementary | 1975 E. Cornell Dr | 85283 | 480-897-6228 | 441 | 14.8 |
| KG | 05 | Performing Plus | Holdeman Elementary | Tempe Elementary | 1326 W. 18th St | 85281 | 480-966-9934 | 602 | 16.5 |
| KG | 05 | Highly Performing | Hudson Elementary | Tempe Elementary | 1325 E. Malibu Dr | 85282 | 480-897-6608 | 503 | 15.8 |
| KG | 05 | Excelling | Kyrene De La Mariposa | Kyrene Elementary | 50 E. Knox Rd | 85284 | 480-783-3200 | 518 | 18.5 |
| KG | 05 | Highly Performing | Kyrene Del Norte | Kyrene Elementary | 1331 E. Redfield Rd | 85283 | 480-783-3300 | 413 | 12.6 |
| KG | 05 | Performing Plus | Laird Elementary | Tempe Elementary | 1500 N. Scovel St | 85281 | 480-941-2440 | 539 | 16.2 |
| KG | 05 | Highly Performing | Meyer Elementary | Tempe Elementary | 2615 S. Dorsey Ln | 85282 | 480-829-8002 | 400 | 16.6 |
| KG | 05 | Excelling | Rover Elementary | Tempe Elementary | 1300 E. Watson Dr | 85283 | 480-897-7122 | 531 | 16.2 |
| KG | 05 | Performing | Scales Professional Development | Tempe Elementary | 1115 W. 5th St | 85281 | 480-929-9909 | 490 | 16 |
| KG | 05 | Performing Plus | Wood School | Tempe Elementary | 727 W. Cornell Dr | 85283 | 480-838-0711 | 638 | 17.3 |
| 06 | 08 | Performing Plus | Connolly Middle | Tempe Elementary | 2002 E. Concorda Dr | 85282 | 480-967-8933 | 971 | 17.8 |
| 06 | 08 | Performing | Fees Middle | Tempe Elementary | 1600 E. Watson Dr | 85283 | 480-897-6063 | 1068 | 17.3 |
| 06 | 08 | Performing | Gilliland Middle | Tempe Elementary | 1025 S. Beck Ave | 85281 | 480-966-7114 | 1019 | 17.5 |
| 06 | 08 | Excelling | Kyrene Middle | Kyrene Elementary | 1050 E. Carver Rd | 85284 | 480-783-1000 | 1097 | 18.7 |
| 06 | 08 | Performing | Mckemy Middle | Tempe Elementary | 2250 S. College Ave | 85282 | 480-921-9003 | 952 | 15.5 |
| 09 | 12 | Excelling | Corona Del Sol High | Tempe Union High | 1001 E. Knox Rd | 85284 | 480-752-8888 | 2755 | 22 |
| 09 | 12 | Highly Performing | Marcos De Niza High | Tempe Union High | 6000 S. Lakeshore Dr | 85283 | 480-838-3200 | 1955 | 20.4 |
| 09 | 12 | Highly Performing | Mcclintock High | Tempe Union High | 1830 E. Del Rio Dr | 85282 | 480-839-4222 | 1797 | 18.7 |
| 09 | 12 | N/a | Tempe Accelerated High (C) | Tempe Accelerated Public Charter High | 5040 S. Price Rd | 85282 | 480-831-6057 | 445 | N/a |
| 09 | 12 | Performing | Tempe High | Tempe Union High | 1730 S. Mill Ave | 85281 | 480-967-1661 | 1363 | 17.1 |

**CAREFREE & CAVE CREEK**

| Low Grade | High Grade | Achievement Profiles | School Name | District | Street Address | Zip | Phone | Students | Student/Teach Ratio |
|---|---|---|---|---|---|---|---|---|---|
| PK | 05 | Highly Performing | Black Mountain Elementary | Cave Creek Unified | 33016 N. 60th St | 85327 | 480-575-2100 | 617 | 19.5 |
| PK | 05 | Excelling | Desert Sun Elementary | Cave Creek Unified | 27880 N. 64th St | 85327 | 480-575-2900 | 719 | 20.7 |
| KG | 05 | Highly Performing | Desert Willow Elementary | Cave Creek Unified | 4322 E. Desert Willow Pkwy | 85327 | 480-575-2800 | 708 | 21.1 |
| | | | | Cave Creek Unified | 5250 E. Montgomery Rd | 85327 | 480-437-3000 | 667 | 21.1 |

| GL | GH | Status | School | District | Address | Zip | Phone | Enroll | Ratio |
|---|---|---|---|---|---|---|---|---|---|
|  |  |  |  | Cave Creek Unified | 3341 N. 60th St | 85327 | 480-575-2300 | 663 | 20.1 |
| 06 | 08 | Highly Performing | Sonoran Trails Middle | Cave Creek Unified | 33606 N. 60th St | 85327 | 480-575-2200 | 612 | 18.7 |
| 08 | 12 | Excelling | Cactus Shadows High /psh | Cave Creek Unified | 5802 E. Dove Valley Rd | 85327 | 480-575-2400 | 1402 | 20.4 |
| **FOUNTAIN HILLS** | | | | | | | | | |
| UG | UG | N/a | Evit Fountain Hills Voc Ctr | East Valley Institute of Technology | 14605 N. Del Cambre | 85268 | 480-461-4101 | 383 | N/a |
| PK | 03 | N/a | Mcdowell Mountain Elementary | Fountain Hills Unified | 14825 N. Fayette Dr | 85268 | 480-664-5200 | 449 | 17.5 |
| KG | 08 | Highly Performing | Fountain Hills Charter (C) | Fountain Hills Charter | 15055 N. Fountain Hills Blvd | 85268 | 480-837-0046 | 243 | N/a |
| 03 | 06 | Highly Performing | Four Peaks Elementary | Fountain Hills Unified | 17300 E. Calaveras | 85268 | 480-664-5100 | 486 | 17.6 |
| 06 | 08 | Highly Performing | Fountain Hills Middle | Fountain Hills Unified | 15414 N. McDowell Mtn Rd | 85268 | 480-664-5400 | 719 | 18.9 |
| 09 | 12 | Highly Performing | Fountain Hills High | Fountain Hills Unified | 16100 E. Palisades Blvd | 85268 | 480-664-5500 | 888 | 19.8 |
| **PARADISE VALLEY** | | | | | | | | | |
| PK | 06 | Excelling | Cherokee Elementary | Scottsdale Unified | 8801 N. 56th St | 85253 | 480-484-8700 | 638 | 18.5 |
| KG | 06 | Excelling | Kiva Elementary | Scottsdale Unified | 6911 E. McDonald Dr | 85253 | 480-484-2200 | 705 | 19.5 |
| 09 | 12 | Excelling | Chaparral High | Scottsdale Unified | 6935 E. Gold Dust | 85253 | 480-484-6500 | 1795 | 21.3 |
| **AVONDALE** | | | | | | | | | |
| PK | 02 | N/a | Avondale Elementary | Avondale Elementary | 45 W. 3rd Ave | 85323 | 623-772-5100 | 905 | 20.6 |
| PK | 08 | Highly Performing | Garden Lakes Elementary | Pendergast Elementary | 10825 W. Garden Lakes Pkwy | 85323 | 623-772-2520 | 1129 | 19.8 |
| PK | 08 | Performing Plus | Rio Vista Elementary | Pendergast Elementary | 10237 W. Encanto Blvd | 85323 | 623-772-2670 | 630 | 18.8 |
| KG | 08 | Performing Plus | Canyon Breeze Elementary | Pendergast Elementary | 11675 W. Encant Blvd | 85323 | 623-772-2610 | 781 | 21.2 |
| KG | 08 | Performing Plus | Collier Elementary | Littleton Elementary | 350 S. 118th Ave | 85323 | 623-478-5900 | 922 | 23.1 |
| 05 | 06 | Performing | Lattie Coor | Avondale Elementary | 220 W. La Canada Blvd | 85323 | 623-772-4400 | 582 | 17.1 |
| 07 | 08 | N/a | Avondale Middle | Avondale Elementary | 1406 N. Central Ave | 85323 | 623-772-4505 | 934 | 20.8 |
| 09 | 12 | Performing | Agua Fria High | Agua Fria Union High | 530 E. Riley Dr | 85323 | 623-932-7301 | 1678 | 22.2 |
| 09 | 12 | N/a | Estrella High (C) | Estrella Public Charter High | 510 N. Central | 85323 | 623-932-6561 | 471 | N/a |
| 09 | 12 | Highly Performing | Westview High | Tolleson Union High | 10850 W. Garden Lakes Pkwy | 85353 | 623-877-2438 | 2385 | 21.9 |
| **BUCKEYE** | | | | | | | | | |
| PK | 08 | Performing Plus | Buckeye Elementary | Buckeye Elementary | 210 S. 6th St | 85326 | 623-386-4487 | 1077 | 19.5 |
| PK | 08 | Performing Plus | Liberty Elementary | Liberty Elementary | 19818 W. Hwy 85 | 85326 | 623-327-2810 | 748 | 17.6 |
| KG | 06 | Underperforming | Bales Elementary | Buckeye Elementary | 210 S. 6th St | 85326 | 623-386-4487 | 389 | 17.1 |
| KG | 08 | Performing Plus | Rainbow Valley Elementary | Liberty Elementary | 19716 W. Narramore Rd | 85326 | 623-386-5180 | 588 | 15.7 |
| 09 | 12 | Performing | Buckeye Union High | Buckeye Union High | 902 Eason Ave | 85326 | 623-386-9714 | 1078 | 19.1 |
| **GOODYEAR** | | | | | | | | | |
| PK | 06 | Performing | Wildflower | Avondale Elementary | 325 S. Wildflower Dr | 85338 | 623-772-5200 | 606 | 20.9 |

NORTH EAST VALLEY

WEST VALLEY

**WEST VALLEY**

| Low Grade | High Grade | Achievement Profiles | School Name | District | Street Address | Zip | Phone | Students | Student/Teach Ratio |
|---|---|---|---|---|---|---|---|---|---|
| KG | 06 | Performing Plus | Desert Star | Avondale Elementary | 2131 W. 157th Ave | 85338 | 623-772-4600 | 819 | 21.8 |
| KG | 08 | Highly Performing | Estrella Mountain Elementary | Liberty Elementary | 10301 S. San Miguel | 85338 | 623-327-2820 | 734 | 18.1 |
| 03 | 04 | Performing | Pioneer | Avondale Elementary | 540 E. La Pasada | 85338 | 623-772-4300 | 603 | 20.1 |
| 09 | 12 | Performing Plus | Desert Edge High School | Agua Fria Union High | 15778 W. Yuma Road | 85338 | 623-932-7500 | 354 | 22.4 |
| 09 | 12 | Performing Plus | Millennium High | Agua Fria Union High | 14802 W. Wigwam Blvd | 85338 | 623-932-7200 | 1625 | 23.5 |
| **LAVEEN** | | | | | | | | | |
| PK | 08 | Performing | Laveen Elementary | Laveen Elementary | 5001 W. Dobbins Rd | 85339 | 602-237-9110 | 760 | 19.3 |
| KG | 12 | N/a | Country Gardens Charter (C) | Higley Unified | 6313 W. Southern Ave | 85339 | 602-237-3741 | 348 | N/a |
| 07 | 08 | Performing Plus | Vista Del Sur Middle | Laveen Elementary | 3908 W. South Mountain Ave | 85339 | 602-237-3046 | 425 | 20 |
| 09 | 12 | Performing | Cesar Chavez High | Phoenix Union High | 3921 W. Baseline Rd | 85339 | 602-764-4000 | 2370 | 19.4 |
| **LITCHFIELD PARK** | | | | | | | | | |
| PK | 06 | Excelling | Litchfield Elementary | Litchfield Elementary | 13825 W. Wigwam Blvd | 85340 | 623-535-6100 | 1154 | 24.6 |
| PK | 06 | Excelling | Palm Valley Elementary | Litchfield Elementary | 2801 N. 135th Ave | 85340 | 623-535-6400 | 809 | 20 |
| KG | 06 | Performing Plus | Corte Sierra Elementary | Litchfield Elementary | 3300 N. Santa Fe Tr | 85340 | 623-547-1000 | 883 | 22.4 |
| KG | 06 | Performing | Scott L Libby Elementary | Litchfield Elementary | 18701 W. Thomas Ave | 85340 | 623-535-6200 | 570 | 19.3 |
| KG | 08 | Performing Plus | Rancho Santa Fe Elementary | Litchfield Elementary | 2150 Rancho Santa Fe Blvd | 85340 | 623-535-6500 | 697 | 20.5 |
| 06 | 08 | Performing Plus | Western Sky Middle | Litchfield Elementary | 4095 N. 144th Ave | 85340 | 623-535-6300 | 972 | 22.3 |
| 06 | 08 | Performing Plus | Wigwam Creek Middle | Litchfield Elementary | 4150 N. 127th Ave | 85340 | 623-547-1100 | 1146 | 21.8 |
| **TOLLESON** | | | | | | | | | |
| PK | 08 | Underperforming | Union Elementary School | Union Elementary School | 3834 S 91st Ave | 85353 | 623-478-5000 | 372 | 21.9 |
| PK | 08 | Performing Plus | Porfirio H. Gonzales Elementary | Tolleson Elementary | 9401 W. Garfield | 85353 | 623-907-5181 | 795 | 17.5 |
| KG | 08 | Underperforming | Arizona Desert Elementary School | Tolleson Elementary | 8803 W. Van Buren St | 85353 | 623-907-5260 | 441 | 18.4 |
| 09 | 12 | Performing Plus | La Joya Community High | Tolleson Union High | 11650 W. Whyman Ave | 85353 | 623-478-4400 | 1054 | 19.9 |
| 09 | 12 | Performing Plus | Tolleson Union High | Tolleson Union High | 9419 W. Van Buren | 85353 | 623-478-4200 | 2048 | 19.4 |
| **EL MIRAGE** | | | | | | | | | |
| PK | 08 | Performing | Dysart Elementary | Dysart Unified | 11405 N. Dysart Rd | 85335 | 623-876-7100 | 1340 | 21.8 |
| PK | 08 | Performing Plus | El Mirage | Dysart Unified | 13500 N. El Mirage Rd | 85335 | 623-876-7200 | 897 | 19.3 |
| PK | 08 | Underperforming | Surprise Elementary | Dysart Unified | 12907 W. Greenway Rd | 85335 | 623-876-7400 | 850 | 18.9 |
| 09 | 12 | Performing | Dysart High | Dysart Unified | 11425 N. Dysart Rd | 85335 | 623-876-7500 | 1270 | 18.4 |

| | | | | | | | | |
|---|---|---|---|---|---|---|---|---|
| PK | Excelling | Arrowhead Elementary | Deer Valley Unified | 7490 W. Union Hills Dr | 85308 | 623-376-4100 | 896 | 19.2 |
| PK | Performing | Arroyo | Washington Elementary | 4535 W. Cholla | 85304 | 602-896-5100 | 455 | 15.9 |
| PK | Performing | Bellair Elementary | Deer Valley Unified | 4701 W. Grovers Ave | 85308 | 602-467-5700 | 707 | 18.9 |
| PK | Excelling | Copper Creek Elementary | Deer Valley Unified | 7071 W. Hillcrest Blvd | 85310 | 623-376-3900 | 831 | 18.7 |
| PK | Performing | Glenn F Burton | Glendale Elementary | 4801 W. Maryland Ave | 85301 | 623-842-8270 | 567 | 19.7 |
| PK | Excelling | Greenbrier Elementary | Deer Valley Unified | 6150 W. Greenbriar Dr | 85308 | 602-467-5500 | 563 | 14.7 |
| PK | Highly Performing | Las Brisas Elementary | Deer Valley Unified | 5805 W. Alameda | 85310 | 623-445-5500 | 767 | 18.4 |
| PK | Performing Plus | Mirage Elementary | Deer Valley Unified | 3910 W. Grovers | 85308 | 602-467-5300 | 731 | 16.1 |
| PK | Highly Performing | Mountain Shadows Elementary | Deer Valley Unified | 19602 N. 45th Ave | 85308 | 623-445-4300 | 937 | 20.2 |
| PK | Highly Performing | Park Meadows Elementary | Deer Valley Unified | 20012 N. 35th Ave | 85308 | 623-445-4100 | 736 | 19.2 |
| PK | Performing | Sunburst | Washington Elementary | 14218 N. 47th Ave | 85306 | 602-896-6400 | 776 | 19.3 |
| PK | Performing Plus | Sunset | Washington Elementary | 4626 W. Mountain View Rd | 85302 | 602-347-3300 | 560 | 22.2 |
| PK | Performing | Barcelona Middle | Alhambra Elementary | 6130 N. 44th Ave | 85301 | 623-842-8616 | 917 | 18.3 |
| PK | Excelling | Canyon Elementary | Peoria Unified | 5490 W. Paradise ln | 85306 | 623-412-5050 | 478 | 12.2 |
| PK | Performing | Coyote Ridge | Glendale Elementary | 7677 W. Bethany | 85303 | 623-842-8215 | 945 | 21.5 |
| PK | Performing | Desert Garden Elementary | Glendale Elementary | 7020 W. Ocotillo Rd | 85303 | 623-842-8214 | 1041 | 23.8 |
| PK | Performing | Desert Mirage Elementary | Pendergast Elementary | 8605 W. Maryland Ave | 85305 | 623-772-2550 | 1043 | 20.5 |
| PK | Performing | Desert Palms Elementary | Peoria Unified | 11441 N. 55th Ave | 85304 | 623-412-4600 | 803 | 18 |
| PK | Performing | Discovery | Glendale Elementary | 7910 W. Maryland Ave | 85303 | 623-842-8213 | 837 | 20.3 |
| PK | Performing Plus | Foothills Elementary | Peoria Unified | 15808 N. 63rd Ave | 85306 | 623-412-4625 | 869 | 18.6 |
| PK | Performing Plus | Glendale American | Glendale Elementary | 8530 N. 55th Ave | 85302 | 623-842-8280 | 964 | 20.1 |
| PK | Performing | Glendale Landmark Middle | Glendale Elementary | 5730 W. Myrtle Ave | 85301 | 623-842-8304 | 1004 | 17.7 |
| PK | Performing | Isaac E Imes | Glendale Elementary | 6625 N. 56th Ave | 85301 | 623-842-8220 | 546 | 17.4 |
| PK | Performing | Luke School | Dysart Unified | 7300 N. Dysart Rd | 85307 | 623-876-7300 | 901 | 20.5 |
| PK | Performing | Melvin E Sine | Glendale Elementary | 4932 W. Myrtle | 85301 | 623-842-8240 | 912 | 22.1 |
| PK | Highly Performing | Sahuaro Ranch | Peoria Unified | 10401 N. 63rd Ave | 85302 | 623-412-4775 | 782 | 16.2 |
| PK | Excelling | Sierra Verde Elementary | Deer Valley Unified | 7241 W. Rose Garden Ln | 85308 | 623-376-4800 | 926 | 20.4 |
| PK | Performing Plus | Sonoran Sky Elementary | Pendergast Elementary | 10150 W. Missouri Ave | 85307 | 623-772-2640 | 880 | 18.3 |
| PK | Highly Performing | Stetson Hills Elementary | Deer Valley Unified | 25475 N. Stetson Hills Loop | 85310 | 623-445-5300 | 1128 | 22.6 |
| KG | Performing | Carol G. Peck Elementary | Alhambra Elementary | 5810 N. 49th Ave | 85301 | 623-842-3889 | 736 | 20.4 |
| KG | Performing | William C Jack | Glendale Elementary | 6600 W. Missouri Ave | 85301 | 623-842-8250 | 964 | 25.2 |

NORTH WEST VALLEY

# Schools

## NORTH WEST VALLEY

| Low Grade | High Grade | Achievement Profiles | School Name | District | Street Address | Zip | Phone | Students | Student/Teach Ratio |
|---|---|---|---|---|---|---|---|---|---|
| KG | 06 | Excelling | Challenge Charter | Challenge, Inc. | 5801 W. Greenbriar Dr | 85308 | 602-938-5411 | 577 | N/a |
| KG | 06 | Excelling | Desert Sage Elementary | Deer Valley Unified | 4035 W. Alameda | 85310 | 623-445-4700 | 878 | 20.7 |
| KG | 06 | Excelling | Legend Springs Elementary | Deer Valley Unified | 21150 N. Arrowhead Loop Rd | 85308 | 623-376-4500 | 694 | 19.3 |
| KG | 08 | Excelling | Copperwood | Peoria Unified | 11232 N. 65th Ave | 85304 | 623-412-4650 | 825 | 17.9 |
| KG | 08 | Performing Plus | Desert Heights Charter (C) | Partnership With Parents | 5821 W. Beverly Ln | 85306 | 602-896-2900 | 354 | N/a |
| KG | 08 | Underperforming | Desert Spirit | Glendale Elementary | 7355 W. Orangewood | 85303 | 623-842-8216 | 629 | 19.4 |
| KG | 08 | Highly Performing | Desert Valley Elementary | Peoria Unified | 12901 N. 63rd Ave | 85304 | 623-412-4750 | 722 | 14.4 |
| KG | 08 | Performing | Harold W Smith | Glendale Elementary | 6534 N. 63rd Ave | 85301 | 623-842-8230 | 889 | 21 |
| KG | 08 | Highly Performing | Heritage | Peoria Unified | 5312 W. Mountain Vw | 85302 | 623-412-4525 | 861 | 19.3 |
| KG | 08 | Highly Performing | Highland Lakes | Deer Valley Unified | 19000 N. 63rd Ave | 85308 | 623-376-4300 | 1050 | 20.6 |
| KG | 08 | Performing Plus | Horizon | Glendale Elementary | 8520 N. 47th Ave | 85302 | 623-842-8200 | 865 | 19.8 |
| KG | 08 | Highly Performing | Kachina | Peoria Unified | 5304 W. Crocus | 85306 | 623-412-4500 | 670 | 15.5 |
| KG | 08 | Highly Performing | Marshall Ranch Elementary | Peoria Unified | 12995 N. Marshall Ranch Dr | 85304 | 623-486-6450 | 864 | 18.9 |
| KG | 08 | Highly Performing | Pioneer | Peoria Unified | 6315 W. Port Au Prince | 85306 | 623-412-4550 | 787 | 16.8 |
| KG | 08 | Performing Plus | Sweetwater | Washington Elementary | 4602 W. Sweetwater | 85304 | 602-896-6500 | 465 | 13.7 |
| 02 | 08 | Performing | Bicentennial North | Glendale Elementary | 7237 W. Missouri Ave | 85303 | 623-842-8290 | 759 | 20 |
| 04 | 08 | Performing Plus | Don Mensendick | Glendale Elementary | 5535 N. 67th Ave | 85301 | 623-842-8260 | 672 | 19.5 |
| 06 | 08 | Performing | Challenger Middle | Glendale Elementary | 6905 W. Maryland Ave | 85303 | 623-842-8314 | 1100 | 20.4 |
| 07 | 08 | Performing | Desert Sky Middle | Deer Valley Unified | 5130 N. Grovers Ave | 85308 | 602-467-6500 | 1045 | 20.7 |
| 07 | 08 | Excelling | Hillcrest Middle | Deer Valley Unified | 22833 N. 71st Ave | 85310 | 623-376-3300 | 1015 | 23.8 |
| 09 | 11 | Highly Performing | Sandra Day O'Connor High | Deer Valley Unified | 25250 N. 35th Ave | 85310 | 623-445-7100 | 1666 | 24.4 |
| 09 | 12 | Performing | Apollo High | Glendale Union High | 8045 N. 47th Ave | 85302 | 623-435-6300 | 1734 | 23 |
| 09 | 12 | Highly Performing | Cactus High | Peoria Unified | 6330 W. Greenway | 85306 | 623-412-5000 | 1829 | 19.9 |
| 09 | 12 | Highly Performing | Deer Valley High | Deer Valley Unified | 18424 N. 51st Ave | 85308 | 602-467-6700 | 2188 | 22.7 |
| 09 | 12 | Performing Plus | Glendale High | Glendale Union High | 6216 W. Glendale Ave | 85301 | 623-435-6200 | 1495 | 21.3 |
| 09 | 12 | Performing Plus | Independence High | Glendale Union High | 6602 N. 75th Ave | 85303 | 623-435-6100 | 1706 | 21.3 |
| 09 | 12 | Excelling | Ironwood High | Peoria Unified | 6051 W. Sweetwater Ave | 85304 | 623-486-6400 | 2119 | 20.7 |
| 09 | 12 | Excelling | Mountain Ridge High | Deer Valley Unified | 22800 N. 67th Ave | 85310 | 623-376-3000 | 2746 | 26.9 |

## PEORIA

| Low Grade | High Grade | Achievement Profiles | School Name | District | Street Address | Zip | Phone | Students | Student/Teach Ratio |
|---|---|---|---|---|---|---|---|---|---|
| PK | 08 | Performing | Alta Loma | Peoria Unified | 9750 N. 87th Ave | 85345 | 623-412-4575 | 976 | 18.5 |

| | | Status | School | District | Address | Zip | Phone | Enrollment | Ratio |
|---|---|---|---|---|---|---|---|---|---|
| PK | 08 | Performing | Cotton Boll | Peoria Unified | 8540 W. Butler Dr | 85345 | 623-412-4700 | 902 | 19.4 |
| PK | 08 | Performing Plus | Desert Harbor Elementary | Peoria Unified | 15585 N. 91st Ave | 85382 | 623-486-6200 | 1008 | 19.7 |
| PK | 08 | Highly Performing | Parkridge Elementary | Peoria Unified | 9970 W. Beardsley Rd | 85382 | 623-412-5400 | 518 | 18 |
| PK | 08 | Pending | Paseo Verde Elementary | Peoria Unified | 7880 W. Greenway Rd | 85381 | 623-412-5075 | 936 | 17.6 |
| PK | 08 | Performing Plus | Peoria Elementary | Peoria Unified | 11501 N. 79th Ave | 85345 | 623-412-4450 | 801 | 15.6 |
| PK | 08 | Performing Plus | Sky View Elementary | Peoria Unified | 8624 W. Sweetwater | 85381 | 623-412-4850 | 680 | 14.4 |
| PK | 08 | Performing Plus | Sundance Elementary | Peoria Unified | 7051 W. Cholla St | 85345 | 623-412-4675 | 777 | 18.2 |
| KG | 08 | Performing | Country Meadows Elementary | Peoria Unified | 8409 N. 111th Ave | 85345 | 623-412-5200 | 1344 | 20 |
| KG | 08 | Highly Performing | Coyote Hills Elementary | Peoria Unified | 21180 N. 87th Ave | 85382 | 623-412-5225 | 1466 | 22.7 |
| KG | 08 | Highly Performing | Frontier Elementary | Peoria Unified | 21258 N. 81st Ave | 85382 | 623-412-4900 | 1424 | 22.4 |
| KG | 08 | Performing | Ira A Murphy | Peoria Unified | 7231 W. North Ln | 85345 | 623-412-4475 | 723 | 18.1 |
| KG | 08 | Excelling | Oakwood Elementary | Peoria Unified | 12900 N. 71st Ave | 85381 | 623-412-4725 | 798 | 17.9 |
| KG | 08 | Highly Performing | Oasis Elementary | Peoria Unified | 7841 W. Sweetwater | 85381 | 623-412-4800 | 828 | 20.6 |
| KG | 08 | Performing | Paramount Academy | Paramount Education Studies Inc. | 8987 W Olive Ave | 85345 | 623-977-0614 | 400 | N/a |
| KG | 08 | Performing Plus | Santa Fe Elementary | Peoria Unified | 9880 N. 77th Ave | 85345 | 623-486-6475 | 898 | 17.6 |
| KG | 08 | Performing Plus | Sun Valley | Peoria Unified | 8361 N. 95th Ave | 85345 | 623-412-4825 | 1022 | 19.7 |
| KG | 08 | Highly Performing | Terramar Elementary | Deer Valley Unified | 7000 W. Happy Valley Rd | 85383 | 623-445-7600 | 648 | 20.3 |
| 09 | 12 | Excelling | Centennial High | Peoria Unified | 14388 N. 79th Ave | 85381 | 623-412-4400 | 2048 | 21.9 |
| 09 | 12 | N/a | Peoria Accelerated High (C) | Peoria Accelerated Public Charter High | 8885 N. Peoria Ave | 85345 | 623-979-0031 | 571 | N/a |
| 09 | 12 | Highly Performing | Peoria High | Peoria Unified | 11200 N. 83rd Ave | 85345 | 623-486-6300 | 2750 | 19.8 |
| 09 | 12 | Excelling | Sunrise Mountain High | Peoria Unified | 21200 N. 83rd Ave | 85382 | 623-487-5125 | 2305 | 22.2 |

**SUN CITY**

| | | Status | School | District | Address | Zip | Phone | Enrollment | Ratio |
|---|---|---|---|---|---|---|---|---|---|
| KG | 08 | Performing Plus | Zuni Hills Elementary | Peoria Unified | 10851 W. Williams | 85373 | 623-412-5275 | 1016 | 20.8 |

**SURPRISE**

| | | Status | School | District | Address | Zip | Phone | Enrollment | Ratio |
|---|---|---|---|---|---|---|---|---|---|
| PK | 08 | Performing Plus | Kingswood Elementary | Dysart Unified | 15150 W. Mondell Rd | 85374 | 623-876-7600 | 1013 | 20.7 |
| KG | 08 | Performing | Ashton Ranch Elementary | Dysart Unified | 14898 W. Acoma Dr | 85379 | 623-523-8300 | 991 | 28.5 |
| KG | 08 | Performing Plus | Cimarron Springs Elementary | Dysart Unified | 17032 W. Surprise Farms Loop | 85374 | 623-523-8600 | 571 | 19.5 |
| KG | 08 | Performing | Countryside Elementary | Dysart Unified | 15034 N. Parkview Pl | 85379 | 623-876-7800 | 1152 | 22.2 |
| KG | 08 | Performing Plus | Paradise Education Center | Paragon Management, Inc. | 15533 W. Paradise Ln | 85374 | 623-975-2646 | 899 | N/a |
| KG | 08 | Performing Plus | West Point Elementary | Dysart Unified | 13700 W. Greenway Rd | 85374 | 623-876-7700 | 1190 | 21.5 |
| 09 | 12 | Performing Plus | Willow Canyon High | Dysart Unified | 17901 W. Lundberg St | 85374 | 623-523-8000 | 858 | 22.6 |

**NORTH WEST VALLEY**

# Schools in the Spotlight

Schools

The Valley has some excellent public, private and charter schools — several are even nationally recognized. With the open enrollment laws, a little luck and a large bank account for the private schools, your child could attend any of them.

In addition to consistent and outstanding academic records, the following schools either have unique educational programs or extracurricular opportunities that are a cut above. The schools are diverse: public and private, west side and East Valley, traditional and not so traditional. Unfortunately, not all of the Valley's excellent schools could be featured here, so many unmentioned options are available for those looking beyond their neighborhood school.

## Public Schools

**Alhambra Traditional School, 3736 W. Osborn Rd., Phoenix, 85019 (602) 484-8816, www.alhambra.k12.az.us**

Alhambra Traditional School considers itself "the best alternative" to standard public schools. A public school itself within the Alhambra Elementary District, Alhambra Traditional School is a back-to-basics program that promotes academic excellence through a traditional curriculum for kindergarten through eighth grade students.

There are no parents sitting on the sidelines at Alhambra Traditional School. Parents and staff work together to develop curriculum, choose textbooks, and provide educational direction. Parents are encouraged to volunteer in the classroom, at PTO-sponsored events, and on committees. In fact, the school employs a part-time volunteer coordinator to ensure that parents can be involved.

Alhambra Traditional School also offers parents a "parent's academy" with classes that relate to school curriculum and a resource center where parents can check out materials (flashcards, etc.) to help students master the basic skills they need to know. As part of the school's plan to create a partnership between home and school, parents can also check out computers to take home for students to use on assignments.

Alhambra Traditional School's goal is to shape students into graduates who are respectful, self-disciplined, conscientious, and motivated. With high standardized test scores and an "excelling" rating, the school seems to be meeting that goal.

## Basha High School, 5990 S. Val Vista Dr., Chandler, 85249
## (480) 224-2100, www.chandler.k12.az.us/bhs

What makes Basha High School unique is a partnership between the City of Chandler and the Chandler Unified School District that has resulted in enhanced facilities for the high school students. One example of this is the Basha Branch of the Chandler Public Library, located on the high school's campus, which serves both the high school students and public. Now, a $6.2 million aquatics center is set to open in May 2007 as a result of this partnership. Mesquite Groves Aquatic Center will feature a resort-style pool with waterfalls, rapids, two water slides and an interactive water feature for public use and an eight-lane, 25-yard pool for high school practices and meets. The complex will be built on six acres directly west of the campus.

Opened in 2002, Basha High School is the district's newest school. The 2005/2006 school year is the first that all four grade levels have been on campus and already the school is approximately 300 students over capacity. Students complain about crowded hallways at this "excelling" school.

The growth has also impacted the school's sports teams, which have moved from Division 4A to 5A in 2005. Many teams, like the school's football team, are playing their first year with seniors. Although many of the teams are doing well, it may be years before the athletics department takes root and flourishes.

With eight computer labs and a media studio, Basha High School is able to provide career-oriented classes like TV production, digital imaging, marketing, and Web design. The school also offers culinary arts, fashion design, and medical professions classes.

## Chaparral High School, 6935 E. Gold Dust Ave., Scottsdale, 85253
## (480) 484-6500, www.susd.org/chaparral/default.asp

Chaparral High School is representative of most of the schools in the Scottsdale Unified District. Standardized test results are high, students are motivated, and the school is nationally recognized. *Newsweek* recently listed Chaparral as one of the top 1,000 schools in the United States.

The school emphasizes a college preparatory curriculum. Eighty percent of all seniors enroll in Advanced Placement (AP) courses, and Chaparral seniors take more than one third of all AP tests administered in the State. Chaparral's students—like those at Arcadia High School, the district's other "excelling" high school—score well above the State and national averages on SAT and ACT tests. Over 90 percent of Chaparral's graduates enroll in higher education, 71 percent in four-year universities.

Technology is important at Chaparral. In addition to the typical computer lab, the school has 24 computers available for use in the library. There is also an LCD projector and scanner available for student use. Beginning with the class of 2004, all students have needed to either pass a computer proficiency test or complete a computer basics course before graduation.

Approximately 1,800 students attend Chaparral. There are 19 intramural sports teams and more than 55 clubs. Some of the clubs—calculus club, chemistry club, and philosophy club, for example—reflect the school's strong academics. Many have an environmental bent, like Sierra Club, or are service-oriented clubs. There are also many one-of-a-kind clubs like the Simpsons appreciation club (yes, the cartoon), swing club for dancers, and free kosher lunch club that raises money for and provides free kosher lunches. The school also has one of four gay-straight alliance high school groups in the State.

## Desert Arroyo Middle School, 33401 N. 56th St., Cave Creek, 85331 (480) 575-2300

Desert Arroyo Middle School is one of three "excelling" schools in the Cave Creek Unified District (the rest are "highly performing"). These schools are rich in resources, Desert Arroyo in particular. Desert Arroyo has state-of-the-art technology, closed circuit TV, and a 20-acre desert education preserve on campus.

The school also has a unique approach to education. Desert Arroyo is a member of the Accelerated School Plus program that focuses on providing gifted-quality instruction for all students. Developed by Professor Henry M. Levin at Stanford University, the program is based on the premise that students thrive in an atmosphere of high expectations and engaging curriculum. Desert Arroyo treats all of its students as gifted students and teaches lesson plans based on students' interests.

Desert Arroyo has an art club, drama club and yearbook. Its music program includes a jazz band, a rock group, and a musical theater group. Athletics feature a three-season sports program.

Students attend Desert Arroyo from sixth through eighth grade. The school sends home weekly progress reports and has a homework hotline.

## Eagleridge Enrichment Program, 737 W. Guadalupe Rd., #113, Mesa, 85210 www.mpsaz.org/eagleridge

As its name suggests, Eagleridge Enrichment Program is a program, not a school, but for the homeschooling family, it's a must. Nearly 600 homeschooled children from throughout the Valley attend the program. Founded in 1996, Eagleridge provides its students enrichment and social opportunities while creating a supportive network for homeschooling parents.

Kindergarten through ninth grade students can participate in either the block program, the rotation program or a combination of both. The block program can be attended either as a one-day program on Monday or a two-day program on Tuesday and Thursday. Blocks (or electives) include Renaissance, math, architecture, band, Spanish, French, computer keyboarding, karate, dance, and aerobics. For ninth grade students, the block program expands to include science, algebra, world history/geography and English.

The rotation program can be attended either on Wednesday or Friday. Kindergarteners through second grade students actually remain in grade-level classes while third through eighth graders rotate through hour-long classes including art, science, music and computers. Seventh and eighth grade students have additional opportunities for coursework in problem solving or can attend student council.

The program has several additional benefits for participating families. Students go on field trips, and they can attend a Basic Skills Camp for third through eighth grade students. The camp provides additional instruction in math, reading and language skills in small groups. Through the program, parents have access to a curriculum room where textbooks and curricular materials can be checked out for use during home lessons.

To attend, the child must be homeschooled. (For more information on home schooling, visit www.maricopa.gov/schools.) Tuition is not charged, but an application must be completed.

## GPS Technology and Leadership Academy, 55 N. Greenfield Rd., Gilbert, AZ 85296 (480) 497-4024, www.gilbert.k12.az.us

"Integrity first, service before self, excellence in all we do"—these are the core values taught at the GPS Technology and Leadership Academy. The school is a partnership between the Gilbert Unified District (the "GPS" stands for Gilbert Public Schools) and the US Air Force. Opened in 2003 to ninth and 10th grade students, the academy will graduate its first seniors in 2005/2006.

Although the school provides a structured environment and strict discipline, it is not a public military school for wayward students. The school has a rigorous curriculum of English, math, science, social studies, and art. Students also participate in JROTC and technology classes as well as electives including Spanish, drill and ceremonies, calculus, and physics. For the past two years, the academy has earned an "excelling" rating.

The goal of the academy isn't necessarily to prepare students for a military career. Instead, the staff strives to prepare students for careers in "an ever-increasingly, technology-oriented work environment." Still, the academy has a military bent. Students wear academy uniforms and adhere to a strict dress code. On Tuesdays, they wear JROTC uniforms, that are provided by the Air Force.

To attend, students must have a GPA of 2.0 at their previous school and no major discipline referrals. In addition to completing an application, they must also write an essay on why they want to attend the academy.

Of special note for the student athlete: Currently, there is no athletic program at the academy, but students can compete at their neighborhood public school.

## Kyrene del Pueblo Middle School, 360 S. Twelve Oaks Blvd., Chandler, 85226 (480) 783-2400

It's hard to single out just one school in a district of outstanding schools; all six of the Kyrene Unified School District's middle schools are "excelling" schools. Still, Kyrene del Pueblo Middle School deserves special mention.

Like many of its district counterparts, Kyrene del Pueblo has multiple computer labs—in this case, four 32-station labs. These are equipped with new Dell 280's running Windows XP. Students have the opportunity to learn photo imaging and Web page development while also using presentation and animation software.

Kyrene del Pueblo offers many enrichment programs. The school has a jazz band, a show choir and an orchestra while the theater department has classes in playwriting, pantomime, improvisation and process drama courses. The art department has Native American and African art study courses as well as instruction in 3-D, clay, masks, watercolors, and drawing techniques. Sports are important, too. The school participates in cross country, volleyball, soccer, softball, basketball, cheer, track, and baseball.

For parents, Kyrene del Pueblo's parent education series offers programs on issues facing parents of middle school students. Recent topics have included drug-related issues, ADD/ADHD, and a course titled "Developing a Culture of Character in Your Home." Parents are often presented with opportunities to win gift baskets or receive freebies like drug test kits at these events.

Although Kyrene del Pueblo ranks among the Valley's best middle school/junior high schools, the district's other middle schools have very similar programs, and some programs that Kyrene del Pueblo does not. For example, Kyrene Akimel A-Al Middle School has a broadcasting club, Kyrene Centennial has a stock market math club and Kyrene Altadena's musical groups have earned in and out of state recognition.

## Magnet Traditional School, 2602 N. 23rd Ave., Phoenix, AZ 85009 (602) 257-6281, www.phxelem.k12.az.us

Commitment makes Magnet Traditional School one of the Valley's most successful urban schools. It begins with the school's staff, which is committed to providing an "A+ education for all students." The staff's goal is to become an "excelling" school although it has been consistently rated as "highly performing" in recent years.

Parents make a commitment, too, by signing a contract that they will attend all parent conferences, volunteer a minimum of 10 hours, and attend a minimum of seven PTO meetings. A parent's failure to fulfill these obligations will result in the student being removed from Magnet Traditional School.

Students are also required to sign a contract. The student contract commits the student to bringing all notes to and from school and adhering to the dress code. Although students wear uniforms, the code is detailed and specific. For example, in the winter, students can only wear button down cardigans in the classroom, no pullover sweaters. If their clothes have belt loops, students must wear a belt. It's no surprise that extreme hairstyles or colors are not permitted, but colored contacts and make-up, including foundation, are not allowed either.

Magnet Traditional School's strict approach with parents, students and staff earns it high marks with many Phoenicians. The school provides a back-to-basics education in a highly structured classroom environment for kindergarten through eighth grade. Students have nightly homework beginning in kindergarten. To maximize educational opportunities, Magnet Traditional School has a longer school day and school year than other schools in the Phoenix Elementary School District.

### Mountain Ridge High School, 22800 N. 67th Ave., Glendale, 85310 (623) 376-3000, www.mrhs.dvusd.org

Students at Mountain Ridge High School strive to "Live Above the Line." What began as a character development program has evolved into a service-oriented movement into the community. "Living Above the Line" characterizes Mountain Ridge High School, whose mission is not only to graduate adults prepared for success but ones prepared to contribute positively to society. Students learn in class about the power of one individual to make a difference (in history, for example) and put that idea into practice by participating in projects like building a "Habitat for Humanity" home, picking citrus to support the Westside Food Bank or gathering goods for the T.J. Pappas clothing drive.

Academics do not take a backseat to service at this "excelling" school. Twenty-seven percent of the Class of 2005 received scholarships for a total of $6.3 million received. The Class also had two National Merit Finalists and three Academy appointments (US Air Force Academy, US Naval Academy, US Military Academy). Advanced placement courses are available in subjects ranging from physics and calculus to studio art. Mountain Ridge also partners with Rio Salado Community College to offer dual enrollment courses where students can concurrently earn high school and college credits.

Mountain Ridge has a strong athletic program of traditional sports like football, baseball, basketball, and soccer, to name a few. Regional and State tournament appearances are the norm with 13 regional championship teams in 2004. Ten students in the Class of 2005 received Division 1 athletic scholarships.

Mountain Ridge celebrates its 10th anniversary this year. It has a media center, a technology plaza, and a mobile computer lab with 19 iBook laptops. Clubs include such diverse offerings as an athletic trainers club, clay club, and ice hockey club.

### Westview High School, 10850 W. Garden Lakes Parkway, Avondale, AZ 85323 (623) 877-2438, www.tuhsd.org/WHS

Although it might have been just one among many outstanding schools in Scottsdale or the East Valley, Westview High School stands out as one of the West Valley's better high schools. Emphasizing a "real world curriculum," Westview is pledged to the personal, social and intellectual growth of every student, and that has led the way to ever improving standardized test results. The school is ranked as "highly performing."

Westview offers traditional extracurricular activities including speech and debate, newspaper, and a drama club/theatre company. For the music lover, there is band, choir and a music club. There's even the NASA Science club that worked to design a packaging system for Pringle potato chips. Several of the clubs are career-oriented. A culinary arts club explores the food service/hospitality industry, the Distributive Education Clubs

of America (DECA) explores marketing and distribution, and the fashion plus club explores the fashion industry.

Athletics are strong at Westview, too. The school has 42 teams in 12 sports including football, baseball, soccer, rugby, and basketball. Many of these teams compete in State championship tournaments. In recent years, the pom and cheer squads have won State championship and runner-up titles, respectively.

Of course, you can't mention Westview without mentioning the Marine Junior ROTC program, one of the most successful in the United States. It has received national recognition, including designation as the best Marine JROTC unit in the nation. In 2004, the unit was the State drill team champions.

## Private / Charter Schools

**Arizona School for the Arts, 1313 N. 2nd St., Phoenix, AZ 85004
(602) 257-1444, www.goasa.org**

Arizona School for the Arts is one of the State's finest schools. *US News and World Report* called the school "a specialized education powerhouse," Sen. Joe Lieberman mentioned it in a *Reader's Digest* article "Schools That Succeed," and the *Wall Street Journal* rated it as one of the top four schools in Arizona. Add to that prestige designation as a National Blue Ribbon School in 2005.

Besides high academic achievement, what sets Arizona School for the Arts apart is the opportunity given to students to work with professional artists. The arts curriculum includes ballet, band/strings, vocal, music, classical guitar, drama and piano.

Admissions requirements reflect the blend of academics and fine arts emphasized at the school. In addition to taking an academic placement test, all students are required to complete a vocal audition. Students interested in ballet will also have to specifically audition for the ballet program.

Ninety percent of graduates go on to a four-year college. Of the remaining 10 percent, many go directly into ballet or other fine arts companies. Recent graduates have been accepted to Johns Hopkins University, Notre Dame, and Vassar College.

Because it focuses so much on fine arts, the school offers little else in the way of extracurricular activities. There are a few clubs including a science fiction club and an Academic Decathlon team. (The Academic Decathlon team was the first charter school team to make it to the State finals.) The school does not have a sports program.

Arizona School for the Arts is a sixth through 12th grade public charter school. No tuition is charged.

**Arizona Agribusiness & Equine Center, (Mesa Community College),
1350 S. Longmore, #39, Mesa, 85202
(480) 833-8899, www.aaechighschools.com**

This school is known as "the horse school" because of its equine science and veterinarian studies programs, but the Arizona Agribusiness & Equine Center (AAEC) is about much more than horses and FFA projects. With four campuses located on or within walking distance of community college campuses, the school offers students the opportunity to take college preparatory and community college classes. AAEC's goal is to help students identify and pursue a passion through advanced coursework by combining an intimate high school environment with a realistic college experience.

Although the school does provide hands-on instruction that actually includes horses, AAEC's programs are not limited to agriculture or animal studies. The school has state-of-the-art biotechnology facilities and programs, and students can study college preparatory programs in fields like technology and business. AAEC studies labor projections to keep its courses in line with the professions future businesses will demand.

AAEC believes high school students are able to take college-level courses. When academically ready, students attend college courses in addition to their high school classes. They earn college credits that apply toward high school graduation. Motivated students can graduate high school with up to two years of transferable college credits or an associate's degree from the school's community college partner (Mesa Community College, for example). Students have college IDs and often have access to the entire college facility including the library, recreational facilities and college advisors. College courses are free as long as the student earns a C or better.

Other locations:

Paradise Valley (Paradise Valley Community College), 17811 N. 32nd St., Phoenix, AZ 85032 (602) 569-7701

South Mountain (South Mountain Community College), 7050 S. 24th St., Phoenix, 85040 (602) 243-8004

Red Mountain (Mesa Community College at Red Mountain), Coming soon. Currently at Mesa campus

## Brophy College Preparatory, 4701 N. Central Ave., Phoenix, 85012 (602) 264-5291, www.brophyprep.org

Sons of Phoenix's rich and powerful attend Brophy College Preparatory. Founded in 1928 by the Society of Jesuits, this high school has more than 1,200 students from 130 primary schools. Although Brophy is committed to the beliefs of the Roman Catholic Church, approximately 40 percent of the student body is not Catholic.

Brophy stresses a liberal arts education that seeks to develop an intimate relationship with God. All courses are college preparatory in nature. As a result, students average 1200 on the SAT test.

Ninety-nine percent of graduates go on to higher education, 97 percent at four-year institutions including some of the nation's most prestigious like Yale, Cornell, Northwestern and Baylor.

Brophy typically receives 500 to 700 applications each year for its freshman class. Admittance is based on seventh and eighth grade achievements, extracurricular activities, letters of recommendation, an entrance exam and interviews. Roughly half of the students that apply are admitted; the class of 2009 has 340 students. Tuition is not cheap. Expect to pay nearly $10,000 for a full school year. Historically, 20 to 30 percent of Brophy's students receive some form of financial aid.

Brophy students can participate in more than 70 clubs. Nearby, the school has a 10-acre sports complex that includes one of the premier swimming/training facilities in the nation. One pool has two underwater viewing rooms for stroke analysis and filming. Brophy is a dominant swim team with multiple state championships. The team has received national recognition as one of the best—if not the best—high school swim team in the country.

## Challenge Charter School, 5801 W. Greenbriar Dr., Glendale, 85308 (602) 938-5411, www.challengecharterschool.net

Challenge Charter School operates based on the principles of Core Knowledge Sequence, a program developed by Ed Hirsch, Jr., editor of the "What Your First Grader (Second Grader, etc.) Needs to Know" series. Hirsch believes that students must achieve a "basic core knowledge" at each grade level before moving on to the next level. When Challenge Charter School opened in 1996, it was the first school in the State to be based on Hirsch's ideas.

As an "excelling" school, Challenge Charter School stamps its own science and technology emphasis on the Core Knowledge curriculum. The school has a computer lab with 24 laptops, and every four classrooms shares a mini computer lab. As part of its science program, the school has a weather station and a weather club. Enrichment programs like dance, foreign language, and karate are available, some as after school programs for a fee.

Depending on the grade level, class sizes are limited to between 22 and 26 students. All classroom teachers are certified, something not all charter schools can say. Because it's a charter school, there is no tuition fee; however a $25 extracurricular activity fee is requested. Parents are advised to complete a preregistration form prior to registration on April 15th. All students will be assessed to ensure they are registered at the proper grade level based on the Core Knowledge Sequence program.

Challenge Charter School adheres to a strict Environmental Heath Policy. No pesticides are used on campus, the building itself was constructed from non-toxic materials, and only unscented, environmentally sound cleaning products are used. Additionally, no students or visitors (even those dropping off or picking up students) are allowed to wear scented personal products like perfume.

### Foothills Academy College Preparatoy, 7191 E. Ashler Hills Dr., Scottsdale, AZ 85262
**(480) 488-5583, www.foothillsacademy.com**

As the saying goes, the idea behind Foothills Academy is that of a small school "where everybody knows your name." An "excelling" school, Foothills Academy is capped at 250 students, and the school claims it is not uncommon to see friendships that cross grade levels or teachers socializing with students during lunch.

Established in 1993 as a private, co-ed college preparatory school, Foothills Academy strives to encourage leadership, enrich lives, and promote academic excellence through a highly personalized learning environment that it labels "self-directed learning." In 1995, Foothills Academy became one of the State's first charter schools. Tuition is free; however, the school requests the donation of a $475 Program Support Fee per student to cover extracurricular activities.

Since beginning in a two-room building with 30 students, Foothills Academy has adhered to two ideals—a low teacher-to-student ratio and variety of field experiences. Although the school has many more students, 12 classrooms, and a modern lab now, it has maintained small class sizes. For sixth through eighth grade, the average class size is 22 students; for ninth through 12th grade, it is 21 students.

Past field experiences have included trips to Chapel Rock and Prescott, participation in advanced language study in Mexico and a hands-on ecological study of Catalina Island, including snorkeling.

Students have the opportunity to participate in several extracurricular activities such as photography, weight training, guitar, sign language and chess. For athletes, there is flag football, baseball, volleyball, basketball, softball, and golf.

### Keystone Montessori, 1025 E. Liberty Lane, Phoenix, 85048
**(480) 460-7312, www.keystonemontessori.com**

Keystone Montessori is admittedly not for everyone. Based on the controversial educational theories of Maria Montessori, the school provides an environment where students teach themselves and are not confined to desks. Students learn "naturally," often through manipulation of age-appropriate, hands-on materials.

The school must be doing something right, though. For the past two years, the school has received an "excelling" rating. Founded in 1995 with 13 students, Keystone Montessori has grown to 300 children ranging in age from 18 months to 12 years (seventh grade). Parents are encouraged to enroll their children as early as possible to optimally develop the child through the Montessori method.

Classrooms are multi-age based on a three-year cycle that corresponds with the developmental stages of children. In other words, three- to six-year-olds will be placed in classrooms together while six- to nine-year-olds and nine- to 12-year-olds will be placed together. Two teachers trained in the Montessori method are in each classroom.

Keystone Montessori strives to provide a challenging college preparatory curriculum. In addition to traditional math and science, students study anthropology, civics, architecture, and "peace education," i.e. conflict resolution. The school has a global perspective and says in its mission statement that "contemporary society must embrace pluralist beliefs."

An application and interview are required. Tuition ranges from $500 to $800 depending on the student's age. Extended care is available for an additional fee.

## Northwest Christian School, 16401 N. 43rd Ave., Phoenix, 85053 (602) 978-5134, www.nwccschool.org

God is central to the education offered at Northwest Christian School. Students learn through a Bible-based program and have opportunity for prayer, devotion, and Bible study. The school has two campuses. The main campus on 43rd Avenue instructs students from pre-kindergarten through 12th grade while the Peoria campus only goes to sixth grade. The school is the largest Christian school in the State with more than 1,400 students.

Students score well above national test score averages, and Northwest Christian School has produced its share of National Merit Finalists and Semi-Finalists. Honors classes are available, and high school students can earn college credit through dual enrollment in courses at Wayland Baptist University.

At the high school level, Northwest Christian School has a strong athletic program that has produced State championship or runner-up teams in eight different sports. It has a rich elective program that includes typical electives like band, choir and drama but adds electives with a Christian focus like Christian Leadership, Contemporary Moral Issues, Law and Historical Simulations.

Tuition ranges from $1,300 for the two-day pre-kindergarten program to nearly $6,000 for high school students. Discounts are provided for families with more than one student attending, and there are additional fees for science labs and sports. Also, additional registration, application, and enrollment fees may apply.

Admission requires that one parent be a Christian involved in a local, Bible-believing church. (See the Web site for the school's statement of faith and beliefs.) Students cannot have been expelled from another school.

Northwest Christian School, Peoria Campus, 8133 W. Cactus Rd., Peoria, 85381, (623) 487-1601

## Tempe Prep Academy, 1251 E. Southern Ave., Tempe, 85282
## (480) 839-3402, www.tempeprep.org

Imagine an Eastern, blueblood preparatory school minus the bluebloods and dormitories, and you won't be far off when it comes to Tempe Preparatory Academy. Founded in 1996 by a group of Tempe professors, engineers, and businessmen, Tempe Preparatory is a liberal arts school based on the legacy of the renowned Trinity network of preparatory schools in the Midwest and East.

Education is based on the great works of Western Civilization. Each grade level builds on the next. By graduation, students are expected to appreciate art and culture, understand the intellectual foundations of the world they live in and know advanced math and science. Tempe Preparatory insists that it is not a school for gifted students, though; it is a school for students curious about learning.

Classes are small—the student/teacher ratio is 10 to one—and even though the classes are considered honors level, grades are not weighted. Students attending sixth through 12th grade will study six years of fine arts including music performance and theory, calculus, biology, chemistry, physics, and two years of Latin. In ninth through 12th grade, English and History are combined into "Humane Letters Seminars," a two-hour daily seminar conducted in the Socratic method.

Tempe Preparatory Academy is considered by many to be one of the best charter schools not only in the State but also in the southwestern United States. For the past two years, 20 percent of the senior class has qualified as either a National Merit Finalist or Semi-Finalist. Students average over 1200 on their combined ACT/SAT scores.

As a public charter school, Tempe Preparatory Academy does not charge tuition. It has two "spin off" schools, Veritas Preparatory Academy and Chandler Preparatory Academy.

Veritas Preparatory Academy, 2131 E. Lincoln Dr., Phoenix, 85016
(602) 263-1128, www.veritasprepacademy.org

Chandler Preparatory Academy, 2020 N. Arizona Ave., Chandler, 85225

(480) 855-5410, www.chandlerprep.org

## Valley Academy, 1520 W. Rose Garden Lane, Phoenix, 85027
## (623) 516-7747, www.valleyacademy.com

Valley Academy is all about the basics. It's the kind of school Grandma and Grandpa might have attended. No pat-on-the-back, "here's an A for trying" at this school. Valley Academy is dedicated to high academic achievement and rewards accomplishment, not effort.

Opened in 1995 as a back-to-basics school, the classes are "teacher-led" and "textbook based." Instruction begins at the kindergarten level with Spalding phonics. By the end of the year, kindergartners are not only reading but also memorizing and reciting short poems.

Memorization plays a key role in the education process. Students continue to memorize poems and classical literature such as Shakespeare's sonnets throughout their educational careers at Valley Academy. First and second graders learn 30 to 40 new spelling words each week, and older students memorize all 50 states and capitals. Memorization becomes even more intense at the seventh and eighth grade level as students begin studying Greek and Latin word origins and algebra.

Students at all levels participate in "Special Area" classes including physical education, art, and music. Beginning in third grade, students add computers/technology and Spanish (more memorization) to the list.

Valley Academy is a public charter school. No tuition is charged. Extracurricular activities such as band, chorus, sports and clubs are available as resources allow.

## Xavier College Preparatory, 4710 N. Fifth St., Phoenix, AZ 85012
## (602) 277-3772, www.xcp.org

Xavier College Preparatory is the female counterpart to the all-boys Brophy College Preparatory. In fact, the two schools share several buildings like the Piper Performing Arts Center where students collaborate on co-ed productions. Like Brophy, Xavier is a Catholic high school. Eighty percent of the students are Catholic, and Xavier holds several school-wide masses and prayer days throughout the school year.

Founded in 1943 by Founding Sisters of Charity of the Blessed Virgin Mary, Xavier promotes a curriculum that emphasizes women. Students learn of women's roles in history, science, literature, fine arts, science and the church. Women hold every leadership position at Xavier, and women serve as Eucharistic ministers and readers of the Word.

The Catholic High School Honor Roll recognizes Xavier as one of 50 best Catholic high schools in the United States. Over past 10 years, the school has had 82 National Merit Scholars, 143 Commended Scholars, 36 National Hispanic Scholars and five National Black Scholars.

More than 500 eighth grade students apply, but only 320 are accepted. Admission is based on grades, standardized test results, and letters of recommendation. Tuition costs nearly $10,000. Some financial aid is available, but this will never cover the entire tuition. Students sometimes work part time jobs to pay for part of their tuition.

Like Brophy, Xavier has a strong swim team and more than 70 clubs. At Xavier, those clubs include the equestrian club, Toastmasters club, and several clubs rooted in Christianity like St. Agnes Club and Loudres pilgrimage.

# Index & Acknowledgements

## INDEX

## ACKNOWLEDGEMENTS

Our acknowledgement and sincere thanks to the many professionals who have provided their time and advice to *Where to Live in Phoenix and the Valley of the Sun*, especially these good folks:

Terry Erickson, City of *Scottsdale Parks & Recreation Department.*

Debbie Driscol, *City of Mesa*

Amy Morales, *City of Mesa*

Laura McMurchie, *Scottsdale Convention & Visitors Bureau*

Viva Ashcroft, *Coldwell Banker Success Realty Camelback*

Earlene Nelson, *Coldwell Banker Success Realty Scottsdale*

Judy Perrin-Crone, *Coldwell Banker Success Realty Biltmore*

Ann Morgan, *Coldwell Banker Success Realty Ahwatukee*

Gary Oman, *Coldwell Banker Success Realty Mesa*

Jo Haitbrink, *Coldwell Banker Success Realty Cave Creek*

Terri Helmick, *Coldwell Banker Success Realty Mesa*

Reggie Sanchez, *Coldwell Banker Success Realty Mesa*

Frank McConnell, *Coldwell Banker Success Realty Mesa*

Harold Poirier, *Coldwell Banker Success Realty Goodyear*

Tom Bourdo, *Keller Williams Realty, East Valley*

Buddy Early, *Echo Magazine*

Steven Vargo, *MCO Realty, Inc., Fountain Hills*

Leon Chusid, *Sterling Fine Homes & Land*

Kenny Klaus, *ReMax Achievers, Mesa*

Doris French, *Baseline Realty*

Helen Prier, *Urban Living Properties*

Debora Bridges, *The Phoenician*

Sally Cooper, *Sally Cooper & Company representing The Royal Palms Resort & Spa*

Amy Rezzonico, *Arizona Department of Education*

James Larsen, *Moon Valley Homeowners Association*

Jennifer Brillowsky, *Suncor Development Corporation*

Carl Giordano, *ReMax Achievers Goodyear*

Charlotte Diaz, *First USA Realty, El Mirage*

Katy Bruehl, *Realty Executives, Buckeye*

Bobby Lieb, *Realty Executives, Phoenix*

Edward Gowan, *Arizona Golf Association*